MIKE MEYERS' CERTIFICATION
Passport ⋆

MCSA Managing a
Windows® 2000
Network Environment

Exam 70-218

WALTER GLENN
with PET...

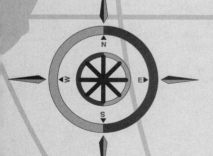

D1446040

Mc
Graw
Hill

New York • Chicago • San Francisco
Lisbon • London • Madrid • Mexico City
Milan • New Delhi • San Juan
Seoul • Singapore • Sydney • Toronto

McGraw-Hill/Osborne
2600 Tenth Street
Berkeley, California 94710
U.S.A.

To arrange bulk purchase discounts for sales promotions, premiums, or fund-raisers, please contact **McGraw-Hill/Osborne** at the above address. For information on translations or book distributors outside the U.S.A., please see the International Contact Information page immediately following the Contents of this book.

Mike Meyers' MCSA Managing a Windows® 2000 Network Environment Certification Passport (Exam 70-218)

34567890 DOC DOC 0198765432

Book p/n 0-07-0-07-222480-0 and CD p/n 0-07-0-07-222481-9
parts of
ISBN 0-07-222482-7

Publisher Brandon A. Nordin	**Copy Editor** Robert Campbell
Vice President & Associate Publisher Scott Rogers	**Proofreader** Linda Medoff
Editorial Director Gareth Hancock	**Indexer** Jack Lewis
Senior Acquisitions Editor Nancy Maragioglio	**Computer Designers** Carie Abrew, Mickey Galicia
Project Editors Jennifer Malnick Jenn Tust	**Illustrators** Kelly Stanton-Scott, Lyssa Wald, Michael Mueller
Acquisitions Coordinator Jessica Wilson	**Series Design** Peter Hancik, epic
Technical Editor Rob Scrimger	**Cover Series Design** Ted Holladay

This book was composed with Corel VENTURA™ Publisher.

About the Authors

Walter Glenn is a Microsoft Certified System Administrator (MCSA), Microsoft Certified Systems Engineer (MCSE), and Microsoft Certified Trainer (MCT). He holds certifications in various products, including Windows NT 4, Windows 2000, and Exchange Server.

Walter has been working in the computer industry for 15 years, starting as a computer technician and moving to network administration and engineering. He is president of Glenn & Associates, where he provides network administration and technical support for medium-sized enterprise organizations. Walter is currently the author or co-author of 14 books, including *Exchange 2000 Server Administrator's Companion*, *Windows XP Tips and Techniques*, and several certification guides. He also trains in a classroom environment and has created several Web-based certification courses. He lives with his family in Huntsville, Alabama.

You can reach Walter with questions or comments about this book at passport@walterglenn.com. You can find more information on his background and services at his Web site: www.walterglenn.com.

Peter Bruzzese (MCSE, MCT, CCNA) is an independent training consultant working within CommVault Systems, EMC, and New Horizons. He has written several books on Windows 2000 certification and has just completed *Windows 2000 Enterprise Storage Solutions* for Sybex. Peter has been working within the IT industry for nearly 10 years. His love for training and public speaking was rewarded this year when he was accepted as part of the MCP Magazine Techmentor Conference tour and had the opportunity to speak at their fall session in San Francisco.

Working for CommVault Systems has allowed Peter to test his national and international training skills as a traveling corporate trainer that has pulled him around the U.S. and Europe. Courses that CommVault required included Cisco training, SAN/NAS course development and training, Exchange 5.5/2000 disaster recovery, and administration and CommVault's Galaxy product administration course, in addition to his standard Windows 2000 Microsoft Official Curriculum (MOC) courses.

About the Tech Editor

Rob Scrimger first learned about computers when his tenth grade teacher brought in an Apple II; a week later he was programming. Over the last 20 years Rob has become a renaissance man of computers as an operator, a programmer, a trainer, a network administrator, a DBA, a field service technician and doing nearly every thing else computer related. Rob currently resides in Ottawa, Canada—known as Silicon Valley North—and works as an independent contractor. He splits his time between training, writing, Web development, and network administration. Rob now has three MCSE designations to his credit, NT3.5, NT 4.0, and Windows 2000 (Charter Member), in addition to being an MCT, MCDBA, MCSE+I, MCP+SB, CTT, A+ Certified Technician, and Network+ certified. He has published many books on Windows, TCP/IP, databases, and Internet technologies. He has also been teaching others "how to" for over 12 years, and for most of that time has concentrated on teaching technical courses to the folks that keep networks running. Rob is particularly noted for his networking, database, and Internet courses.

Dedication

I'd like to dedicate this book to Richard Moore, my wife Susan's father. You raised a great girl.

Acknowledgments

I'd like to thank Nancy Maragioglio for trusting me with this project, for her advice along the way, and for helping to make sure the book got done. I'd also like to thank Peter Bruzzese for his help in writing the book. Thanks, also, to Rob Scrimger, Jessica Wilson, Jennifer Malnick, Jenn Tust, and all the other editors who worked on this book for their dedication. And, as always, I'd like to thank Neil Salkind at Studio B for his continued support.

—*Walter Glenn*

Contents

4 Managing Dynamic Host Configuration Protocol (DHCP) 85

5 Managing Windows Name Resolution 107

V Configuring, Securing, and Troubleshooting Remote Access 355

13 Configuring Remote Access 357

INTERNATIONAL CONTACT INFORMATION

AUSTRALIA
McGraw-Hill Book Company Australia Pty. Ltd.
TEL +61-2-9417-9899
FAX +61-2-9417-5687
http://www.mcgraw-hill.com.au
books-it_sydney@mcgraw-hill.com

CANADA
McGraw-Hill Ryerson Ltd.
TEL +905-430-5000
FAX +905-430-5020
http://www.mcgrawhill.ca

GREECE, MIDDLE EAST,
NORTHERN AFRICA
McGraw-Hill Hellas
TEL +30-1-656-0990-3-4
FAX +30-1-654-5525

MEXICO (Also serving Latin America)
McGraw-Hill Interamericana Editores S.A. de C.V.
TEL +525-117-1583
FAX +525-117-1589
http://www.mcgraw-hill.com.mx
fernando_castellanos@mcgraw-hill.com

SINGAPORE (Serving Asia)
McGraw-Hill Book Company
TEL +65-863-1580
FAX +65-862-3354
http://www.mcgraw-hill.com.sg
mghasia@mcgraw-hill.com

SOUTH AFRICA
McGraw-Hill South Africa
TEL +27-11-622-7512
FAX +27-11-622-9045
robyn_swanepoel@mcgraw-hill.com

UNITED KINGDOM & EUROPE
(Excluding Southern Europe)
McGraw-Hill Education Europe
TEL +44-1-628-502500
FAX +44-1-628-770224
http://www.mcgraw-hill.co.uk
computing_neurope@mcgraw-hill.com

ALL OTHER INQUIRIES Contact:
Osborne/McGraw-Hill
TEL +1-510-549-6600
FAX +1-510-883-7600
http://www.osborne.com
omg_international@mcgraw-hill.com

Check-In

May I See Your Passport?

What do you mean you don't have a passport? Why, it's sitting right in your hands, even as you read! This book is your passport to a very special place. You're about to begin a journey, my friend, a journey toward that magical place called *certification!* You don't need a ticket; you don't need a suitcase—just snuggle up and read this passport. It's all you need to get there. Are you ready? Let's go.

Your Travel Agent: Mike Myers

Hello! My name's Mike Meyers, and I'm proud to introduce myself to you as the series editors for the Mike Meyers' Exam Passport series and this book. I've written a number of popular certification books, and this is my dream of the perfect certification book! Certifications are important to me as I am first and foremost a real techie. On any given day, you'll find me replacing a hard drive, setting up a Web site, or configuring a server or writing code. I love every aspect of this book you hold in your hands. Every book in this series combines easy readability with a condensed format—in other words, the kind of book I always wanted when I did my certifications. Putting this much information in an accessible format is an enormous challenge, but I think we have achieved our goal, and I am confident you will agree.

I designed this series to do one thing and only one thing: to get you the only information you need to achieve your certification. You won't find any fluff in here; your author, Walter Glenn, packed every page with nothing but the real nitty-gritty of the certification exam. Every page is packed with 100 percent pure concentrate of knowledge! But we didn't forget to make the book readable. I hope you enjoy the casual, friendly style; I want you to feel as though Walter is speaking to you, discussing the certification—not just spewing facts at you.

My e-mail address is mikem@totalsem.com. Please feel free to contact me directly if you have any questions, complaints, or compliments.

Your Destination: MCSA Managing a Windows 2000 Network Environment

This book is your passport to the Microsoft MCSA Managing a Windows 2000 Network Environment exam. This exam tests your skills as an administrator of many aspects of a Windows 2000 network. You'll learn about configuring and monitoring Windows 2000, setting up and managing a TCP/IP network infrastructure, sharing network resources, monitoring security, managing Active Directory, and controlling remote access. It's a lot of information, but then administering a Windows 2000 network is a big job! I am confident that, with this book in hand, you'll be a better administrator and certification holder in no time.

Your Guide: Walter Glenn

Between his training, writing, and course design, Walter Glenn has helped thousands of people obtain certifications of one kind or another. He's the author of *Exchange 2000 Server Administrator's Companion,* a book considered the standard for administrators of Exchange server. He's written books on certifications including *Windows 2000; Windows NT 4, TCP/IP, Exchange Server;* and general networking. You won't get too far into this book before you realize that he can help you get your MCSA too.

Walter wants you to know your input is very important to him. You can contact him at passport@walterglenn.com to discuss issues regarding this book.

Why the Travel Theme?

One of my favorite topics is the parallel of gaining a certification to taking a trip. All the elements are the same: preparation, an itinerary, and a route—even mishaps along the way. Let me show you how it all works.

This book is divided into 15 chapters. Each chapter begins with an Itinerary of objectives covered in the chapter and an ETA to give you an idea of the time involved in learning the skills presented in the chapter. Each chapter is broken down by real exam objectives, as published by Microsoft. Also, each chapter contains a number of helpful items to bring out points of interest.

Exam Tip	
Points out critical topics you're likely to see on the exam.	

Travel Assistance	
Points you to additional sources such as books and Web sites to give you more information.	

Local Lingo	
Describes special terms in detail in a way you can easily understand.	

Travel Advisory	
Warns you of common pitfalls, misconceptions, and downright physical peril!	

The end of the chapter gives you two handy tools. The Checkpoint reviews each objective covered in the chapter with a handy synopsis—a great way to review quickly. Plus, you'll find end-of-chapter questions and answers to test your newly acquired skills.

But the fun doesn't stop there! After you've read the book, pull out the CD-ROM and take advantage of the free practice questions. Use the full practice exam to hone your skills and keep the book handy to check answers. When you're passing the practice questions, you're ready to take the exam, so go get certified!

The End of the Trail

The IT industry grows and changes constantly—and so should you. Finishing one certification is just a step in an ongoing process of gaining more and more certifications to match your constantly changing and growing skills. Read the Career Flight Path (Appendix B) at the end of the book to see where this certification fits into your personal certification goals. And remember: in the IT business, if you're not moving forward, you're way behind!

Good luck on your certification! Stay in touch!

Mike Meyers
Series Editor
Mike Meyers' Certification Passport

Managing, Securing, and Troubleshooting Servers and Client Computers

Configuring Client and Server Computers

CHAPTER 1

	NEWBIE	SOME EXPERIENCE	EXPERT
ETA	3 hours	2 hours	1 hour

One of your primary duties as a system administrator is to keep servers and client computers running smoothly. Since Windows 2000 Professional and the various Windows 2000 Server editions share an identical interface, there are many tasks that you will face on both your server and client computers. You must understand how to determine whether specific hardware is compatible with Windows 2000, and how to install and configure that hardware. You must also know how to troubleshoot a computer that isn't starting properly. Finally, you must know how to apply the periodic updates to the Windows 2000 operating system that come from Microsoft in the form of service packs and hot fixes.

Install and Configure Server and Client Computer Hardware

Objective 1.01

Most of the hardware available for Windows-based computers today is much more sophisticated than what was available even a couple of years ago. With the advent of Microsoft's Plug and Play standard, you rarely have to configure a piece of hardware manually; you simply plug it into the computer and watch while Windows recognizes and configures it for you. Even though the process has gotten much easier, there are still some things you need to understand about installing and configuring hardware in Windows 2000.

Travel Advisory

This chapter, like the exam itself, does not focus on the physical installation of hardware. Rather, it focuses on the installation of drivers and any resource configuration that takes place after you install the hardware in a computer. For details on physical installation, you should always consult the hardware documentation.

Assessing Compatibility

Before you install any hardware in a computer running Windows 2000, you should determine whether that device has been tested by Microsoft for compatibility. The easiest way to do this is to look for the "Designed for Windows 2000" logo on the device packaging. If this logo is not present, or if you don't have the packaging, you can consult Microsoft's Windows 2000 Compatibility Site at http://www.microsoft.com/windows2000/server/howtobuy/upgrading/compat/default.asp.

This site presents a searchable database of computer systems, hardware devices, and software that have been tested and found to be compatible with Windows 2000. Of course, it is possible that a particular device not represented on this list is compatible and simply has not been tested. If this is the case, and you do not have the choice to use a device that is on the list, you should test the hardware on an isolated computer (i.e., a nonproduction computer that is not part of your network) before installing it on a server or client computer.

Viewing and Configuring Resource Settings

Every device connected to a computer uses resources that let the device communicate smoothly with the rest of the computer. For most modern devices, Windows configures the resources used by the device automatically using its Plug and Play technology. On legacy devices, such as ISA cards and some serial and parallel port devices, you may need to configure the resource settings on the hardware manually using jumpers, DIP switches (the little plastic two-position switches on some hardware), or software from the manufacturer.

The following resources are used by most hardware:

- **I/O address**   A hexadecimal number that identifies the location of a memory buffer for a particular device. This buffer is used for storing requests by the device while the CPU processes them. All I/O addresses assigned on a computer must be unique.

- **Interrupt (IRQ)**   Any of 16 channels used by devices to signal the processor that they need its attention. PCs have 16 interrupt settings, numbered 0–15. Many Plug and Play–compatible devices can share an interrupt, and Windows will set these devices up for you. Most legacy devices will not share an interrupt, so you must configure an interrupt that does not conflict with another device.

- **DMA (direct memory access) channel**   Any of six channels used by a limited number of devices that need to have direct access to a computer's memory. DMA is used for transferring data from memory to a device without passing it through the CPU, thus speeding up the process greatly. Your floppy drive always takes DMA 2. Other devices may need to be configured manually.

- **Memory addresses**   Some devices use specific addresses in your computer's memory to transfer information to the processor.

Each piece of hardware on your computer also has a *driver,* a piece of software that serves as a liaison between the hardware and Windows. The resources used by the driver must be the same as the resources configured on the hardware device. Most of the time, Windows can detect the resources used by the hardware and configure its driver automatically. With some legacy devices, you must determine the resource settings used by the hardware and configure the driver manually using Device Manager, which is shown in Figure 1-1. You can get to Device Manager by opening the System Control Panel utility, switching to the Hardware tab, and clicking Device Manager.

All devices installed on the computer are displayed in the Device Manager window, grouped into hardware categories such as Disk Drives and Modems. The icon associated with a device lets you know the device's status:

- A working device has a normal icon.
- A disabled device has a red "x" over the icon.
- A device with a problem has an exclamation point over the icon. Problems can be bad or missing drivers, resource conflicts, or some other problem.

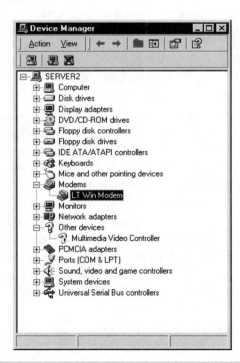

| **FIGURE 1.1** | Use Device Manager to configure resources for hardware devices. |

- A device without a driver has a yellow question mark for an icon.
- A device that has the Use Automatic Settings option disabled (its resources are manually assigned) has a blue "i" over the icon.

Double-click any device to open its Properties dialog box. Use the Resources tab, shown in Figure 1-2, to modify the resources used by the device driver to match those used by the device itself.

Travel Advisory

You can determine all the resources in use by devices on a computer using Device Manager. This is helpful when figuring out what resources to use for a particular device. Choose View | Resources By Type and then expand the node for the type of resource you want to examine.

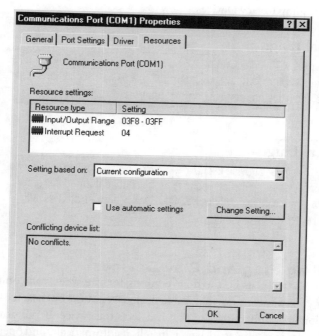

FIGURE 1.2   You can disable the automatic resource settings used by Windows if you need to manually configure a device.

Installing Hardware in Windows 2000

Installing hardware in Windows 2000 is not difficult. After following the manufacturer's directions for physically installing the hardware, you will see one of two things happen:

- If you have connected a Plug and Play device, Windows 2000 should notice automatically. In some cases, Windows installs the driver for you without any interaction required; in other cases, Windows opens a wizard that steps you through the process of installing the driver and configuring the hardware. If the device is hot-pluggable, this wizard opens when you plug the device in. If the device is not hot-pluggable, this wizard opens when you start Windows. Using the Add/Remove Hardware wizard is described in the section "Installing Plug and Play Devices."

- If you installed a device that is not Plug and Play compatible, Windows 2000 may or may not detect it during startup. If the device is not detected automatically, you'll need to use the Add/Remove Hardware wizard to configure the device. We'll cover this in the section "Installing Legacy Devices."

Local Lingo

Hot pluggable A device that can be connected to and disconnected while the computer is running is a *hot-pluggable* device. You must have a device and a system that support this feature.

Local Lingo

Legacy A *legacy* device is one a company or individual already owns. It is typically an older device and may or may not conform to current standards. In the case of Windows 2000, legacy devices are typically not Plug and Play compatible.

Installing Plug and Play Devices

Windows 2000 tries its best to do everything for you when you connect a new device. If you connect a hot-pluggable device, Windows opens a tool tip in the notification area informing you that it detects the device. If Windows already has an appropriate software driver, it installs it automatically and opens another tool tip letting you know when the device is ready to use.

If Windows does not have the specific driver, you are presented with the Found New Hardware wizard, which walks you through the steps for installing a driver and configuring the device. As you step through this wizard, you can show Windows where to search for a driver (or specify a location manually) or choose a specific type of hardware from a list of manufacturers and models for which Windows 2000 includes drivers. Often, you can use a driver for a similar device, though you should do this only if the manufacturer suggests it.

Once a hardware driver is located, Windows 2000 determines whether the driver has been tested for compatibility and digitally signed. If it has not, you can still install the driver, but you should monitor the hardware closely until you feel comfortable that the driver is not causing any problems. You'll learn more about drivers in the later section "Working with Device Drivers."

Installing Legacy Devices

If Windows does not detect the hardware device automatically, you must use the Add/Remove Hardware wizard available in the Control Panel. During the first stages of the wizard, your system is scanned for new Plug and Play–compatible hardware. Since this type of hardware is usually detected automatically, the wizard rarely finds anything new at this point.

Travel Advisory

If the hardware you are installing comes with an installation disk, there may be an installation program for the device. Try using it to install the hardware before using the Add/Remove Hardware wizard. Often, the installation program provided by the manufacturer is quicker and more reliable than using the Add/Remove Hardware wizard to install drivers.

The wizard next presents a list, shown in Figure 1-3, of any new Plug and Play devices found, along with any devices already installed on your computer. This includes devices that are not functioning for whatever reason—improper drivers, conflicting resources, and so on. If you select a nonfunctioning device, the wizard suggests that you go find a troubleshooter and ends. If a new Plug and Play device was found (and it is the device you are trying to install), select it and click Next to continue the installation. This routine follows the same procedure covered in the preceding section.

If the desired device is not included on the initial list, choose the Add A New Device entry and click Next to have the wizard search your computer for legacy devices that are not Plug and Play compatible, but for which Windows does come with drivers. If the wizard does not detect your device, you'll have to set it

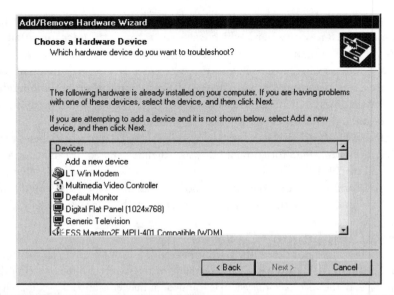

FIGURE 1.3   The Add/Remove Hardware wizard starts by searching for new Plug and Play devices.

up yourself by choosing a device type, as shown in Figure 1-4. Following this, you'll select a manufacturer and model for the device.

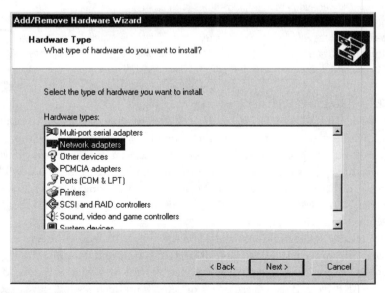

FIGURE 1.4   If the Add/Remove Hardware wizard cannot find a device, you can set the device up manually.

Once a device is selected and a driver is installed, Windows tries to detect the device, determine what hardware resources the device uses, and configure the driver to use those same settings. If Windows cannot make this determination, you are given the chance to set the resources manually. To do this, you must know what settings the device is configured to use. This often requires examining the device itself (usually jumpers or DIP switches are used to configure settings) or using a software utility provided by the manufacturer (often included on the driver disk). If you know the settings, you can enter them during the last phase of the Add/Remove Hardware wizard. Otherwise, you will have to end the wizard, figure out the settings, and then change the driver settings using Device Manager.

Travel Advisory

If a device is configured with settings that conflict with another device in the system, you must change the configuration of one of the devices. Use Device Manager to determine open resource settings, consult the manufacturer's documentation for instructions on configuring the device itself, and then use Device Manager again to configure the resources used by the driver.

Working with Device Drivers

Most hardware that you install on your computer also requires a software component to let Windows and the processor know what to do when the device is used; this software component is called a *driver*. Windows comes with a huge number of drivers for common hardware built in, which is why Windows usually doesn't have much trouble configuring your hardware during installation. Nonetheless, some devices, especially those manufactured after the release of Windows 2000, require that you supply the driver software.

Microsoft offers a driver testing program to all manufacturers. Once a driver is fully tested by Microsoft, it is digitally signed. This signature lets you know that the driver has been tested and that it has not been modified since testing. If you attempt to install a driver that has not been signed, Windows presents a warning, though you can continue the installation.

Travel Advisory

You can change the way Windows notifies you when it detects an unsigned driver. On the Hardware tab of the System Properties dialog box, click Driver Signing. You have three options: ignore unsigned drivers and install them without notifying you, warn you when unsigned drivers are detected, or block unsigned drivers from being installed at all.

You can manage drivers for a device using that device's Properties dialog box, available by double-clicking the device in Device Manager. In the Properties dialog box, switch to the Driver tab, shown in Figure 1-5.

The Driver tab provides basic information concerning the driver, such as the provider, date, and version, and lets you perform three actions:

- **View driver details** Click Driver Details to view a list of actual driver files used by the device.
- **Update the driver** Click Update Driver to launch a wizard that walks you through updating the driver. This process is almost identical to installing a driver for a new device.
- **Uninstall the driver** Uninstalling the driver removes the device from your computer.

Using the System File Checker

Windows 2000 protects critical system files so that they cannot be accidentally deleted and so that applications cannot overwrite them with their own versions of the

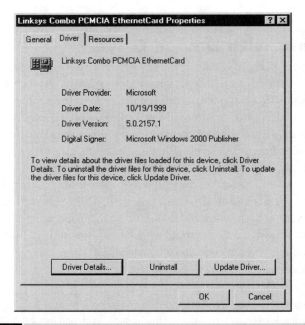

FIGURE 1.5 Use the Driver tab of a device's Properties dialog box to view and manage driver details.

files. Two features of Windows 2000 provide this protection. The first feature is named Windows File Protection (WFP). WFP runs in the background, monitoring changes to system files. When it detects a change, WFP compares the file signature of the new version of the file with its own database to determine whether it is a valid file version. If it is not valid, WFP replaces the problem file with one from a file cache named Dllcache (found in %SystemRoot%\System32\Dllcache) or from the original installation files.

The second feature used for file protection is named System File Checker (SFC). SFC is a command-line utility that lets you verify the digital signatures of files. It also checks the Dllcache folder and repopulates it with valid versions of files, if needed.

Use the following syntax to run the SFC:

```
SFC [/scannow] [/scanonce] [/scanboot] [/cancel] [/quiet] [/enable]
[/purgecache] [/cachesize=x]
```

The following switches are used with the SFC command:

- **/scannow**   Scans all protected files immediately
- **/scanonce**   Scans all protected files the next time Windows starts
- **/scanboot**   Scans all protected files each time Windows starts
- **/cancel**   Cancels all pending scans, such as from using the /scanboot switch
- **/quiet**   Replaces invalid files without prompting the user
- **/enable**   Returns WFP to normal operation
- **/purgecache**   Purges the Dllcache folder and scans all protected files immediately
- **/cachesize=x**   Sets the file cache size, in megabytes

Using the File Signature Verification Utility

The File Signature Verification utility is used to verify the digital signature on a file or group of files. You can use it to scan automatically for unsigned system files (which may have been overwritten by applications but remain undetected by the SFC) or to scan a specified set of files. To run the utility, use the following steps:

1. Click Start | Run and enter **sigverif** in the Run dialog box.
2. Once the Signature Verification utility opens, click Start to scan all system files.

3. Alternatively, to specify search parameters for files and the folder in which to scan, click Advanced and select the Look For Other Files That Are Not Digitally Signed option. This is a useful way of scanning driver files before you actually install them.

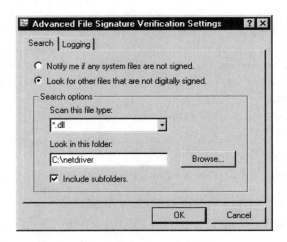

A simple dialog box informs you when the scan is complete, if no unsigned files were found. However, if unsigned files are found, a Signature Verification Results window opens to alert you to their presence. If unsigned files are discovered, you will need to decide what action to take. You can try to find updated drivers, remove the devices using the unsigned drivers, or take no action at all.

You won't be able to take any action from within the utility—it is just for finding the files. You should uninstall or update the drivers using the techniques discussed earlier in this section.

Troubleshoot Starting Servers and Client Computers

Many of the problems that occur in Windows happen during the startup process, especially following Windows installation or the installation of new hardware. This section examines the startup process and then looks at some of the tools used to troubleshoot startup problems.

Understanding the Startup Process

Understanding how Windows 2000 starts is an important part of understanding Windows. There are two distinct phases to the startup process. First, the computer itself boots, and then Windows starts. The process happens something like this:

1. When you apply power to the computer, the basic input/output system (BIOS) performs a power-on self-test (POST) routine that checks the basic hardware on the computer.

2. The BIOS then checks out the remaining hardware in your system, applies configuration settings, and then determines what device to boot from (floppy, CD-ROM drive, hard disk, and so on). The order of selection is specified in the BIOS settings. If the hard disk is the selected device, BIOS then loads the Master Boot Record (MBR) on your disk into memory.

3. The Master Boot Record, typically found on the first sector of a hard drive, contains information on the physical layout for a disk and its partition table. Based on this information, a program named NT Loader (NTLDR) is loaded into memory. NTLDR, in turn, is responsible for loading several other elements of Windows into memory during the startup process.

4. NTLDR uses the information in a file named boot.ini to determine what operating system to start your computer with. If multiple operating systems are installed, a menu is displayed at this point allowing you to choose the system to boot into. If only one operating system is installed (such as Windows 2000), the menu is skipped and Windows continues to start.

5. If Windows 2000 is selected to load, NTLDR loads a file named ntdetect.com that performs another hardware test to make sure basic devices such as processors and memory are functioning properly so that Windows can be started. NTDETECT also builds the HKEY_LOCAL_MACHINE\Hardware key of the Windows Registry.

6. NTLDR loads the NTOSKRNL into memory, which in turn loads the rest of the Windows files and device drivers. NTLDR then starts any Windows services scheduled to start automatically.

7. The graphic interface of Windows starts and a logon dialog box is displayed, requesting a username and password.

Starting Windows Using Advanced Boot Options

Windows provides a number of alternative startup methods that can be used to troubleshoot different kinds of problems. To access these advanced boot options, press the F8 key right at the beginning of Windows startup (right after the initial POST screen clears and the Starting Windows 2000 message appears). Windows displays an Advanced Startup Options menu with a number of startup options, which include the following:

- **Safe Mode** This option loads only the basic drivers, services, and programs needed to get Windows running and allow access to your disks. It also loads a simple VGA driver running at 640×480 resolution in 16 colors. Safe mode is designed for when configuring something in Windows (such as installing a new driver) causes Windows not to start properly. You can boot into safe mode, restore the original settings or make other changes, and then hopefully restart Windows in normal mode again. You can also boot a safe mode with networking enabled and a safe mode that does not load the Windows GUI but leaves you at the command prompt instead.

- **Enable Boot Logging** This option causes Windows 2000 to start in normal mode, but also to create a log file that displays all the drivers and services loaded when Windows starts. This log file is found at \Windows\ntbtlog.txt.

- **Enable VGA Mode** This option starts Windows 2000 normally but uses a standard VGA driver; it is particularly useful if you have installed a video adapter driver that doesn't display correctly.

- **Last Known Good Configuration** This option starts Windows 2000 using the hardware configuration that was saved the last time a user successfully logged on to Windows 2000. If you have installed a new device and driver only to find out that Windows can no longer start, you can shut down your computer, remove the device, and then restart using the last known good configuration.

- **Directory Services Restore Mode** This option starts Windows in a mode that allows you to restore the Active Directory database from an external backup. This option is available only on computers running editions of Windows 2000 Server that function as a domain controller.

- **Debugging Mode** This option starts Windows normally but sends debugging information to another computer through a serial cable. This option is primarily useful when developing software for Windows 2000 and when a Microsoft product support specialist is helping to diagnose a problem.

Creating a Parallel Installation

A parallel installation is essentially a second copy of Windows 2000 that is installed onto the same computer, but into a different disk partition or folder. If a problem prevents you from booting into the normal Windows 2000 installation, you can boot into the parallel installation in order to access information on hard drives, particularly those formatted using NTFS. Of course, this assumes that the startup failure is particular to the normal installation of Windows 2000 (such as a faulty driver) and not a hardware problem that would affect both installations.

Local Lingo

The **NT File System (NTFS)** is an advanced disk system used by Windows NT, Windows 2000, and Windows XP. Technically superior to the file allocation table (FAT) file system, NTFS supports such advanced features as file encryption, file-level security, and compression.

To create a parallel installation of Windows 2000, you simply install Windows 2000 a second time the same way you performed the initial installation. During the second installation, however, you'll specify a different disk partition or folder into which to install Windows.

Travel Advisory

While you can create a parallel installation of Windows 2000 in a different folder on the same disk partition as the original installation, it's usually not a good idea. Both installations will share the same root directory, Program Files folder, and Documents and Settings folder, and they will run the risk of interfering with one another if not carefully controlled. It is always best to specify another disk partition for the parallel installation.

Using the Recovery Console

The Recovery Console is a command-line program with a variety of trouble-shooting and recovery tools. Starting the Recovery Console instead of starting Windows normally lets you perform actions like starting and stopping services, formatting hard disks, accessing local drives, and managing disk partitions.

You can run the Recovery Console either by booting from the Windows 2000 installation CD-ROM or by installing the Recovery Console so that it appears on a special OS Choices menu before Windows starts. This is the same menu that lets you select an operating system to start if more than one is installed on the computer, but it is displayed when Recovery Console is installed even if you have only one operating system. Note that should a hardware problem prevent you from starting Windows from your hard drive, you may be forced to run Recovery Console from the CD-ROM anyway.

To run Recovery Console from the Windows 2000 installation CD-ROM, insert the disk and boot the computer. Some computers boot from CD-ROM automatically when a CD-ROM is present during startup; others require you to press a key to specify that you want to boot using the CD-ROM. On the initial setup screen, press R to select the Repair A Windows 2000 Installation option. On the Repair Options screen that opens, press C to start the Recovery Console. Enter the number of the installation you want to repair (number one if there is only one installation) and enter the password for the local administrator account.

Travel Advisory

If your computer does not have a bootable CD-ROM drive, you can boot the computer using Windows 2000 startup floppy disks. You will still need to have the installation CD-ROM handy to install or run Recovery Console, but you won't have to boot your computer using it. If you don't have startup floppy disks, you can create them using the makebt32.exe program in the Bootdisk folder on the installation CD-ROM. Note that this is a Windows program, so you will have to use an existing installation of Windows to create the disks.

To install Recovery Console so that you can start it from the hard disk, run the winnt32.exe program in the \I386 folder on the Windows 2000 Installation CD-ROM using the /cmdcons parameter. The easiest way to do this is to type **X:\i386\winnt32.exe /cmdcons** (where *X* is your CD-ROM drive) in the Run dialog box. Once it is installed, restart your computer and a Boot Manager menu appears before Windows starts, giving you the chance to start the Recovery Console.

The Recovery Console looks like a normal Windows 2000 command prompt. The following commands are available from the Recovery Console:

- **Chdir (cd)**   Displays the name of the current folder or changes folders
- **Chkdsk**   Scans a hard drive and reports the status of the drive
- **Cls**   Clears the screen
- **Copy**   Copies a file to another location
- **Delete (del)**   Deletes one or more files
- **Dir**   Lists the files in the current folder
- **Disable**   Disables a service or device driver
- **Enable**   Enables a service or device driver
- **Exit**   Exits the Recovery Console and restarts the computer
- **Fdisk**   Starts a program used to manage disk partitions
- **Fixboot**   Writes a new partition boot sector onto the system partition
- **Fixmbr**   Repairs the Master Boot Record on the partition boot sector
- **Format**   Formats a partition
- **Help**   Lists the commands available in the Recovery Console
- **Logon**   Logs on to a Windows 2000 installation
- **Map**   Displays a list of drive letter mappings
- **Mkdir (md)**   Creates a folder
- **Rmdir (rd)**   Deletes a folder
- **Rename (ren)**   Renames a file
- **Systemroot**   Sets the current folder to the system root folder
- **Type**   Displays a text file

Objective 1.03 # Install and Manage Windows 2000 Updates

Another important task you will have as an administrator is making sure that the installations of Windows are up to date on client and server computers. Microsoft provides periodic updates that implement new software features, fix bugs discovered in the software since its release, and most importantly, patch security holes.

These updates come in two forms:

- *Service packs* are collections of new features and patches that can be installed all at once. These have been tested to ensure that all new updates work together.
- *Hot fixes* are individual updates that are released between issuances of service packs. Most of the time, hot fixes are security patches that can't wait for a Service Pack release.

Travel Advisory

Actually, Microsoft uses a third method to distribute security patches, called a *security rollup package*. A security rollup package provides a cumulative collection of security updates that have been released since the last publicly released service pack.

Installing Windows 2000 Service Packs

A *service pack* is a collection of all the patches and new features that have been released since the release of Windows 2000. This includes any updates in previous service packs; so if you install Windows 2000, you can then install Service Pack 2 (for example) without having to install Service Pack 1 first. A Windows 2000 service pack covers installations of Windows 2000 Professional and all editions of Windows 2000 Server, so there is no need to track separate service packs.

Travel Advisory

You can determine what service pack is installed on a computer using the winver.exe command in the Run dialog box or at the command prompt. This command displays an About Windows dialog box showing the current Windows version, service pack information, and licensing information.

Finding Service Packs

There are two ways to obtain a service pack: you can download it for free or order it on CD-ROM for a nominal shipping charge. If you order the CD-ROM, you will receive the full network installation of the service pack, which contains all the service pack files and can be used to update any Windows 2000 computer on your network.

You can also download the service pack from Microsoft's site at http://www.microsoft.com/windows2000/downloads. If you download the service pack, you have two options. You can download the full network in-stallation of the service pack, which is appropriate if you have a network full of computers you need to upgrade. The full download usually runs over 100MB. You can also download an express installation of the service pack. Choosing this option actually downloads a small application that scans a single computer, de-termines what service pack files that computer needs, and then downloads and applies them. The advantage to an express download is obviously that it takes much less time to download, as it downloads a service pack customized for that computer. The disadvantage is that it updates only that one computer.

Deploying Service Packs

There are a number of ways to deploy service packs to the computers on your network. Before you ever install a service pack on a production computer, though, you should test it on an isolated computer first. Sometimes, service packs introduce as many bugs as they fix, and you'll often find yourself trading a bug you can live with for a bug you can't. While you are testing the service pack (or if you can't, for some reason), you should at least give the service pack a little time to settle after its release. Let other people do the testing and then see what the IT community is saying about it in trade magazines, on the Web, or in public newsgroups.

Once you are certain that you want to deploy a service pack, there are several ways to do it:

- Install it on each computer manually using the CD-ROM or a network share of the downloaded installation files. This method is really appropriate only on small networks, where you can either do the upgrades yourself or rely on users to upgrade their own computers.

- Use the Microsoft Windows Installer Service. Windows 2000 service packs include a package file named update.msi, which can be used to update networked computers automatically by assigning a group policy. This policy will cause each computer to which it is assigned to install the service pack the next time Windows is started. You'll learn more about using group policies in Chapter 11, "Using Group Policies."

- Use a program like Microsoft System Management Server (SMS) to distribute the service pack to any networked computer. You can configure SMS to notify client computers that the service pack is ready to be installed and then let users install it, or you can push the installation to client computers and even schedule the installation to run at a particular time.

Travel Advisory

In Windows NT, only installed operating system components were upgraded when you installed a service pack. If you added a new component following a service pack installation, you had to reinstall the service pack. Windows 2000 service packs store their update files on your local disk during installation, so that Windows 2000 can automatically update components when they are added to Windows. You do not have to reinstall a Windows 2000 service pack.

Installing Service Packs During a Windows 2000 Installation

Another way to deploy a service pack is along with an installation of Windows 2000, a practice often referred to as *slipstreaming*. When you slipstream a service pack, the original files in the Windows 2000 installation location are replaced with the updated files from the service pack. When Windows 2000 is installed, the service pack is installed along with it.

To slipstream a service pack, use the following steps:

1. Use the Run dialog or the command prompt to extract the service pack archive file. You do this by appending the -x switch to the executable service pack file. For example, to extract the archive file for Windows 2000 Service Pack 2, you would type **w2ksp2.exe -x**. When prompted, enter the name of a directory where you want the extracted service pack files to reside.

2. Once the files are extracted, you will find the subfolder named \I386\update in the extraction folder. Using the Run dialog or command prompt, enter the following command in that directory: **update.exe -s:***drive_letter***:\win2kdist**, where *win2kdist* is the location of the Windows 2000 installation files.

Once the update program is finished integrating the service pack into the installation files, you can use those installation files to install Windows 2000 along with the service pack in one step.

Installing Windows 2000 Hot Fixes

A *hot fix* is an update that addresses a single problem, such as a security hole, discovered in Windows. Hot fixes are issued between service pack releases. Unlike service packs, individual hot fixes are not tested to verify that they work well together (at least, not until they are included in a service pack). For this reason, you should investigate and test hot fixes fully before installing them on a production computer, and install hot fixes only on computers that need them to fix a particular problem.

Hot fixes are also available for free on the Windows 2000 download site at http://www.microsoft.com/windows2000/downloads and are grouped as critical updates, advanced security updates, and recommended updates. You can download each hot fix individually, as well as read information about the problem the hot fix addresses.

Hot fixes are given a long, but logical, name that helps to identify them. An example of a hot fix name is

   Q314147_W2K_SP3_X86_EN.exe

Broken down, the components of this example hot fix name are

- **Q314147**   Indicates the Microsoft Knowledge Base article that addresses the problem solved by the hot fix.
- **W2K**   Indicates that the hot fix is for Windows 2000.
- **SP3**   Indicates the service pack in which the hot fix is (or will be) included.
- **X86**   Indicates the hardware platform for which the hot fix is intended. X86 indicates the Intel processor platform.
- **EN**   Specifies that the hot fix is for the English language installation of Windows 2000.

Using Windows Update

Another method of keeping a Windows 2000 computer updated is to use the Windows Update Web site, shown in Figure 1-6. Clicking the Product Updates link installs a small program that scans the computer for installed components and then lists the available updates. You can choose and install any updates from this site. Windows Update is a wonderful resource for updating a single computer but can become tedious if you need to apply updates to a large network of computers. For this reason, Windows Update is best suited to small networks where you can rely on users to install updates as they are needed.

Viewing and Removing Updates

You can use the Add/Remove Programs utility in the Windows Control Panel to determine the hot fixes and service packs that have been applied to a computer

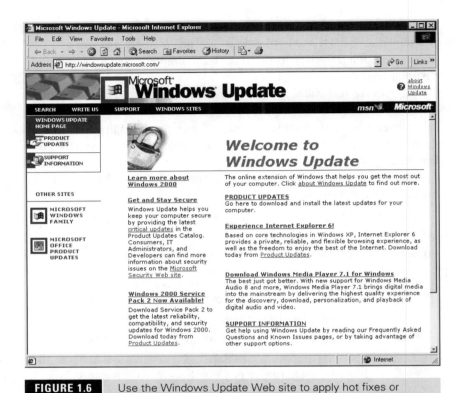

FIGURE 1.6 Use the Windows Update Web site to apply hot fixes or service packs to a single computer.

and, in most instances, to remove them as needed. Figure 1-7 shows a list of installed hot fixes in the Add/Remove Programs window.

You can uninstall any hot fix from a computer by selecting it and clicking Change/Remove. You can often uninstall service packs using the same method, but there are a few things you should be aware of when uninstalling service packs:

- You cannot uninstall a service pack that was slipstreamed with a Windows installation.

- You should not uninstall a service pack if any other applications have been installed since the service pack installation.

- By default, a backup directory is created when a service pack is installed. This backup directory is filled with files that allow the service pack to be uninstalled, should you need to do so for some reason (such as discovering that it causes problems with your system). If you disabled the creation of this backup directory during the service pack installation, you cannot uninstall the service pack.

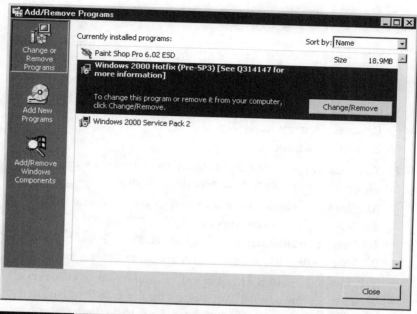

FIGURE 1.7 Use Add/Remove Programs to see what updates have been installed and to remove them.

CHECKPOINT

✔ **Objective 1.01: Install and Configure Server and Client Computer Hardware**
This objective looked at how to determine whether hardware is compatible with Windows 2000 and how to install both Plug and Play and legacy hardware in Windows after the physical installation is complete. The objective also covered advanced methods for working with device drivers.

✔ **Objective 1.02: Troubleshoot Starting Servers and Client Computers** This objective examined the Windows 2000 startup process and showed a number of ways to troubleshoot a failed startup, including advanced boot options and the System Recovery Console.

✔ **Objective 1.03: Install and Manage Windows 2000 Updates** This objective looked at the difference between Windows 2000 service packs and hot fixes. It also showed how to deploy both types of updates and how to remove them, if necessary.

REVIEW QUESTIONS

1. What hardware resource is used to signal a processor that a device needs its attention?

    A. I/O address

    B. Interrupt (IRQ)

    C. Direct memory access (DMA)

    D. Memory address

2. You open Device Manager and see that the entry for your modem has a blue "i" over the icon. What does this indicate?

    A. That there is an interrupt conflict with another device

    B. That the device driver is not installed

    C. That an updated driver has been detected and should be installed

    D. That the device is using manually assigned resources

3. You have just installed a new driver for a sound card and Windows 2000 has become unstable. You suspect the driver to be at fault and would like to remove it. What is the best way to do that?

    A. Use the Add/Remove Programs utility to remove the driver from your system.

    B. Use the Add/Remove Hardware wizard to roll back to the previous driver.

    C. Use the device's properties page in Device Manager to roll back to the previous driver.

    D. Use Device Manager to remove the device and uninstall the new driver. Reinstall the device using the old driver.

4. Which of the following commands would you use to scan all the protected system files on a computer the next time Windows starts?

    A. wfp /scanboot

    B. sfc /scanboot

    C. wfp /scanonce

    D. sfc /scanonce

5. You have downloaded a new driver for a network adapter and would like to determine whether the driver has been digitally signed before attempting to install it. How can you do this?

    A. Use the sfc /scannow command and indicate the location of the file.

B. Put the file into the %systemroot%\system32 folder and use the sigverif utility to scan all system files.

C. Use the sigverif utility and indicate the location of the file.

D. Use the Check Driver button on the device's Properties dialog box and indicate the location of the file.

6. What Windows 2000 startup file contains information about the operating systems installed on a computer and their locations?

   A. ntldr

   B. boot.ini

   C. ntdetect.com

   D. ntoskrnl

7. What Windows 2000 startup file is responsible for loading device drivers into memory?

   A. mbr

   B. ntldr

   C. ntdetect.com

   D. ntoskrnl

8. What command is used to install the Recovery Console?

   A. Winnt32 /cmdcons

   B. Winnt32 /console

   C. Winnt32 /instcmd

   D. Winnt32 /csetup

9. You have recently installed a new device driver and find that Windows will not start correctly. How could you start Windows and remove the driver?

   A. Boot into safe mode.

   B. Boot into the Recovery Console.

   C. Boot using the last-known good configuration.

   D. Remove the hardware device and start Windows normally.

10. Which of the following commands would you use to extract a service pack archive with an executable file named w2ksp2.exe?

   A. w2ksp2.exe -e

   B. w2ksp2.exe -extract

   C. w2ksp2.exe -x

   D. w2ksp2.exe -xarc

REVIEW ANSWERS

1. **B**   An IRQ is a channel used to signal that a device needs the processor's attention. PCs have 16 interrupt settings, numbered 0–15. Many Plug and Play–compatible devices can share an interrupt, and Windows will set these devices up for you. Most legacy devices will not share an interrupt, so you must configure an interrupt that does not conflict with another device.

2. **D**   A device with a blue "i" on the icon has its Use Automatic Settings option disabled, meaning that you have manually assigned resource settings. This will sometimes be the case with legacy devices.

3. **D**   If you experience problems with an updated driver, uninstall the driver and reinstall the previous driver. C is wrong because the Roll Back Driver feature is not available in Windows 2000, though it is in Windows XP.

4. **D**   The System File Checker (sfc) is used to scan protected files. The /scanonce switch causes the files to be scanned the next time Windows starts. The /scanboot switch would cause the files to be scanned every time Windows boots.

5. **C**   The File Signature Verification utility is used to verify the digital signature on a file or group of files. You can use it to scan automatically for unsigned system files (which may have been overwritten by applications but remain undetected by the SFC) and to scan a specified set of files.

6. **B**   The boot.ini file contains a list of operating systems into which you can boot and the disk location of each of those systems. During startup, NTLDR uses information from the boot.ini file to display a menu of boot choices.

7. **D**   During the final phase of system startup, NTLDR loads NTOSKRNL into memory. NTOSKRNL then loads the remaining Windows files and device drivers into memory.

8. **A**   winnt32 /cmdcons is used to install the Recovery Console so that it can be accessed during Windows startup. The other commands listed do not exist.

9.   **A** **B** **C**   Booting into safe mode may work, except that even in safe mode, certain drivers must be loaded. It is possible that the driver causing the problem may prevent loading into safe mode, but it is worth a try. Booting using the last-known good configuration is the best option if the suspect driver did not load after the last user logged on to Windows (the point at which the last-known good configuration is saved), because it will use the previous driver to start Windows. You can then use the driver rollback feature to remove the faulty driver for good. B should also work because the Recovery Console can be used to disable and enable drivers. You could then update the driver with a better version. D won't work because removing the hardware will not necessarily prevent the faulty driver from continuing to cause problems. In addition, it may be hardware necessary for Windows to start.

10.   **C**   To extract a service pack archive, use the executable filename followed by the -x switch. You will be prompted for a directory into which to extract the files. The other commands listed do not exist.

Monitoring Server
Health and Performance

ETA	NEWBIE	SOME EXPERIENCE	EXPERT
	4 hours	2 hours	1 hour

While this chapter covers only one objective, it is an important one. The performance of the servers on your network is critical, because they are used to provide most of the functions on a network, from logging in users to serving files, printers, web pages, databases, and more.

Monitor and Troubleshoot Server Health and Performance

I n this chapter, we'll look at a number of tools for monitoring the health and performance of servers running Windows 2000. Event Viewer is used to check up on logged events related to security, applications, and system activity. You'll use Task Manager to get a quick overview of current performance and to monitor the applications and processes running on a system. Finally, we'll look at the Performance tool, which has sophisticated tools for gathering and charting performance data on a system.

Using Event Viewer

Windows 2000 automatically records events that occur in various log files. Using the Event Viewer, you can view these logs for the local computer and for remote computers, as well.

> **Exam Tip**
>
> You can connect to a remote computer and view its event logs using Event Viewer. In the main Event Viewer window, make sure the Event Viewer entry is selected and choose Action | Connect To Another Computer. You can also use the Computer Management snap-in to view events for a remote computer.

Windows 2000 always maintains three distinct logs:

- **Application log**   This is a record of events generated by applications. Most Windows services write their status information to this log; some services, such as DNS, write to a specialized log. Events written to the Application log are determined by the developer of an application.
- **System log**   This is a record of events that concern components of the system itself, including such events as device driver, service, and network failures. This is the most valuable log for watching over the

general health of a server. Windows 2000 determines what events are written to this log.

● **Security log** This is a record of events that result from audit settings you configure on the computer. Depending on the way you set up auditing, this log details the successes and failures of such events as users logging on to Windows or accessing resources. We'll cover auditing in Chapter 11.

In addition to these basic logs, computers operating as Windows 2000 domain controllers maintain three other logs:

● **Directory Services log** This log contains information about Active Directory events.

● **File Replication Service log** This is a record of replication activities between domain controllers. We'll talk about this more in Chapter 13.

● **DNS Server log** This log holds events regarding the Domain Name System (DNS) service, which is discussed in Chapter 6.

Working with an Event Log

You can run Event Viewer from the Administrative Tools folder on your Programs menu. The main Event Viewer window is shown in Figure 2-1. As you can see, the various logs are shown at the left; the events associated with the selected log are shown on the right.

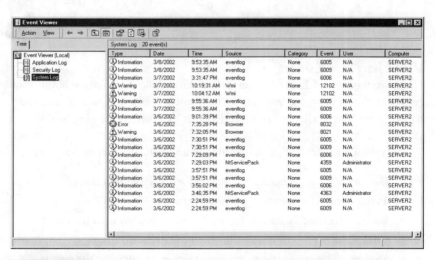

FIGURE 2.1 You should use Event Viewer to scan logs for problems on a regular basis.

Each event in a log is assigned a particular type. The types of events you see include

- **Information**   Describes a successful event, such as the loading of a service or driver.
- **Warning**   Describes an event that is not critical, but that may need your attention. An example of such an event might be a failed connection to a network service. This could be due to something as simple as a server that was temporarily unavailable, or it could indicate a more serious situation. Normally, a warning event is something you need to keep an eye on because it could turn into something serious.
- **Error**   Describes a critical event, such as the failure of a service to load. These are events that need immediate attention.
- **Success audit**   Found only in the Security log, this event is logged when an audited security function, such as a user logon, is performed successfully.
- **Failure audit**   Also found only in the Security log, this event is logged when an audited security function is not performed successfully.

Travel Advisory

Checking up on logs with Event Viewer should become a daily part of your routine as administrator. It is the single best way to monitor the health of your server and to spot problems before they grow out of hand.

Viewing an Event

The main window of Event Viewer shows some basic information about each event in column view, but you can see the same information and a detailed description by double-clicking an event to open its Properties dialog box, shown in Figure 2-2.

The following information is included in an Event Properties dialog box:

- **Date and Time**   The exact date and time the event occurred
- **Type**   The type of event (warning, error, and so on)
- **User**   The specific user account, if any, associated with the event
- **Computer**   The computer on which the event occurred
- **Source**   The application, service, or driver that logged the event

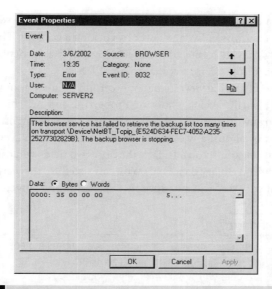

The Event Properties dialog box displays a description of the event.

- **Category**   A category for the event as defined by the source that logged the event
- **Event ID**   An event number that uniquely identifies a particular event
- **Description**   A detailed description of the event that is often useful in identifying the cause of the event
- **Data**   A binary output for the event that can be used by developers to track the cause of an event

---

Travel Advisory

The ID associated with an event is primarily intended to help technical support personnel troubleshoot problems, but these IDs are also useful to you. Using Microsoft's Knowledge Base at http://support.microsoft.com, you can search using an event ID and often find support articles on dealing with whatever problem you may be having.

Filtering and Finding Events

A typical Windows 2000 event log may have more events than you can effectively sort through just by scanning. Fortunately, Event Viewer provides some handy tools for helping to locate events. To begin with, you can sort the logs using any of the columns in Event Viewer by clicking a column. This allows you, for example, to quickly locate all the events logged by a particular source, at a particular time, or that share a common event ID.

You can also filter a log view so that only certain events are shown. Do this by right-clicking a particular log, choosing Properties, and switching to the Filter tab of the dialog box that opens, shown in Figure 2-3. You can use this dialog to filter a log view by almost any of the fields associated with an event (event type, category, event ID, and so on). In fact, the only two fields you can't sort by are the Description and Binary data fields. You can also filter the view to show only the events that occurred within a specified date and time range.

Travel Advisory

You can apply a different filter to each log file. Also, filters are persistent only within a single Event Viewer session. If you switch to another log and come back, a filter will still be in effect. If you close Event Viewer and reopen it, all filters are turned off.

Finding events works in almost the same way as filtering events. Select a log, and then choose View | Find to open a Find dialog box similar to the one shown

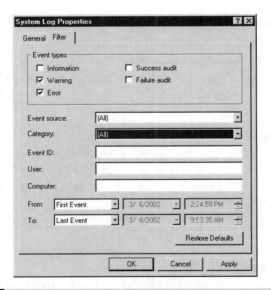

FIGURE 2.3 You can apply a filter to each log file so that only certain events are shown.

in Figure 2-4. Fill in any of the fields you want to search on, and then choose whether to search up or down relative to a currently selected event (if no event is selected, searching starts from the top or bottom of the log). Click Find Next to jump to the next event in the log that matches your criteria. The Find dialog box stays open so you can keep searching.

Saving and Loading Log Files

Event Viewer allows you to archive logs so that you can keep them around for review and reference. When you archive (save) a log file, it does not affect the events in the current file in any way. You can save a log in one of three formats:

- **Log-file format (.evt)**   Enables you to view the archived log again in Event Viewer.
- **Text-file format (.txt)**   Lets you view the information using Notepad, or any other program capable of viewing or importing text files.
- **Comma-delimited text-file format (.csv)**   Lets you import the information easily into a program that uses tables or spreadsheets, such as Excel.

To archive a log file, select the log in Event Viewer and choose Action | Save Log File As. Specify the type of file you want to create and the location and click Save.

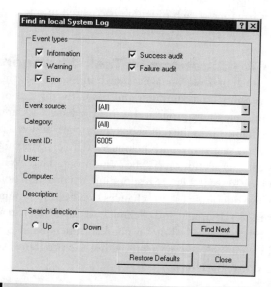

FIGURE 2.4   You can search for events using almost any event criteria.

To open a log file saved as an event log (.evt file), choose Action | Open Log File and locate the file you want to open. You must also specify what type of log it is (Application, Security, or System). A display name is suggested to match the type of log, but you can change it to whatever you like. The loaded log is displayed as a separate log in Event Viewer and is named using the display name.

Using Task Manager

Most people are familiar with using Task Manager for ending applications that have frozen up on them, but Task Manager provides a lot more than that. It lets you view and manage not only the applications running on your computer, but also the various processes that make up those applications and Windows 2000 functions. Task Manager even gives you a quick, easy way to check up on the current performance of your processor and memory.

You can start Task Manager in a number of ways:

- Press CTRL-ALT-DEL and then click Task Manager in the Windows Security dialog box.
- Press CTRL-SHIFT-ESC.
- Right-click the Windows taskbar and choose Task Manager from the shortcut menu.

The Task Manager window is divided into three tabs—Applications, Processes, and Performance—each of which is covered in one of the following sections.

Managing Applications in Task Manager

The Applications tab of Task Manager, shown in Figure 2-5, shows each program (or task) running on a computer and the status for that program. From this tab, you can start a new program by clicking New Task and entering the name of an executable file in the dialog box that opens, and you can switch to a running program by selecting it and clicking Switch To. Switching to a program is the same as clicking its button on the Windows taskbar. Windows queries programs regularly to see if they are responding. If a program does not respond to three successive queries, its status changes to Not Responding, and you can end the program by selecting it and clicking End Task. You can also end a program that is running normally, but it is not recommended. It is much better to exit a normally running program from within the program itself to give it a chance to shut down gracefully.

FIGURE 2.5   Use the Applications tab of Task Manager to end programs that are not responding.

Managing Processes in Task Manager

You can use the Processes tab of Task Manager, shown in Figure 2-6, to monitor and control the processes running on a computer. Each program that runs in Windows 2000 may run as a single process, or it may create multiple processes to carry out different functions. Windows 2000 also runs a number of processes in the background, so the list on the Processes tab is often pretty long.

Each process is listed, along with the username under which the process is running. The usernames SYSTEM and NETWORK SERVICE indicate Windows 2000 processes, while application processes usually have an actual username associated with them (because someone runs them). By default, four other columns are displayed on the processes list, each of which represents a piece of statistical data called a *counter* that indicates a particular aspect of the process. You'll learn other uses for counters later in the chapter, in the section "Using System Monitor."

The default process counters shown in Task Manager include

- **PID**   The process identifier is a unique number assigned to a process to distinguish it from other processes.

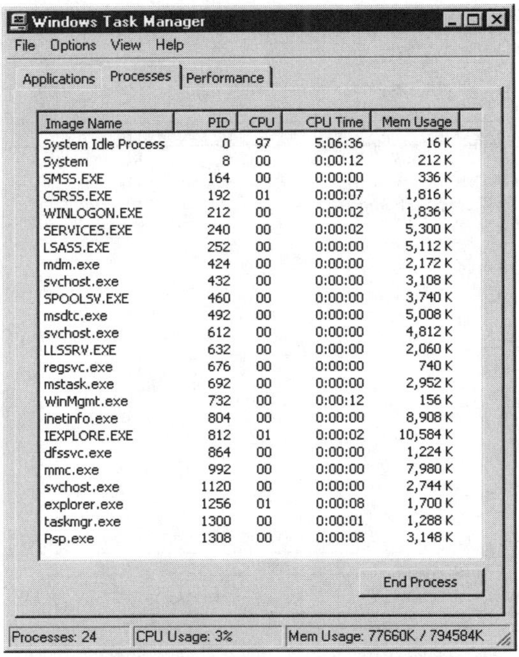
Windows Task Manager
File Options View Help
Applications Processes Performance
Image Name PID CPU CPU Time Mem Usage
System Idle Process 0 97 5:06:36 16 K
System 8 00 0:00:12 212 K
SMSS.EXE 164 00 0:00:00 336 K
CSRSS.EXE 192 01 0:00:07 1,816 K
WINLOGON.EXE 212 00 0:00:02 1,836 K
SERVICES.EXE 240 00 0:00:02 5,300 K
LSASS.EXE 252 00 0:00:00 5,112 K
mdm.exe 424 00 0:00:00 2,172 K
svchost.exe 432 00 0:00:00 3,108 K
SPOOLSV.EXE 460 00 0:00:00 3,740 K
msdtc.exe 492 00 0:00:00 5,008 K
svchost.exe 612 00 0:00:00 4,812 K
LLSSRV.EXE 632 00 0:00:00 2,060 K
regsvc.exe 676 00 0:00:00 740 K
mstask.exe 692 00 0:00:00 2,952 K
WinMgmt.exe 732 00 0:00:12 156 K
inetinfo.exe 804 00 0:00:00 8,908 K
IEXPLORE.EXE 812 01 0:00:02 10,584 K
dfssvc.exe 864 00 0:00:00 1,224 K
mmc.exe 992 00 0:00:00 7,980 K
svchost.exe 1120 00 0:00:00 2,744 K
explorer.exe 1256 01 0:00:08 1,700 K
taskmgr.exe 1300 00 0:00:01 1,288 K
Psp.exe 1308 00 0:00:08 3,148 K
End Process
Processes: 24
CPU Usage: 3%
Mem Usage: 77660K / 794584K

FIGURE 2.6 Use the Processes tab in Task Manager to view and end processes.

- **CPU** This is the percentage of elapsed time that all threads of this process have used the processor to execute instructions.
- **CPU Time** This is the total amount of time that the process has been running.
- **Mem Usage** This is how much virtual memory the process is using.

Travel Advisory

You can select from a host of other counters (22 in all) to display on the Processes tab of Task Manager. Select View | Select Columns to open a dialog box displaying the choices. We can't explain all the counters here (because of limited space and because they are not necessary for the exam), but you can find out what they are all for within System Monitor.

Ending Processes   You can end any process by selecting it and clicking End Process. Be careful when doing this, though. While Windows 2000 won't normally let you end a process that is vital to its own operation, it is easy to cause system instability by ending other processes. It is always best to let Windows 2000 and running applications manage their own processes.

You can also end a process along with all other related processes by right-clicking the process and choosing End Process Tree. For example, you could end all the processes associated with a particular application. Ending a process tree, however, is even more dangerous to system stability than ending a single process.

Changing Process Priority   The Processes tab also lets you change the priority of a process, though for the most part you will never need to do this unless you are testing programs during development. Each process is given a priority that governs how much processor time it is given related to other running processes. There are six priorities available:

- Real-time
- High
- AboveNormal
- Normal
- BelowNormal
- Low

The priorities are listed in descending order. The threads of a process with a High priority would be given processor time before a process with Normal priority. By default, the vast majority of processes are run with a Normal priority setting. The only time I can think of that you might want to assign a priority during the normal use of a server is to assign a Low or BelowNormal priority to an application that will need a lot of processor time, but that is not performing a critical task. For example, you might want to perform certain database operations in the background so that they do not interfere with other, more critical, applications.

Travel Advisory

Be extremely careful about assigning the Real-time priority, as it essentially gives a process access to the processor whenever it wants it. A greedy application can freeze out all other operations and effectively crash a system. Only administrators can assign the Real-time priority.

> ### Exam Tip
> Be sure you are familiar with the various priorities and how they relate to one another. You should also understand the ramifications of using the Real-time priority.

Monitoring Performance in Task Manager

The Performance tab, shown in Figure 2-7, features four gauges that help you check out the current performance of a computer. These four gauges include

- **CPU Usage**   This graph indicates the percentage of processor cycles that are not idle at the moment and is the prime indicator of processor activity. If this graph displays a high percentage continuously, your processor may be overloaded and you should perform some more sophisticated monitoring with System Monitor, covered later in this chapter. While Task Manager is running, an accurate miniature of this graph appears in the System Tray. Placing your mouse over it opens a pop-up tip with the percentage value.

- **MEM Usage**   This is the percentage of the paging file used for virtual memory that is currently being used. If this value runs near 100 percent continuously, you may need to increase the size of the paging file or decide whether you need more memory.

- **CPU Usage History**   This graph shows how busy the processor has been recently, although it shows only values since Task Manager was opened. You can use View | Update Speed to specify how often the values are refreshed. The High value updates about twice per second, Normal once every two seconds, and Low once every four seconds. You can also pause the updates and update the view manually by pressing F5—a useful method if you want to monitor some specific activity. The length of time shown by the graph varies depending on the update speed selected, but it is never more than a few minutes unless the update is paused. If more than one CPU is present on a system, you can set Task Manager to show a separate graph for each CPU or to show all CPUs on the same graph. Do this using the View | CPU History submenu.

- **Memory Usage History**   This graph shows how full the page file has been over time, although it shows only values since Task Manager was opened. Values set using the Update Speed command affect this history as well.

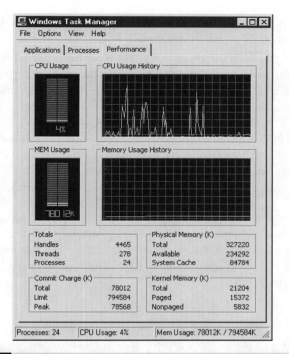

FIGURE 2.7 The Performance tab of Task Manager lets you monitor several minutes' worth of performance data.

Using System Monitor

While Task Manager is good for getting a quick overview of the current performance of your system, it pales in comparison to the functionality provided by System Monitor. System Monitor is one of two parts of an MMC snap-in named Performance, the other part being the Performance Logs and Alerts tool.

System Monitor is used to measure the statistical data generated by various components of your computer. System Monitor breaks down that data into three distinct pieces:

- **Object**   An object represents a major system resource that is either physical or logical in nature. Examples of physical objects are physical disks, processors, and memory. An example of a logical object is TCP, which represents one of the major networking protocols of the TCP/IP suite.

- **Instance**   A separate instance of an object exists for every component of the type the object represents on your computer. For example, if you have two processors installed on a computer, there would be three instances of the processor object.

- **Counter** Each instance of an object is further broken down into counters, which are the actual aspects of the object that you can measure. For example, the processor object includes counters such as %Processor Time and Interrupts/sec.

To open System Monitor, select Start | Programs | Administrative Tools | Performance. The Performance snap-in opens with the System Monitor window displayed, as shown in Figure 2-8.

The following elements are part of the System Monitor window:

- A toolbar with capabilities such as copying and pasting counters, clearing counters, adding counters, and so on. The toolbar buttons provide the quickest way to configure monitoring, but you can also use a shortcut menu (just right-click in the display) to add counters and configure properties.

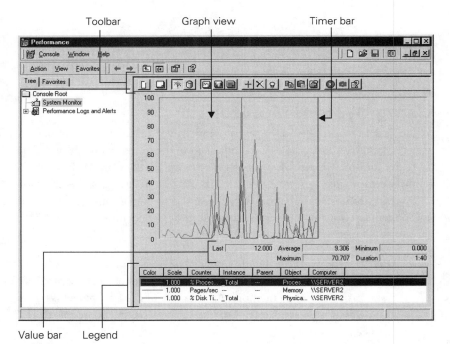

FIGURE 2.8 System Monitor is part of an MMC snap-in named Performance.

- The Graph view, where counter values are displayed as graph lines. You can vary the line style, width, and color of these lines. You can also change the color of the window and of the chart within the window.

- A Timer bar that moves across the graph, indicating the passage of each update interval. Regardless of the update interval, the view shows up to 100 samples. System Monitor compresses log data as necessary to fit it in the display. For example, if there are 1,000 samples, the display might show every tenth sample.

- A Value bar, where you see the Last, Minimum, Maximum, and Average values for the counter that is currently selected. The Value bar also shows a Duration value that indicates the total elapsed time displayed in the graph (based on the update interval).

- A legend showing the selected counters and associated data such as the computer name, parent object, and instances.

Adding Performance Counters to System Monitor

When you first open System Monitor, it doesn't look like much—just a blank window. In order to start monitoring performance, you have to add the counters you want to monitor. To do this, click the Add Counter button on the toolbar. This opens the Add Counters dialog box shown in Figure 2-9.

If you want to monitor a remote computer, make sure the Select Counters From Computer option is selected and type the full network path to the computer (i.e., **computername**). Monitoring a remote computer is a great way to make sure that the overhead created by the graphical display of System Monitor itself is not included in the performance results being graphed.

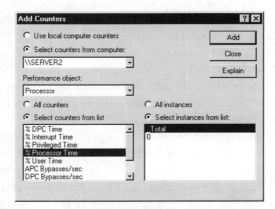

FIGURE 2.9   Add the counters you want to monitor to System Monitor.

Travel Advisory

You can launch multiple instances of the Performance snap-in. Each open version of System Monitor can be configured to monitor a different computer on the network. Many people dedicate a computer to running multiple instances of System Monitor to track the performance of various servers or workstations on their network.

Next, you'll select a performance object to be monitored (such as Physical Disk for a hard drive), an instance of that object (if there is more than one), and a particular counter to be measured. Select any counter and click Explain to open a window with a description of the counter.

You can continue to add as many counters to the display as you want, but it is best to keep the number to a minimum just to make the display easier to read. If you want to record the performance of a number of different objects and counters, it is usually better to create a log, as is described in the upcoming section "Using Performance Logs and Alerts."

When you have finished adding counters, click Close to return to the System Monitor window, which should already be graphing the counters you have selected.

Establishing a Baseline and Identifying Bottlenecks

After becoming familiar with System Monitor and the process of configuring graphs and logs, you are ready to start monitoring. The first thing you will want to do is establish a baseline of performance. A *baseline* is a measurement of performance over a reasonably long period of time that encompasses various times during which a computer is used. The baseline is a good indicator of how a computer's resources are used during periods of normal activity and also gives you a good idea of the normal performance of the computer. Once you have created a baseline (which you can do using the Performance Logs and Alerts tool described in the next section), you can then monitor current system activity occasionally using System Monitor and compare the results to your baseline to detect when bottlenecks are developing or to watch for long-term changes in performance patterns.

A *bottleneck* is a single system resource that performs more slowly than other resources. This slowest performer governs the performance of the whole computer in most instances—the weakest link in the chain, as it were. All computers have bottlenecks; after all, something has to be slowest. Performance monitoring is a matter of determining what the bottlenecks are and whether they truly present a problem.

Typically, you will monitor five major areas that tend to become bottlenecks:

- Memory
- Processor
- Disk
- Network
- Applications

Of course, identifying a bottleneck is not usually as simple as noting poor performance of a single one of these areas, as the different subsystems work together extensively. For example, a lack of memory would force the excessive use of the paging file, which in turn would result in poor disk performance. For this reason, it is important that you establish a baseline against which to compare performance results and that you compare enough results to get a clear picture.

Table 2-1 lists many of the most important objects in System Monitor, along with some of the more useful counters for each. Note that this is not a complete list of available objects and counters; this is a minimum list of items you should monitor to get a good picture of the performance of your hardware.

> ### Exam Tip
>
> For the exam, you should know the five primary areas that tend to become bottlenecks and the major counters used to monitor their performance.

Using Performance Logs and Alerts

The Performance Logs and Alerts tool, also a part of the Performance snap-in, provides a more sophisticated way to monitor performance than watching a real-time graph in System Monitor.

Performance Logs and Alerts provides three basic functions:

- You can create one or more counter logs that track the performance of specified counters over time. A counter log measures data in much the same way as System Monitor, but it logs the data to a comma- or tab-separated value file instead of displaying it. The log file can be opened later in System Monitor to view a graph of performance. You add counters to System Monitor the same way as when monitoring in real time, except that you use the log file as the source instead of the actual computer. You can also import log files into programs like Excel or Access. Logging is the perfect way to establish a performance baseline for a computer because you can log data over a longer period of time and store the results for future comparison.

TABLE 2.1 Important Objects and Counters in System Monitor

Object	Counter	Description
Cache	Data Map Hits %	Indicates the percentage of data maps that can be retrieved directly from physical memory instead of from the paging file. A higher number is better.
LogicalDisk	%Free Space	This counter shows the free space on a drive. Typically, you should watch for it to fall below about 10–15 percent.
Physical Disk	%Disk Time	This counter shows the amount of time the disk is busy servicing read and write requests. Watch for it to stay above 90 percent, indicating that the disk may not be fast enough or that there may not be enough memory on your system. Low memory situations result in large amounts of disk activity, as more paging must take place.
	Disk Reads/sec; Disk Writes/sec	These counter values can be tricky to read. For the most part, you should watch for any drastic changes in these values over time. These often indicate a low memory situation, as described in the preceding entry.
	Current Disk Queue Length	This counter represents the number of requests outstanding on the disk drive at the time the data is collected. Higher requests often mean that the disk cannot keep up with demand. Compare this value to the baseline you have established. As with other disk situations, this can indicate a disk or memory problem.
Memory	Available Bytes	This counter represents the number of bytes available at the time the data is collected. If this value falls below around 4MB, it may indicate a memory bottleneck.
	Pages/sec	This counter represents the number of memory pages written to disk in a second. It's usually recommended that this value remain below 20 pages/sec. Higher values could indicate not enough memory.
Paging File	%Usage	This counter represents the amount of the paging file currently being used. Watch for it to rise frequently above 70 percent. Consistently high values could indicate not enough memory.
Processor	%Processor Time	This counter represents the percentage of time that the processor spends on nonidle threads. Watch for it to rise frequently above 85 percent, which could indicate a processor bottleneck.
	Interrupts/sec	This counter measures the average rate at which the processor receives hardware interrupts. A dramatic increase in this value that is not accompanied by an increase in system activity often indicates that another hardware device (such as a network card or disk controller) is sending spurious interrupts.

- You can create a trace log that records detailed system and application events to a log file when certain performance events occur. This differs from counter logs in that performance is not actually measured; instead, events are recorded in response to predefined triggers. The built-in Windows 2000 kernel trace data provider supports tracing system data; if other data providers are available, developers can configure logs with those providers as appropriate. A parsing tool is required to interpret the trace log output.

- You can create alerts that trigger specified events when they detect that a performance threshold has been crossed. You create alerts by adding counters and specify a trigger value (a high or low value that, when crossed, triggers an alert). When triggered, alerts can log the event to the Windows System log, send a network message, start a counter log, or run a custom program.

The Performance Logs and Alerts tool appears as a node in the Performance snap-in, as shown in Figure 2-10. Inside this node, separate folders contain all counter logs, trace logs, and alerts configured on the system. Selecting any of these folders displays a list of available logs or alerts in the details pane.

Exam Tip

For the exam, you will not need to know details about creating and running counter logs, trace logs, or alerts. It is enough to know what each is used for.

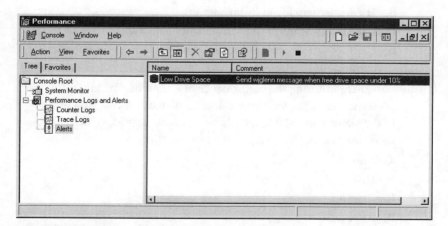

| FIGURE 2.10 | Use Performance Logs and Alerts to establish baselines and to configure alerts. |

CHECKPOINT

✔ **Objective 2.01: Monitor and Troubleshoot Server Health and Performance**
This objective looked at the primary tools used to monitor the health and performance of servers running Windows 2000. These tools include Event Viewer, Task Manager, System Monitor, and Performance Logs and Alerts.

REVIEW QUESTIONS

1. How many data samples does System Monitor display in its graph view, regardless of the timing interval you set for measurements?

   A. 50
   B. 100
   C. 500
   D. 1,000

2. One of your servers running Windows 2000 is scheduled to automatically back up several other computers over the network each night. You are checking the log for the automated backup routine and find that none of the backup jobs scheduled for the night before ran successfully. The backup log leads you to believe that the backup server had a problem accessing the computers over the network. What would you do to find more information?

   A. Use the Application log in Event Viewer.
   B. Use the System log in Event Viewer.
   C. Use System Monitor to chart network activity.
   D. Use the Networking tab of Task Manager to monitor network connections.

3. You are monitoring the performance of a computer running Windows 2000 and notice the following values consistently recorded: Physical Disk\%Disk Time >90% and Memory\Pages/sec >50. Which of the following areas do you suspect may be a bottleneck?

   A. Processor
   B. Disk
   C. Memory
   D. Applications

4. You are configuring an alert to occur whenever the free disk space on a particular drive on a server falls below 5 percent. Which of the following actions can you have the alert perform without using a custom program?

   A. Send you an e-mail message.

   B. Send a pop-up network message to a user account.

   C. Send a message to a pager.

   D. Log the event to the Windows System log.

5. The %Processor time measurement used to gauge the percentage of time the processor is utilized is an example of which of the following?

   A. Object

   B. Instance

   C. Counter

   D. Log

6. You would like to measure the amount of network activity a particular server experiences over a two-day period. What would be the best tool for this job?

   A. Task Manager

   B. Network Viewer

   C. Performance Logs and Alerts

   D. Event Viewer

7. Which of the following values for the %Processor Time counter, when measured consistently, might indicate a processor bottleneck?

   A. Above 85 percent

   B. Below 85 percent

   C. Above 15 percent

   D. Below 15 percent

8. You want to record detailed events to a log file whenever certain performance thresholds are crossed. What type of log would you configure to do this?

   A. Counter log

   B. Trace log

   C. Alert log

   D. Trigger log

9. You have configured auditing on a computer running Windows 2000 and need to examine audit events. Where would you go to do this?

   A. Security log

   B. Audit log

   C. System log

   D. Directory log

10. You would like to determine the CPU resources used by a database application on one of your servers. What tools could you use to do this?

   A. Event Viewer

   B. Task Manager

   C. System Monitor

   D. Trace Log

REVIEW ANSWERS

1. **B**   A Timer bar that moves across the graph indicates the passing of each update interval. Regardless of the update interval, the view shows up to 100 samples. System Monitor compresses log data as necessary to fit it in the display.

2. **B**   The System log of Event Viewer contains events logged by Windows 2000. This includes events related to system services and device drivers. If network access was down the night before, chances are good that the System log contains other events that may lead you to the cause of the problem. A is incorrect because the Application log contains errors logged by applications. While the Application log may contain errors related to the backup program's failure, it probably won't contain the information you need. C is incorrect because measuring the performance of your network will not likely lead you to the cause of the problem. D is incorrect because there is no Networking tab in Task Manager in Windows 2000.

3. **C**   The %Disk Time counter shows the amount of time the disk is busy servicing read and write requests. Measurements consistently above 90 percent can indicate a slow disk or not enough memory. The Pages/sec counter represents the number of memory pages written to disk in a second. Measurements consistently above 20 pages/sec often indicate not enough memory. Taken together, these two values point to memory as the bottleneck.

4. **B** **D** You can create alerts that trigger specified events when they detect that a performance threshold has been crossed. You create alerts by adding counters and specifying a trigger value. When triggered, alerts can log the event to the Windows System log, send a network message, start a counter log, or run a custom program.

5. **C** An object represents a major system resource that is either physical (such as a device) or logical (such as a service) in nature. A separate instance of an object exists for every actual object on your computer. Each instance of an object is further broken down into counters, which are the actual aspects of the object that you can measure.

6. **C** Performance Logs and Alerts can be used to record measurements to a log file over a period of time. You would then use System Monitor to graph counters from those log files. A is incorrect because Task Manager in Windows 2000 does not graph network activity and is not used for logging performance data. B is wrong because there is no such tool as Network Viewer. D is not right because Event Viewer is not used to measure performance.

7. **A** The %Processor Time counter represents the percentage of time that the processor spends on nonidle threads (i.e., when the processor is busy). Watch for it to rise frequently above 85 percent, which could indicate a processor bottleneck.

8. **B** A trace log records detailed system and application events to a log file when certain triggers occur. This differs from counter logs in that performance is not measured; events are recorded in response to predefined triggers. C and D are wrong because there is no such thing as an Alert or Trigger log.

9. **A** The Security log is a record of events that result from audit settings you configure on the computer. Depending on the way you set up auditing, this log details the successes and failures of such events as users logging on to Windows or accessing resources. B and D are incorrect because there is no such thing as an Audit or Directory log. C is wrong because the System log is used to record events generated by Windows 2000.

10. **B** **C**   Many application-specific counters, such as the CPU resources used by a program, are available within System Monitor and as columns on the Processes tab of Task Manager. A is wrong because Event Viewer does not measure performance data. D is wrong because trace logs are used to record events, not to directly record counter activity. For that, you could use a counter log.

Configuring, Administering, and Troubleshooting the Network Infrastructure

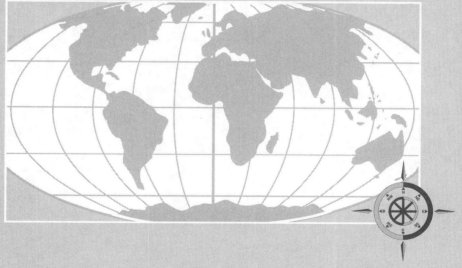

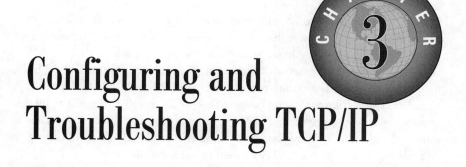

Configuring and Troubleshooting TCP/IP

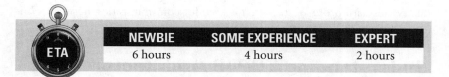

ETA	NEWBIE	SOME EXPERIENCE	EXPERT
	6 hours	4 hours	2 hours

Transmission Control Protocol/Internet Protocol (TCP/IP) is actually a suite of protocols that together offer the most stable and widely accepted networking technology in use today. Almost all network operating systems offer TCP/IP support, and many large networks, including the Internet, rely on TCP/IP for their network traffic. The various protocols in the TCP/IP suite function together to make network communication happen. This process involves a lot of activities, including resolving computer names to Internet Protocol (IP) addresses; determining the locations of communicating computers; and packaging, addressing, and routing data so that it reaches its destination successfully.

This chapter starts with an overview of TCP/IP. We'll look at basic TCP/IP architecture, explore how IP addressing and subnetting work, and examine the routing process. You'll also learn how to configure computers running Windows 2000 to be TCP/IP clients. Finally, we'll look at the various utilities used to troubleshoot routing on a TCP/IP network.

Configure and Troubleshoot TCP/IP on Servers and Client Computers

B efore you dive into setting up clients on a TCP/IP network, it's important that you have a good understanding of how TCP/IP works. TCP/IP is an industry-standard protocol stack that is used for communication between Windows 2000–based computers.

Understanding TCP/IP Architecture

The TCP/IP protocol suite includes a number of different protocols and utilities. The protocols in the TCP/IP suite are organized into four logical layers that help define their roles in the process. These four layers roughly correspond to the seven layers that make up the OSI protocol reference model you may be familiar with, but the TCP/IP model is a bit more flexible for real-world use. The four layers, indicated in Figure 3-1, are the application layer, transport layer, Internet layer, and link layer. Each of these is discussed in detail in the following sections.

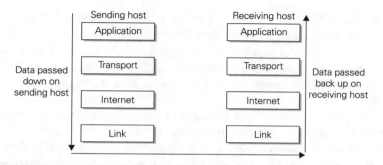

FIGURE 3.1	Packets of data are passed down the layers of the sending host and back up the layers of the receiving host.

Travel Assistance

The OSI reference model for networking protocols defines seven different functional layers, while the TCP/IP model defines four. You can learn more about these models and how applications use them with Douglas Comer's excellent three-volume set, *Internetworking with TCP/IP* (Upper Saddle River, New Jersey: Prentice Hall, 1998–2000).

Exam Tip

For the exam, it is important that you remember the four TCP/IP layers, their order in the suite, and the important protocols that make up those layers. You will not need to know anything about the OSI reference model.

Application Layer

Most applications and utilities are contained in the *application layer* and use this layer to gain access to the network functions of TCP/IP. Windows 2000 provides two interfaces that allow applications to access the rest of the TCP/IP protocol suite:

- **WinSock**   This is the Microsoft version of the Berkeley Sockets application programming interface (API), which is the standard interface used to access TCP/IP protocols.

- **NetBIOS Helper Service** Network Basic Input Output System (NetBIOS) is a legacy interface that was originally based on the DOS BIOS but added a number of functions for network access. It is still used for interprocess communications throughout Windows. The NetBIOS Helper Service manages interactions between NetBIOS and sockets.

These two interfaces form two groups of TCP/IP-enabled applications: WinSock applications and NetBIOS applications. Aside from some Windows functions and Microsoft applications, though, most applications use WinSock. A number of familiar TCP/IP applications run in the application layer; they include the Hypertext Transfer Protocol (HTTP), the protocol used to transfer data between Web servers and browsers; the File Transfer Protocol (FTP), a protocol used for transferring files between computers; and the Simple Mail Transfer Protocol (SMTP), a protocol used for sending e-mail between mail servers and from mail clients to mail servers.

Transport Layer

The *transport layer* orders communication between computers and passes data up to an application in the application layer or down to the Internet layer for network delivery. The transport layer also specifies a unique identifier for each communicating application in the form of a port, which is used to keep track of what data packets are associated with what applications.

Data delivery in the transport layer is controlled by two protocols:

- **Transmission Control Protocol (TCP)** TCP is referred to as a *connection-oriented* protocol because a connection must be established between two computers before any data is transferred. It is also termed a *reliable* protocol because it checks up on the delivery of data to a remote computer by requiring that an acknowledgment be returned. If the remote computer does not return an acknowledgment within a specified period of time, the source computer retransmits the data. Most applications use TCP to transmit data.

- **User Datagram Protocol (UDP)** UDP is a *connectionless* service— it neither establishes a connection before transmitting data nor requires an acknowledgment of receipt. This provides faster data delivery than TCP but does not offer the capability to retransmit data that is not acknowledged. UDP is often used by applications sending very small amounts of data and by applications that stream media over a network, where retransmittal of data would not be useful.

A *port* is associated with either TCP or UDP transport layer protocols and is referred to as a TCP port or a UDP port. A port can have any number between 0 and 65,535. The port numbers from 0 to 1,023 are reserved for common TCP applications. Referred to as the well-known port numbers, these are under the control of the Internet Assigned Numbers Authority. For example, the FTP Server application uses the TCP port numbers 20 and 21.

Travel Assistance

You can find information on all well-known port numbers using the Web site of the Internet Assigned Numbers Authority. The page listing port numbers is http://www.iana.org/assignments/port-numbers.

Internet Layer

The *Internet layer* is responsible for addressing, packaging, and routing the data that is handed down to it from the transport layer. There are three core protocols in this layer: Internet Protocol (IP), Address Resolution Protocol (ARP), Internet Control Message Protocol (ICMP), and Internet Group Management Protocol (IGMP).

Internet Protocol   IP is a connectionless, and therefore unreliable, protocol that is primarily responsible for addressing packets and routing them between networked computers. Although IP always attempts to deliver a packet, a packet may be lost, corrupted, delivered out of sequence, duplicated, or delayed. IP does not attempt to recover from these types of errors by requesting retransmission of the data. Acknowledging the delivery of packets and recovering lost packets is the responsibility of a higher-layer protocol, such as TCP, or of the application itself.

IP also assigns a Time to Live (TTL) value to each packet, which specifies the maximum length of time that the packet can travel on the network before being discarded. The TTL is measured in seconds, which represent the maximum time a packet can survive on a network. Every instance of IP that processes a packet decrements the TTL by at least one. Any instance of IP that examines a packet with a TTL of zero discards the packet.

Address Resolution Protocol   ARP is responsible for mapping IP addresses to the hardware addresses (or MAC addresses) of the network adapters of computers on the network. When IP readies a packet for transmission to a remote computer, it does so using that computer's IP address (you'll learn more about IP addresses later in the chapter). However, the actual network cards (and other network interfaces) on a network transfer data using long hardware addresses that ensure each network interface on a network is uniquely identified, independent of any particular network protocols.

ARP translates between IP addresses and hardware addresses by maintaining a table of mappings known as the *ARP cache*. This table is built dynamically. When ARP receives a request to translate an IP address, it checks for the address in its table. If the address is found, ARP returns the address to the requesting software. If the address is not found in the table, ARP broadcasts a packet to the local subnet; this packet contains the IP address for which the hardware address is needed. If a receiving host identifies the IP address as its own, it responds by sending its hardware address back to the requesting host. The response is then cached in the ARP table.

Internet Control Message Protocol   ICMP provides error reporting and traffic control messaging. With ICMP, computers and routers that use IP communication can report errors and exchange limited control and status information. For example, if IP is unable to deliver a packet to a destination computer, ICMP sends a Destination Unreachable message to the source computer.

Internet Group Messaging Protocol   The Internet Group Messaging Protocol (IGMP) is used by hosts to report multicast group membership to adjacent routers. Multicasting allows one host to send content to multiple other hosts simultaneously. Examples would be streaming high-bandwidth media to multiple computers, updating software on a number of computers at once, and some types of distribution lists. Typically, a group of computers becomes part of a multicast group membership so that they can be sent multicast messages.

Link Layer

The *link layer* is responsible for placing data on the network medium and receiving data off the network medium. This layer contains physical devices such as network cables and network adapters. This layer does not contain the type of software-based protocols that are included in the other three layers, but it does contain such protocols as Ethernet and Asynchronous Transfer Mode (ATM), which define how data is transmitted on the network.

IP Addressing and Routing

Every interface on a TCP/IP network is given a unique IP address that identifies it on that network. I use the term interface instead of computer or device because a single network device may actually have more than one interface on a single network (and interfaces on multiple networks), and thus more than one IP address. The Internet Protocol (IP) handles this addressing, defining how the addresses are constructed and how packets are routed using those addresses. In this section, we're going to talk about how IP addresses are assigned and how to subnet a network into segments using IP addresses and custom subnet masks. First, however, you need to know how an IP address works.

An IP address consists of a set of four numbers, each of which can range from 0 to 255. The reason for this is that each number is actually based on a binary octet, or an eight-digit binary number. Each of these numbers is separated from the others by a decimal point, so a typical IP address in decimal form might look something like 192.168.001.102. This number represented in binary form is 11000000 10101000 00000001 01100110. Computers work with the binary format, but it's much easier for people to work with the decimal representation.

In the same way that a house address has two parts—a street address and a ZIP code (the city and state are not really used anymore)—an IP address also has two parts:

- The network ID identifies the network segment on which a network interface is located. All computers on the same segment must have the same network ID, just as all houses in a specific area must have the same ZIP code.
- The host ID identifies a network interface within a network segment. The host ID for each host must be unique within the network ID, in the same way that the street address for a house must be unique within a ZIP code.

Just as two different postal delivery areas can have the same street address within them, two computers with different network IDs can have the same host ID. However, the combination of the network ID and the host ID must be unique to all computers in communication with each other.

Computers and other network devices depend on a second number called a *subnet mask* to help determine which portion of an IP address is the network ID and which portion is the host ID, as shown next. You'll learn more about subnet masks in the section "Custom Subnetting," later in the chapter. For now, just understand that the host ID is some portion of the IP address, starting at the left and proceeding to the right in the binary representation of the address. The subnet mask defines where the network ID stops and the host ID starts.

	Decimal		Binary
IP address:	185.106.34.56		10111001 01101010 00100010 00111000
Subnet mask:	255.255.0.0		11111111 11111111 00000000 00000000
Network ID:	185.106.0.0		10111001 01101010 00000000 00000000
Host ID:	0.0.34.56		00000000 00000000 00100010 00111000

Classful IP Addressing

IP addresses are organized into classes that help define the size of the network being addressed. This is called *classful* IP addressing. Five different classes of IP addresses define different size networks, capable of holding varying numbers of hosts.

Classful IP addressing is based on the structure of the IP address and provides a systematic way to differentiate network IDs from host IDs. As you learned earlier, there are four numerical segments of an IP address ranging from 0 to 255. Here, we'll represent those segments as w.x.y.z. Based on the value of the first octet (w), IP addresses are categorized into the five address classes outlined in Table 3-1.

Classes A, B, and C are available for registration by public organizations. Actually, all of these addresses were snapped up long ago by major companies and Internet service providers (ISPs), so the actual assignment of an IP address to your organization will likely come from your chosen ISP. Classes D and E are reserved for special use.

TABLE 3.1   IP Address Classes

Class	Network ID	Range of First Octet (w)	Number of Network Segments Available	Number of Hosts Available	Subnet Mask
A	w.0.0.0	1–127	127	16,777,214	255.0.0.0
B	w.x.0.0	128–191	16,384	65,534	255.255.0.0
C	w.x.y.0	192–223	2,097,152	254	255.255.255.0
D	N/A	224–239	N/A	N/A	N/A
E	N/A	240–255	N/A	N/A	N/A

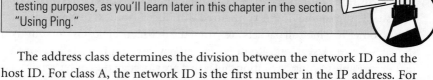

Travel Advisory

You may notice in Table 3-1 that the octet 127 is missing from the list of available IP addresses. The network ID 127.0.0.0 is reserved for testing purposes, as you'll learn later in this chapter in the section "Using Ping."

The address class determines the division between the network ID and the host ID. For class A, the network ID is the first number in the IP address. For class B, it is the first two numbers; and for class C, it is the first three numbers. The remaining numbers identify the host ID.

Network IDs are usually represented using a four-number structure, just like the IP address, but with zeros standing in for the host ID portion. As an example, the IP address 172.16.53.46 would be a class B address because 172 is between 128 and 191. That makes the network ID 172.16.0.0 and the host ID 53.46 (without a period at the end).

Understanding Routing

Routing is the process of moving information along a path from a source to a destination. On a TCP/IP network, the source and destination are called *hosts* and the information is broken apart into small packets that are transmitted between these hosts. The Internet Protocol (IP) handles the routing of all these packets for the network.

Remember that a protocol such as TCP or UDP will hand down a packet of data to IP for transmission to a remote host. IP must determine where the packet goes. First, it compares the network ID of the local host with the network ID of the destination host identified in the packet. If the two network IDs match, the two hosts are on the same network segment and the packet can be sent directly to the destination host.

If IP determines that the network IDs of the local host and the remote host do not match, that means that the two hosts are on different network segments and the packet cannot be sent directly. Instead, IP must send the packet to a gateway, which is a router connecting one network segment to another. When this gateway receives the packet, its IP protocol goes through the process of comparing network IDs to determine the best place to send the packet. If the destination host is on one of the network segments to which the gateway is directly connected, the gateway can forward the packet straight to the destination host. Otherwise, the gateway forwards the packet on to another gateway, and then perhaps another, until the packet finally reaches its destination. Each time a packet crosses a gateway, that is referred to as a *hop*. For example, if a packet must cross three routers to reach its destination, that is considered three hops.

Usually, the source host is configured with the IP address of a default gateway, a router to which all packets are sent if the destination host is not found on the same network segment. Routers (and all devices with IP installed, for that matter) are able to consult routing tables that are stored in the router's memory. A routing table holds information on preferred routes for various network IDs. This way, the router can determine the best gateway to send a packet to based on the network ID of the packet's destination host. There are two ways in which a router can build its routing table:

* **Static** A *static* router has a routing table that is constructed and updated manually. In other words, someone must actually access the routing table to create routes the router can use.

* **Dynamic** A *dynamic* router builds and updates its own routing table as it finds appropriate routes. When it finds shorter routes, it favors those over longer routes. Most important, dynamic routers can also share their information with other routers on the network. Almost all the routers in use today are dynamic routers—manual routers are just too much work. Dynamic routers use one of two common routing protocols: Routing Information Protocol (RIP) and Open Shortest Path First (OSPF).

Custom Subnetting

In the classful method of IP addressing, the number of networks and hosts available for a specific address class is predetermined from the default subnet mask for the class. As a result, an organization that is allocated a network ID has a single, fixed network ID and a specific number of hosts. With the single network ID, the organization can have only one network connecting its allocated number of hosts. If the number of hosts is large, the single network will not be able to perform efficiently. To solve this problem, the concept of custom subnetting was introduced, also known as Classless Internet Domain Routing (CIDR).

Custom subnetting allows a single classful network ID to be divided into smaller network IDs. The idea behind custom subnetting is that you take the default subnet mask used for the class to which your IP address range belongs and then borrow some of the bits used for the host ID to use as an extension of the network ID instead.

You can think of a custom subnet mask as a screen that differentiates the network ID from a host ID in an IP address, but that is not restricted by the same rules used in the classful method. A subnet mask consists of a set of four numbers, similar to an IP address. These numbers range in value from 0 to 255, though only some of the numbers in the range are actually available to use for the mask. To see why this is, we need to jump back to the binary format for just a moment. The default subnet mask for a class B network (255.255.0.0) in binary format would be

11111111 11111111 00000000 00000000

This mask specifies that the first 16 bits of an IP address are to be used for the network ID and the second 16 bits are to be used for the host ID. To create a custom subnet mask, you would extend the mask into the host ID portion. However, you must extend this by adding ones from left to right. For example, a custom subnet mask might look like

11111111 11111111 11110000 00000000

The value 11110000 in decimal format would be 240, making this IP address 255.255.240.0. Table 3-2 shows the possible values for an octet in a custom subnet mask.

In the classful method, each of the four numbers in a subnet mask can be only the maximum value 255 or the minimum value 0. The four numbers are then arranged as contiguous octets of 255 followed by contiguous octets of 0. For example, 255.255.0.0 is a valid subnet mask, whereas 255.0.255.0 is not. The 255 octets identify the network ID, and the 0 octets identify the host ID. For example, the subnet mask 255.255.0.0 identifies the network ID as the first two numbers in the IP address.

TABLE 3.2	Possible Values for Custom Subnet Masks

Binary Value	Decimal Value
10000000	128
11000000	192
11100000	224
11110000	240
11111000	248
11111100	252
11111110	254

When subnetting an existing network ID to create additional subnets, you can use any of the preceding subnet masks with any IP address or network ID. So the IP address 172.16.2.200 could have the subnet mask 255.255.255.0 and network ID 172.16.2.0, as opposed to the default subnet mask 255.255.0.0 with the network ID 172.16.0.0. This allows an organization to subnet an existing class B network ID of 172.16.0.0 into smaller network IDs to match the actual configuration of their network.

Exam Tip

For this exam, you will need to understand the binary representation of IP addresses and subnet masks, as well as the decimal representation. You will also need to know the custom subnet masks and the number of subnets and hosts a particular subnet mask provides.

Using Private Addressing

Every computer that is connected directly to the Internet must have an IP address registered with the Internet Assigned Numbers Authority (IANA). This prevents IP address conflicts between devices. If you are configuring a private network that is not connected to the Internet or one that exists behind a firewall or proxy server, you can configure devices on your network with private addresses.

Each address class has a range of private addresses available for general use:

- **Class A**   10.0.0.0 through 10.255.255.255
- **Class B**   172.16.0.0 through 172.31.255.255
- **Class C**   192.168.0.0 through 192.168.255.255

You can choose whatever range you like to use for your network and implement custom subnets as you see fit. None of these addresses is ever officially assigned to a publicly accessible Internet host.

Configuring Windows 2000 Computers as TCP/IP Clients

Configuring a computer running Windows 2000 (Server or Professional) to be a client on a TCP/IP network is straightforward. In fact, if you have a default installation of Windows 2000 and your network uses Dynamic Host Configuration Protocol (DHCP) to automatically assign IP addresses, you won't need to do any configuration at all. The computer will contact a DHCP server automatically on startup, obtain an IP address along with other TCP/IP information, and be ready to use on the network. DHCP is discussed in detail in Chapter 4.

There are times, however, when you will need to configure TCP/IP client settings yourself (as for servers that need static IP addresses), and it is not hard to do. Each network connection created on a Windows 2000 computer can have its own protocols installed, including TCP/IP. The first step in configuring TCP/IP is to access the correct network connection. Most networked computers will have only one, though some may have more than one. Choose Start | Settings | Network and Dial-Up Connections to open the Network and Dial-Up Connections window, which displays all network connections configured on the computer. Open the Properties dialog box for the connection you want to configure by right-clicking its icon and choosing Properties from the shortcut menu.

The Properties dialog box for a standard local area connection is shown in Figure 3-2. If TCP/IP is installed (as it will be by default), it is listed in this window. If TCP/IP is not listed, you will need to install it. Click Install, choose Protocol from the list of components in the dialog box that opens, and then choose the TCP/IP protocol from the list of available protocols.

To configure the TCP/IP properties for a connection, select Internet Protocol (TCP/IP) and click Properties to open the Internet Protocol (TCP/IP) Properties

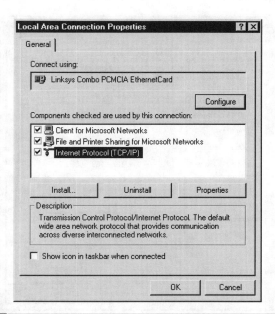

FIGURE 3.2   Use the Properties dialog box for a network connection to adjust TCP/IP settings.

dialog box shown in Figure 3-3. By default, a computer is set to obtain both its IP address and its DNS server addresses automatically. This means one of two things. If a DHCP server is configured for the network, the computer retrieves an IP address from that server during startup. If a DHCP server is not configured, Windows uses a feature called Automatic Private IP Addressing (APIPA) to assign an IP address to itself. If you have a small network and don't use DHCP, all the computers running APIPA will assign themselves IP addresses that should allow for communications between the computers. APIPA uses the IP address range 169.254.0.1 through 169.254.255.255. This range has been reserved by Microsoft so that it cannot be used on the Internet.

Exam Tip

You should familiarize yourself with the private address ranges available, including the APIPA range and the others covered earlier in the chapter in the section "Using Private Addressing." If a client is assigned an address in the APIPA range, for example, it could indicate that a DHCP server could not be contacted.

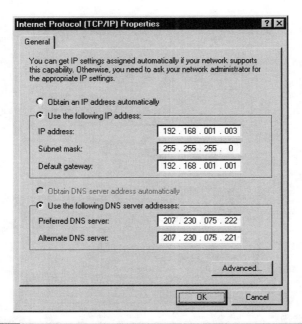

FIGURE 3.3 Choose whether to assign an IP address automatically or manually.

If your network does not use automatic addressing, or if you need a computer to use a specific IP address instead of having one automatically assigned, you can configure TCP/IP manually. Select the Use the Following IP Address option and configure the required information, including the IP address, the subnet mask, and the default gateway. Depending on your situation, you may also need to manually assign the Domain Name System (DNS) servers used by the computer. DNS is covered in detail in Chapter 6.

You can also configure a number of advanced options for TCP/IP by clicking Advanced in the Internet Protocol (TCP/IP) Properties dialog box. Advanced options include the following:

- Setting multiple IP addresses for a network connection. You can configure a single network connection with an unlimited number of IP addresses for advanced networking purposes, such as when multiple logical IP networks are in use and the computer needs a different IP address to communicate with each.

- Setting multiple default gateways. You can configure more than one default gateway to serve as a backup in case the primary default gateway is unavailable for some reason.

- Configuring additional DNS servers as backups and advanced DNS options.

- Configuring Windows Internet Naming Service (WINS) servers, which are used to resolve NetBIOS computer names to IP addresses. WINS is covered in Chapter 5.

- Configuring advanced IP security, which protects the authenticity of IP packets sent between computers on a network, and TCP/IP filtering, which is used to control the type of TCP/IP traffic that reaches a computer.

Objective 3.02 # Troubleshoot Routing

TCP/IP has been around a while and has accumulated a good number of troubleshooting utilities along the way. Most of these are command-line utilities, and you'll find them (or something very much like them) available on the TCP/IP implementation of almost every operating system. The utilities are used to display information about and test the basic functions of TCP/IP, such as routing and IP addressing.

Using Ipconfig

As its name implies, ipconfig is a command-line utility used to display and, to some extent, manage the IP addressing information for network connections. Typing **ipconfig** at the command prompt returns basic TCP/IP information, including the IP address, subnet mask, and default gateway of each network connection on a computer.

For the most part, you will use ipconfig to verify that the IP address assigned to a network connection is what you expect. For example, it could show you whether an IP address was actually obtained from a DHCP server or whether Windows used APIPA to assign an address from its private range. Sometimes, you will also use ipconfig to release the IP address lease assigned to a computer by a DHCP server and to renew that lease.

The options available for use with the ipconfig command are shown in Table 3-3.

Travel Advisory

Windows 95, 98, and Me have a graphical version of the ipconfig utility named winipcfg.exe. You can start it from the Run dialog box or the command line, and it has most of the features of ipconfig.

TABLE 3.3	Available Options for the ipconfig Command

Option	Description
/?	Displays a help message with a description of all options and the syntax for using them.
/all	Displays the full TCP/IP configuration, including DNS and DHCP configurations, and the physical addresses of adapters.
/release	Releases an IP address. If used without specifying a network connection, this option releases IP addresses for all connections. This command is used for connections that obtain IP addresses automatically.
/renew	Releases automatically assigned IP addresses and attempts to renew the address from the DHCP server or APIPA. If you do not specify an adapter to renew, all adapters are renewed.
/flushdns	Purges the DNS resolver cache, which is covered in Chapter 6.
/registerdns	Refreshes all DHCP leases (much like the renew command) and reregisters DNS names.
/displaydns	Displays the contents of the DNS Resolver cache.
/showclassid	Displays all the DHCP class IDs allowed for an adapter. This is discussed in Chapter 4.
/setclassid	Modifies the DHCP class ID.

Using Ping

Ping is one of the simplest and most important troubleshooting tools used in TCP/IP. Ping is a command-line utility that generates an Echo Request message and transmits it to a remote computer. The remote computer responds to this request, letting you know that the transmission arrived and was replied to. The output looks something like the following example:

```
C:\>ping 192.168.1.101

Pinging 192.168.1.101 with 32 bytes of data:

Reply from 192.168.1.101: bytes=32 time<1ms TTL=128
Reply from 192.168.1.101: bytes=32 time<1ms TTL=128
Reply from 192.168.1.101: bytes=32 time<1ms TTL=128

Ping statistics for 192.168.1.101:
    Packets: Sent = 4, Received = 4, Lost = 0 (0%loss),
Approximate round trip times in milli-seconds:
    Minimum - 0ms, Maximum = 0ms, Average = 0ms
```

Here, I've pinged a remote computer on a different network segment on my network (i.e., the packet had to cross a router). The information displayed tells us that three Echo Request messages were received and replied to, that the time was virtually instantaneous, and that no packets were lost.

However, merely being able to ping this remote host tells us so much more. It tells us that TCP/IP settings on both computers are correct (otherwise, neither computer could send or receive a packet). It also tells us that the router is working properly.

Suppose, now, that we had not gotten a successful reply. This could be due to a failure anywhere along the path, but we could likely use ping to isolate the point of failure. For example, if we could ping our default gateway (router) successfully, it would mean the problem lay on the other side of that gateway—perhaps on another gateway or perhaps with the remote computer itself.

You can use a systematic method of pinging hosts to determine where a routing problem lies after determining that there is a problem. Follow these steps:

1. First, try pinging 127.0.0.1. This is a reserved address, known as a local loopback address, that is a way to ping the local computer. If this ping doesn't work, then TCP/IP on the local computer is not installed or did not load properly.

2. Next, try pinging the actual IP address of the local computer. If this doesn't work, it means that TCP/IP may have loaded successfully, but that the protocol is not correctly bound to the adapter. It could be due to an invalid IP address or other TCP/IP information. At this point,

you could likely use ipconfig (discussed in the previous section) to isolate the problem.

3. Next, ping the address of the local computer's default gateway. If this is unsuccessful, it could still mean improper configuration on the local computer (maybe an invalid subnet mask or default gateway configured) or that the gateway itself is having problems. The easiest way to verify the gateway is to try pinging from another computer configured to use that gateway.

4. Finally, ping the address of the remote host. If this is unsuccessful, either one of the other gateways along the path or the remote host itself has a problem. At this point, you should probably give the traceroute command described in the next section a try.

Once you can successfully ping the IP address of the remote host, you can also try pinging the remote host using its host name or computer name. This can help you determine whether the name resolution system used on your network is functioning correctly. This is covered in more detail in Chapter 5.

Using Traceroute

Traceroute is a program that works much like ping, except that it displays information about each hop along the path to the destination computer, including the names of routers used. Traceroute can be useful in determining the exact point at which routing between two hosts fails, once it is determined that the problem actually lies between the hosts.

Run traceroute from the command prompt by typing **tracert** followed by the name or IP address of a remote host. An example of the output from a traceroute command is shown here:

```
C:\>tracert www.yahoo.com

Tracing route to www.yahoo.akadns.net [216.115.102.76]
over a maximum of 30 hops:

  1     1 ms     1 ms     1 ms  192.168.1.1
  2    14 ms    14 ms    29 ms  user-24-214-110-1.knology.net [24.214.110.1]
  3    16 ms    16 ms    16 ms  24.214.0.146
  4    22 ms    24 ms    22 ms  24.214.0.21
  5    24 ms    22 ms    22 ms  POS-1-3.pr1.atl01.netrail.net [205.215.15.93]
  6    21 ms    22 ms    23 ms  ibr01-f2-0.paxa01.exodus.net [216.32.132.113]
  7    22 ms    21 ms    21 ms  bbr01-p3-0.atln01.exodus.net [206.79.9.93]
```

```
 8    24 ms    23 ms    23 ms   bbr02-g5-1.atln01.exodus.net  [216.35.162.130]
 9    42 ms    41 ms    41 ms   bbr02-p7-0.ftwo01.exodus.net  [206.79.9.190]
10    43 ms    41 ms    41 ms   bbr01-g2-0.ftwo01.exodus.net  [216.39.64.1]
11    85 ms    80 ms    84 ms   bbr01-p5-0.sntc04.exodus.net  [209.185.9.109]
12     *        *        *      Request timed out.
13     *        *       86 ms   vl20.bas1.snv.yahoo.com  [216.115.100.225]
14    86 ms    83 ms    84 ms   w4.snv.yahoo.com  [216.115.102.76]

Trace complete.
```

As you can see, each of the numbered lines in the display indicates a router that forwards the packet along the path to its destination. The three-millisecond (ms) values on each line represent the reply time for the three Echo Requests sent to that router (just like the ping command). Finally, each line includes the name and address of the router (sometimes just the address). Lines 12 and 13 in the example show a router that could not be reached (probably because it was too busy) and was tried again.

Using Pathping

Pathping is a new utility to Windows 2000 and is based on both the ping and traceroute commands. Essentially, pathping performs a traceroute command and then pings each router that the traceroute encounters along its path to its intended destination. In addition to returning the computer name and IP address for each hop, it includes the percentage of sent and lost packets to each router. This additional information can help you determine the cause of networking problems more efficiently than using traceroute and ping separately.

Run pathping from the command prompt by typing **pathping** followed by the name or IP address of a remote host. An example of the output from a pathping command is shown here:

```
C:\>pathping www.yahoo.com

Tracing route to www.knology.net [24.214.63.162]
over a maximum of 30 hops:
  0  j [192.168.1.2]
  1  192.168.1.1
  2  user-24-214-40-129.knology.net [24.214.40.129]
  3  24.214.0.146
  4  24.214.0.21
  5  mlp1-0-0.Wspt.GA.US.knology.net [24.214.0.70]
  6  www.knology.net [24.214.63.162]

Computing statistics for 150 seconds...
            Source to Here   This Node/Link
```

```
Hop  RTT      Lost/Sent = Pct  Lost/Sent = Pct  Address
 0                                               j [192.168.1.2]
                                 0/ 100 =  0%    |
 1    1ms     0/ 100 =  0%       0/ 100 =  0%    192.168.1.1
                                 0/ 100 =  0%    |
 2   16ms     0/ 100 =  0%       0/ 100 =  0%    user-24-214-40-129.knology
.net [24.214.40.129]
                                 0/ 100 =  0%    |
 3   16ms     0/ 100 =  0%       0/ 100 =  0%    24.214.0.146
                                 0/ 100 =  0%    |
 4   23ms     0/ 100 =  0%       0/ 100 =  0%    24.214.0.21
                                 0/ 100 =  0%    |
 5   28ms     0/ 100 =  0%       0/ 100 =  0%    mlp1-0-0.Wspt.GA.US.knology.net
[24.214.0.70]
                                 0/ 100 =  0%    |
 6   27ms     0/ 100 =  0%       0/ 100 =  0%    www.knology.net [24.214.63.162]

Trace complete.
```

The full syntax for using the pathping command is as follows:

```
pathping [-n] [-h maximum_hops] [-g host-list] [-p period] [-q num_queries
[-w timeout] [-T] [-R] target_name
```

Table 3-4 defines the options used with the pathping command.

TABLE 3.4	Available Options for the pathping Command
Option	**Description**
-n	Does not resolve addresses to host names.
-h *maximum_hops*	Specifies the maximum number of hops to search. The default is 30 hops.
-g *host_list*	Allows consecutive computers to be separated by intermediate gateways.
-p *period*	Specifies the number of milliseconds to wait between consecutive pings. The default value is 250 milliseconds.
-q *num_queries*	Specifies the number of queries to each computer along the route. The default value is 100 queries.
-w *timeout*	Specifies the number of milliseconds to wait for each reply. The default value is 3,000 milliseconds.
-T	Attaches a layer 2 priority tag to the ping packets sent by the command, helping identify devices that do not have layer 2 priority configured.

TABLE 3.4	Available Options for the pathping Command *(continued)*
Option	**Description**
-R	Determines whether each device on the route supports the Resource Reservation Setup Protocol (RSVP), which allows the host computer to reserve a certain amount of bandwidth for a data stream.
target_name	Specifies the endpoint of the search, the destination IP address.

Using Route

Computers running Windows 2000 can also act as routers if they have interfaces on two or more network segments. Windows 2000 supports both static and dynamic routing. If a Windows 2000 computer is operating as a static router, you can view entries in its routing table using the route command. You can also manipulate the entries with this command, but it is easier and better to use the Routing and Remote Access Service console instead. This is covered in Chapter 13.

The syntax for using the route command is as follows:

```
Route [print][-f] [-p] [command [destination] [netmask] [gateway]
[metriccost]]
```

Table 3-5 defines the options used with the route command.

TABLE 3.5	Available Options for the route Command
Option	**Description**
Print	Displays the contents of the routing table. This option is not used with other options.
-f	Flushes all entries from the routing table.
-p	If used with the Add command, this makes a route persistent. If used with the Print command, this displays all persistent routes.
Command	Three commands are supported. The Add command adds a route to the table. The Delete command removes a route. The Change command edits an existing route.
Destination	This is the network ID to which packets might be sent.
Netmask	This is the subnet mask that tells IP how to calculate the network ID.

TABLE 3.5	Available Options for the route Command *(continued)*

Option	Description
Gateway	This is the IP address to which packets for the network being entered are sent. If this is a network to which the router is attached, the address is one of the router's own interfaces. Otherwise, it will be the IP address of another router.
Metriccost	This is the hop count used to determine the route a packet takes.

Using ARP

As you learned earlier, in the section "Understanding Routing," the Address Resolution Protocol (ARP) is responsible for resolving IP addresses to the hardware addresses of network interfaces. ARP does this initially by broadcasting resolution requests, but it also builds a cache of responses so that it does not always have to rely on network broadcasts. The arp command is used to view and manipulate this ARP cache.

An example of an actual ARP cache is shown here:

```
C:\>arp -a

Interface: 192.168.1.2 --- 0x2
  Internet Address       Physical Address       Type
  192.168.1.1            00-30-ab-08-10-9a       dynamic
  192.168.1.3            00-e0-98-03-65-2d       dynamic
```

Each line includes an IP address, the physical address the IP address is mapped to, and whether the entry is static (fixed) or dynamic (can be changed by the ARP protocol itself). A dynamic entry is automatically removed from the cache after a certain amount of time. The default value is 14,400 seconds. This helps ensure that the ARP cache is up to date by forcing ARP to repeat the resolution of hosts every so often. Though you can configure static entries within an ARP cache, it is not a good idea to do so. Not only does maintaining static entries increase the level of management required, but caches that are not continually maintained run the risk of improper resolution of addresses.

The possible formats for the arp command are

```
arp -s inet_addr eth_addr [if_addr]
arp -d inet_addr [if_addr]
arp -a [inet_addr] [-N if_addr]
```

Table 3-6 defines the options that can be used with the arp command.

TABLE 3.6	Available Options for the arp Command

Option	Description
-a or -g	Displays current ARP entries. If the host has more than one network interface, entries for each ARP table are displayed.
inet_addr	Specifies an Internet address.
eth_addr	Specifies a physical address.
if_addr	Specifies the Internet address of the interface whose address translation table should be modified. If not present, the first applicable interface will be used.
-N	Specifies the ARP entries for the network interface specified by if_addr.
-d	Deletes the host specified by inet_addr.
-s	Adds a static mapping to the ARP cache. Static mappings will remain until the system is restarted.

Using Netstat

The netstat command is actually a powerful compilation of other commands that you can use to get a snapshot view of the current state of network connections on a computer. This includes information such as currently active and listening ports. In fact, netstat is most commonly used as a security tool because it also lists any foreign addresses along with the active port connections. In addition to this information, netstat also displays statistics on network traffic and routes.

The syntax for using the netstat command is as follows:

```
netstat [-a] [-e] [-n] [-s] [-p proto] [-r] [interval]
```

Table 3-7 shows the options that can be used with the netstat command.

TABLE 3.7	Available Options for the netstat Command

Option	Description
-a	Displays all connections and listening ports.
-e	Displays Ethernet statistics. This may be combined with the -s option.
-n	Displays addresses and port numbers in numerical form.
-p protocol	Shows connections for the protocol specified by protocol; protocol may be TCP or UDP. If used with the -s option to display per-protocol statistics, protocol may be TCP, UDP, or IP.
-r	Displays the routing table.

TABLE 3.7	Available Options for the netstat Command *(continued)*
Option	**Description**
-s	Displays per-protocol statistics. By default, statistics are shown for TCP, UDP and IP; the -p option may be used to specify a subset of the default.
interval	Redisplays selected statistics, pausing interval seconds between each display. Press CTRL-C to stop redisplaying statistics. If omitted, netstat will print the current configuration information once.

CHECKPOINT

✔ **Objective 3.01: Configure and Troubleshoot TCP/IP on Servers and Client Computers** This objective took a basic look at how TCP/IP works, including how the core protocols work together, how IP addressing and subnetting work, and how data is routed between computers on a network. The objective also showed you how to configure TCP/IP on a computer running Windows 2000.

✔ **Objective 3.02: Troubleshoot Routing** This objective examined the major TCP/IP utilities used in troubleshooting basic TCP/IP and routing problems. These utilities include ping, pathping, ipconfig, traceroute, arp, route, and netstat.

REVIEW QUESTIONS

1. Which protocol of the TCP/IP suite is used to resolve IP addresses into hardware addresses?

   A. IP

   B. ARP

   C. ICMP

   D. TCP

2. You notice that network communications between a local and remote host are unusually slow and determine that the problem most likely is with a router on the network. Which of the following utilities would you use to find the router with the slow response time?

   A. Route

   B. Tracert

   C. Ping

   D. arp

3. In which of the four layers of the Internet protocol is the routing of packets between source and destination hosts handled?

   A. Application

   B. Transport

   C. Internet

   D. Link

4. The Transmission Control Protocol (TCP) is commonly referred to as which of the following types of service?

   A. Connection oriented

   B. Connectionless

   C. Reliable

   D. Unreliable

5. What are the two ways in which ARP can resolve an IP address to a hardware address?

   A. Consult the local ARP cache for a matching address.

   B. Consult the local routing table for a matching address.

   C. Send an ARP request to the destination host.

   D. Broadcast an ARP request to the local subnet.

6. Which of the following default subnet masks would be used on a computer with the IP address 136.120.004.201?

   A. 255.0.0.0

   B. 255.255.0.0

   C. 255.255.255.0

   D. 255.255.255.255

7. One of your client computers running Windows 2000 can no longer communicate with the network. Your network uses a DHCP server that allocates addresses in the range 192.168.1.1 through 192.168.1.254. You use the ipconfig command and determine that the computer has been assigned the address 169.254.0.1. What is most likely the problem?

   A. The IP address for the computer has been manually assigned.

   B. This IP address has been assigned by a malfunctioning DHCP server.

   C. The DHCP server could not be contacted, so Windows assigned itself an IP address.

   D. The IP address has been assigned by an alternate DHCP server.

8. Which of the following commands would you use to display all active connections to ports on a computer and to display the addresses and port numbers in numerical form?

   A. Netstat -a

   B. Netstat -a -n

   C. Netstat -p

   D. Netstat -p -e

9. Which of the following commands could you use to determine whether TCP/IP was configured correctly on a local computer?

   A. Netstat

   B. Ping your local IP address

   C. Ping 127.0.0.1

   D. Ipconfig /all

10. Which of the following commands could you use to display the routing table on the local computer?

    A. Route -p

    B. Route print

    C. Netstat -r

    D. Netstat -t

REVIEW ANSWERS

1. **B**   Address Resolution Protocol (ARP) is used to resolve IP addresses into hardware (or MAC) addresses. ARP is found in the Internet layer of the TCP/IP protocol suite.

2. **B**   The tracert utility reports the routers that a packet passes through on its way to a destination and the response times of those routers.

3. **C**   The Internet Protocol (IP) handles the routing of packets on a TCP/IP network. IP is the core protocol of the Internet layer.

4. **A C**   TCP is referred to as a connection-oriented service because a connection must be established between two computers before any data is transferred. It is also termed a reliable protocol because it can retransmit data to a remote computer if an acknowledgment is not returned.

5. **A D**   ARP first consults the local ARP cache to find a matching IP address. If one is not found there, ARP broadcasts an ARP request to the local subnet, trying to find a matching address.

6. **B**   IP addresses whose first octet is in the range 128–191 are class B addresses and, as such, use the default subnet mask 255.255.0.0. A and C are wrong because those subnet masks are used in class A and class B, respectively. D is wrong because 255.255.255.255 is not used as a subnet mask.

7. **C**   Windows uses a feature called Automatic Private IP Addressing (APIPA) to assign an IP address to itself when no DHCP server is available. APIPA uses the IP address range 169.254.0.1 through 169.254.255.255.

8. **B**   The -a option for the netstat command is used to display active connections and the -n option is used to order addresses and ports numerically. C and D are wrong because the -p option is used to show connections for a specific protocol and -e is used to display Ethernet statistics.

9. **B D**   Pinging the local IP address will tell you whether TCP/IP is configured correctly and working on the local computer. Using ipconfig /all will also tell you whether the correct IP address and other TCP/IP settings are configured properly. A is wrong because netstat shows you only the current state of connections to a computer. C is wrong because pinging the local loopback address (127.0.0.1) may tell you whether TCP/IP is loaded on a computer, but not whether it is configured properly.

10. **B C**   Both the route print and netstat -r commands can be used to display the local routing table. A is wrong because the -p option is used along with the Add command to make a route persistent. D is wrong because no -t option is available for the netstat command.

Managing Dynamic Host Configuration Protocol (DHCP)

CHAPTER 4

	NEWBIE	SOME EXPERIENCE	EXPERT
ETA	4 hours	2 hours	1 hour

Dynamic Host Configuration Protocol (DHCP) is an industry-standard protocol that allows the automatic assignment of IP addressing information to computers on a network. This saves you the burden of having to manually assign IP addresses and other TCP/IP information to each computer or, worse, expecting computer users to do it themselves. Using DHCP is certainly easier and faster than manual assignment, and it also prevents the introduction of networking errors due to mistyped information.

As usual, this chapter starts with a brief overview of the technology; we'll take a look at how DHCP clients obtain addresses from DHCP servers. We'll also examine how to configure a server running Windows 2000 to be a DHCP server and how to troubleshoot DHCP on your network.

Configure, Administer, and Troubleshoot DHCP on Servers and Client Computers

Objective 4.01

D HCP is an extension of a protocol named BOOTP, which was originally designed to allow diskless clients to start up and automatically configure TCP/IP. DHCP, when properly configured, can ease your administrative chores considerably. Windows 2000 Server provides a robust and scalable DHCP server implementation, and every operating system out there that supports TCP/IP can be configured as a DHCP client.

How DHCP Works

Configuring DHCP is actually a pretty simple process. On the server end, you configure a range of IP addresses, called a *scope*, that a DHCP server is allowed to assign to clients. In addition, you must specify a subnet mask and a default gateway address to be assigned. You can also assign some optional values, such as DNS and WINS server information. On the client end, you simply tell a client that it should obtain its IP address and other information automatically (the default option for Windows 2000–based clients).

Whenever TCP/IP loads on a client computer, a message is broadcast to the local IP subnet looking for DHCP servers. Any DHCP server that receives the request and has a valid scope of IP addresses responds with an offer of configuration. When the client receives and accepts an offer of configuration, it configures itself with the IP address and other information provided by the

DHCP server. This process is called *leasing* (the client leases an IP address from the server).

During the leasing process, a number of messages are sent back and forth between the prospective client and the DHCP server. These messages occur in four basic phases, named for the primary message sent in each: DHCPDISCOVERY, DHCPOFFER, DHCPREQUEST, and DHCPACK. These phases are covered in the following sections and are followed by a discussion of lease renewal.

DHCPDISCOVER

When TCP/IP is first loaded on a client configured to use DHCP, the client broadcasts a DHCPDISCOVER message to the local network segment. These messages may also be relayed to other network segments by specially configured DHCP relay agents (discussed later in the chapter). Since the client does not yet have an IP address, it includes as part of the message its physical hardware address. All DHCP servers that receive the message respond to the DHCPDISCOVER message by sending a DHCPOFFER message to the client's hardware address.

DHCPOFFER

Any DHCP server that receives a DHCPDISCOVER message, and that has an available IP address in a scope appropriate for that client, returns a DHCPOFFER message. This message is broadcast to the local network segment and includes the hardware address of the client so that clients can determine which messages are meant for them.

The DHCPOFFER message includes this information as part of a lease:

- DHCP server IP address
- The IP address being offered to the client
- The subnet mask being offered to the client
- Other DHCP information, such as default gateway and DNS servers
- The lease interval, which is the period in days or hours that the lease lasts

The DHCP Request

When a DHCP client begins receiving DHCPOFFER messages, it tests the offered IP addresses on a first-come, first-served basis. The test involves sending an Address Resolution Protocol (ARP) message to the IP address that is being offered to make sure that no other device on the network already has this address. A prospective DHCP client accepts the first DHCPOFFER message that it receives and that passes this test.

The client then responds by broadcasting a DHCPREQUEST message to the network. This message has two purposes. It serves to confirm the acceptance of a DHCPOFFER from the server whose offer has been accepted and to let other DHCP servers that responded know that another offer has been accepted. The rejected DHCP servers can then put the IP addresses they offered back into their pools of available addresses.

Acknowledgment

The final step in the DHCP lease process is for the DHCP server whose offer is accepted to return a DHCPACK message to the requesting client (ACK stands for acknowledgment). When the server sends this message, it marks the offered IP address as leased in its DHCP scope and will not reassign the IP address to another computer during the lease period. Once the client receives this message, it has officially leased the IP address from the DHCP server. The client then assigns itself the address and any other information obtained, and finishes loading TCP/IP.

Lease Renewal

Since a DHCP lease is a timed event, at some point, the lease expires and clients must either renew the existing lease or obtain a new IP address. Two values that are determined during the initial leasing process govern the renewal of an IP address:

- **T1 value**   Also called the *renewal time value*, this is set to 50 percent of the original lease duration by default. When a client reaches this point in the lease, it sends a DHCPREQUEST message directly to the server that holds the lease. If the server receives the message, it responds with a DHCPACK message (which restarts the lease period) or a DHCPNACK message (which ends the lease and forces the client to start the lease process again).

- **T2 value**   Also called the *rebinding time value*, this is set to 87.5 percent of the original lease duration by default. If a client reaches this point in the lease (because the leasing server has not responded to the message sent at the T1 value), the client enters a rebinding state and begins to broadcast DHCPREQUEST messages looking for any server that can renew its lease.

If a client's lease expires without being renewed, its IP address and other information are removed and the DHCP leasing process must start all over again.

> **Exam Tip**
>
> If, during the original leasing or during the renewal process, a Windows 2000 or XP client is unable to obtain an IP address from a DHCP server, the client assigns itself an IP address using a Windows 2000 feature called Automatic Private IP Addressing. This feature is covered in Chapter 3.

Installing and Configuring a DHCP Server

DHCP runs as a service on computers running any edition of Windows 2000 Server. A DHCP server is simply a Windows 2000 domain controller or member server that has this service installed and has been configured to issue IP addresses to clients.

In this section, you'll learn to install, authorize, and configure the DHCP service on a computer running Windows 2000. You'll also learn about configuring multiple DHCP servers on a network and about using DHCP relay agents.

Installing the DHCP Service

Before you can configure a DHCP server, you must make sure the DHCP service is installed. DHCP is not installed during a default installation of Windows 2000. Fortunately, installation is an easy process.

To install the DHCP service on a computer running Windows 2000 Server, use the following steps:

1. Click Start | Settings | Control Panel.
2. Double-click Add/Remove Programs.
3. Click Add/Remove Windows Components. This starts the Windows Components Wizard.
4. From the list of available components, select Networking Services and click Details.
5. From the list of subcomponents, select Dynamic Host Configuration Protocol (DHCP) and click OK.
6. Click Next. You may be prompted to provide the location of the Windows 2000 installation files.
7. Once files have finished copying, click Finish to close the wizard.

Exam Tip

A DHCP server cannot be a DHCP client. A DHCP server's IP address, subnet mask, and default gateway must be assigned manually.

Travel Advisory

Do not install the DHCP service on a live network without permission or knowledge that you're doing the right thing. An improper DHCP server installation can lead to disrupted network communications and improperly configured clients. Instead, experiment on an isolated computer or network segment.

Authorizing a DHCP Server

Since the DHCP communications between a client and a server happen mostly through network broadcasts, an unauthorized DHCP server (often called a rogue server) can wreak havoc on a network by assigning improper addressing information. DHCP clients assigned improper information will be unable to locate important network services or be unable to communicate on a network at all.

To fix this problem on networks running Active Directory, DHCP servers on a Windows 2000 network must be authorized in the Active Directory before they are allowed to assign IP addresses. This means that the DHCP service must be installed on a domain controller or a member server running Windows 2000.

Whenever the DHCP service on a server running Windows 2000 starts, it accesses Active Directory to find out whether it is authorized. If it is authorized, it broadcasts a DHCPINFORM message that helps it determine whether other DHCP servers are running on the network and whether those servers are authorized. If a server is not authorized (or cannot connect to Active Directory), it will be unable to provide IP addresses to clients.

Once the DHCP service is installed on a server, you can authorize that server using the following procedure:

1. Click Start | Administrative Tools | DHCP to open the DHCP console.

2. Select Action | Manage Authorized Services to open the Manage Authorized Servers dialog shown next.

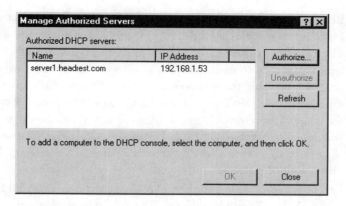

3. Click Authorize to open the Authorize DHCP Server dialog box.

4. Type the name or IP address of the server you want to authorize and click OK.

5. Click Yes to confirm the authorization.

6. Click Close.

Creating a DHCP Scope

Once you have installed and authorized a DHCP server, the next step is to create a DHCP scope, which is the pool of IP addresses that the DHCP server can assign. The creation of a new scope is driven by a wizard, making the process fairly simple. Nonetheless, there are several pieces of information that you must know before creating a new scope:

- **IP address pool** This is the range of IP addresses the server is allowed to assign. If you are using a single DHCP server, this range is easy to determine. If you will have multiple DHCP servers on your network, read the section "Using Multiple DHCP Server" later in the chapter.

- **Excluded addresses** These are IP addresses within the pool that the server is never allowed to assign. Excluded addresses, or simply exclusions, are typically addresses of computers (such as domain controllers) or devices (such as routers) whose address never changes and that do not need to (or cannot) be assigned IP addresses from a DHCP server.

- **Reserved addresses**   These are IP addresses within the pool that are leased out to specific clients according to each client's hardware address. The lease is permanent and does not require renewal. Reservations are typically used for computers such as notebooks that are moved and restarted often, but that you do not want to get a new IP address each time. If multiple DHCP servers are configured with a scope that covers the range of the reserved IP address, the client reservation must be made and duplicated at each of these DHCP servers. Otherwise, the reserved client computer can receive a different IP address, depending on the responding DHCP server.

- **Lease duration**   This is the period of time a client can keep an IP address before it must be renewed. The default lease duration in Windows 2000 is eight days.

- **DHCP options**   These are additional values that you want assigned along with the IP address. Such options include a default gateway, and addresses for WINS or DNS servers.

Once you have this information in hand, use the following steps to create a new scope on a DHCP server:

1. Click Start | Administrative Tools | DHCP to open the DHCP console.

2. Right-click the server for which you want to configure a new scope and choose the New Scope command from the shortcut menu. This starts the New Scope wizard.

3. Click Next on the Welcome page of the wizard.

4. Enter a name and a description for the new scope and click Next. These items are displayed in the DHCP console, so pick a name and description that help identify the scope.

5. Enter the starting and ending IP address for the address pool, as shown in the next illustration. The wizard automatically assigns a subnet mask based on the IP addresses you use. If you need to customize the subnet mask on your network, you can do that here. Click Next when you're done.

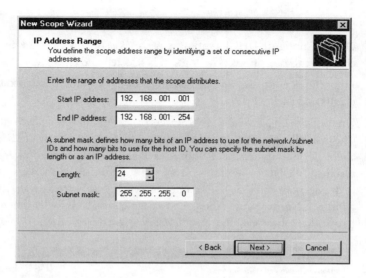

6. You can exclude one address by typing it in the Start IP Address field and clicking Add. You can exclude a range of addresses by specifying starting and ending IP addresses. You can exclude multiple addresses or ranges from a single pool. When you've finished adding exclusions, click Next.

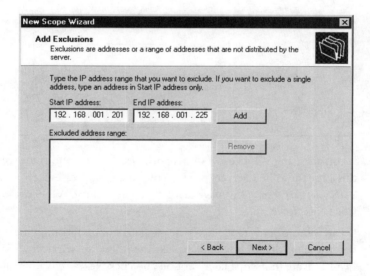

7. Set a duration for IP leases and click Next.

8. On the Configure DHCP Options page, make sure the "Yes, I want to configure these options now" option is selected and click Next.

9. Enter the IP addresses for any default gateways you want assigned to clients and click Next.

10. On the Domain Name and DNS Servers page, you can specify two settings. The first is the parent domain name that you want passed down to DHCP clients. The second is the IP addresses of any DNS servers you want assigned to DHCP clients. If you are not sure of the DNS servers' IP addresses, you can type their names and click Resolve to look up those addresses. Normally, the values on this page are used only when you need to override values set at the server level. Click Next when you're done.

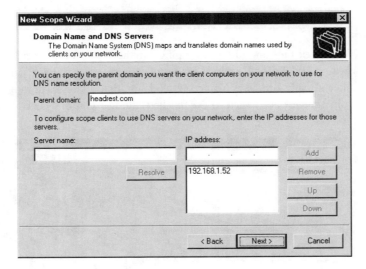

11. If you are using WINS on your network (see Chapter 5 for more on this), use the WINS Servers page to enter the IP addresses for your WINS servers. Leave this page blank if you do not use WINS servers. Click Next to go on.

12. If you want to activate the scope immediately upon finishing the wizard, select that option and click Next. Otherwise, select the "No, I will activate this scope later" option and click Next. Activating and deactivating scopes outside the wizard's interface are discussed in the upcoming section "Activating and Deactivating a Scope."

13. Click Finish to return to the DHCP console.

Managing Scopes

Once you have created one or more scopes, you'll manage them using the DHCP console, shown in Figure 4-1. As you can see, a container for each scope appears inside the container for the server on which the scope is configured. Right-click the scope container and choose Properties from the shortcut menu to open a Properties dialog box that lets you change many of the options you set during the creation of the scope, including the scope's name, description, address range, lease duration, and DNS information.

Within a scope container, you'll find four entries:

- **Address Pool**   Select this to display the IP addresses configured for the scope. Right-click the Address Pool entry and choose New Exclusion Range to add exclusions to a scope.

- **Address Leases**   Select this entry to display information on all IP addresses currently leased out to clients. Information includes the client's name and IP address, and the duration of the lease.

- **Reservations**   Select this entry to display all the reserved IP addresses in effect for the scope. Right-click the entry and choose New Reservation to add IP addresses to the reservation list.

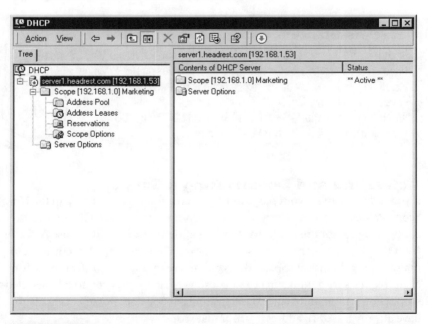

FIGURE 4.1   Use the DHCP console to manage all the scopes on a server and even to manage scopes on other servers.

- **Scope Options** Select this entry to view the optional TCP/IP information (i.e., everything besides the IP address and subnet mask) that the DHCP server is configured to assign to clients. Right-click the entry and choose Configure Options to choose from a long list of additional options you can assign to clients.

The Server Options entry doesn't fall under a particular scope. Rather, it is associated with a server and applies to all scopes on the server. The options you can configure using this entry are the same as the options configured using the Scope Options entry. The difference is that scope options apply only to the scope for which they are configured; server options act as the default options for all scopes unless conflicting scope options are set. In this case, scope options override server options. Table 4-1 list the important options supported by Microsoft clients, though this is a small subset of the actual options available.

Exam Tip

On the exam, pay attention to whether a question specifies scope or server options.

Travel Assistance

In addition to the basic options, such as default gateways and DNS information, there are a huge number of options you can assign using DHCP. While you don't need to know all the scope options for the exam and may never need to apply them on your own network, you can find detailed information on all the options in the "Standard DHCP and BOOTP Options" section of the built-in DHCP help files.

Activating and Deactivating a Scope

If you did not activate your scope during its creation (as the last step of the New Scope Wizard), you can easily activate it from within the DHCP console after configuring its options. To activate a scope, right-click it and choose Activate from the shortcut menu. For a scope that is already active, a Deactivate command appears in the same place that you can use to stop a scope from accepting client requests without having to stop a server. This allows you to take selected scopes down for maintenance. Deactivating a scope does not affect clients that have already leased IP addresses from that scope.

TABLE 4.1	Important DHCP Options
Option	**Description**
003 Router	The IP address of the default gateway to be used by the client.
006 DNS	The IP address of the DNS server.
015 Domain Name	The DNS domain name the client should use.
044 WINS/NBNS Servers	The IP address of the WINS server.
046 WINS/NBT Node Type	The NetBIOS node type. Node types are discussed in Chapter 5.
047 NetBIOS Scope ID	The NetBIOS scope ID. NetBIOS over TCP/IP will communicate only with other NetBIOS clients using the same scope ID.

Using Multiple DHCP Servers

Unless you are managing a small network on a single subnet, you will likely have to use multiple DHCP servers on your network. Even if you are managing a single subnet, you may want to use more that one DHCP server to provide a level of fault tolerance should one DHCP server fail.

There are a few general rules you need to be familiar with when using multiple servers. First, you must create a scope on every DHCP server. If you are configuring two or more DHCP servers, even on a single subnet, each must have its own scope and you should plan the division of available IP addresses accordingly. DHCP servers do not share scope information, so you must make sure that addresses are not duplicated in the IP address pools you allocate for each server.

You must also create a separate scope for each subnet on a network. You can create multiple scopes for a subnet, but you can create only one scope for each subnet on a particular server. To configure multiple scopes for a subnet, you must configure each scope on a different server.

Exam Tip

One recommended practice is that each DHCP server should be configured with one scope that includes 75 percent of the available IP addresses for the local subnet and one scope that includes 25 percent of the available IP addresses for one remote subnet. This way, the available IP addresses for a subnet are not managed by a single server and a client can still retrieve an IP address even if the DHCP server on the local subnet is down. This practice requires that routers between the subnets be configured as DHCP relay agents, as described in the next section.

Microsoft recommends the use of *superscopes* when you have more than one DHCP server on a subnet. A superscope is a feature of the Windows 2000 implementation of DHCP that lets you use more than one scope for a single subnet. A superscope contains a collection of child scopes that are manageable as a single entity. You can manage the IP address assignment of all child scopes from within the superscope, but you must manage other scope options within the child scopes themselves.

Superscopes are useful in the following situations:

- When more DHCP clients are added to a network than were originally planned, requiring the addition of a new scope
- When the IP addresses on a network must be renumbered
- When two or more DHCP servers exist on the same subnet, such as for the purpose of fault tolerance

Using DHCP Relay Agents

Since most of the communications between DHCP servers and clients rely on network broadcasts, those communications are restricted to the local subnet unless the routers between subnets are configured to relay those broadcasts. For the most part, you will probably be using dedicated hardware routers on your network. If this is the case, you must make sure that those routers are able to pass DHCP/BOOTP broadcast messages.

Travel Assistance

In order to pass DHCP/BOOTP broadcasts, routers must conform to the RFC (Request for Comment) 1542. You can find more information on this at http://www.ietf.org/rfc.html. You can determine support for particular hardware by consulting your hardware documentation.

Windows 2000 computers that have network interfaces on more than one subnet can be configured as routers that can pass DHCP/BOOTP broadcasts. Computers configured this way are called DHCP Relay Agents. To configure a Windows 2000 computer that is already set up as a router to also be a DHCP Relay Agent, use the following steps:

1. Click Start | Programs | Administrative Tools | Routing and Remote Access.

2. In the console tree, click the *servername*\IP Routing\General entry.

3. Right-click General and choose New Routing Protocol from the shortcut menu. This opens the Select Routing Protocol dialog box.

4. Select DHCP Relay Agent and click OK.

Troubleshooting DHCP

For the most part, you won't have to do too much troubleshooting of your DHCP service. Assuming that your network is in good working order (i.e., clients and servers can communicate with one another) and that you have configured your DHCP servers and clients correctly, the service should experience few problems. Nonetheless, you may occasionally experience problems with DHCP that require a bit of troubleshooting. The following sections describe how you can use Event Viewer and System Monitor to check up on DHCP and some advanced DHCP troubleshooting tools.

Finding DHCP Events in Event Viewer

Any errors or warnings that occur within the DHCP service (such as the failure of the service to load) are logged to the Windows 2000 system log, just as with any other service. When you check up on your event logs each day (you are doing that, right?), you should see any problems noted with the DHCP service. See Chapter 2 for more on using Event Viewer.

Monitoring DHCP with System Monitor

System Monitor, which is also discussed in detail in Chapter 2, lets you measure the performance of many different aspects of your system using counters. System Monitor includes a large number of counters that can be used to monitor DHCP server activity. While the full list is too large to include here, Table 4-2 lists some of the more important DHCP counters.

DHCP Logging

DHCP on Windows 2000 includes the ability to generate an audit log for the DHCP service. These logs include detailed descriptions of DHCP activity, including leases and renewals, starting and stopping the DHCP service, and server error messages. Events in the log also indicate the date and time of the event, as well as the full identity of the client involved (IP address, name, and hardware address).

DHCP logging is enabled by default. You can enable and disable logging by right-clicking a DHCP server in the DHCP snap-in and choosing Properties from the shortcut menu. On the General tab of the Properties dialog, use the Enable DHCP Audit Logging option.

TABLE 4.2	Important DHCP Server Counters in System Monitor

Counter	Description
Object\Packets Received/sec	The average number of DHCP messages received by the server. You should compare this number against a baseline measurement to determine unusual levels of DHCP activity.
Object\Packets Expired/sec	The average number of DHCP messages that expire each second because they were held in the DHCP server's queue for too long before being serviced. If this number is high compared to a baseline measurement, it may indicate a problem with server response time.
Object\Nacks/sec	The average number of negative acknowledgments per second. A high number could indicate that many computers are moving between network segments (such as with notebooks) or that there is a configuration problem.
Object\Declines/sec	The average number of declines received from clients because an invalid IP address was offered. A high number might indicate conflicting assignments from DHCP servers.

By default, DHCP logs are stored in the %systemroot%\system32\dhcp folder, and you can open them using Notepad. You can also change the storage location by right-clicking a server in the DHCP console and choosing Properties. In the Properties dialog box that opens, switch to the Advanced tab and indicate a new audit log file path.

Conflict Detection

Conflict detection is a useful tool for determining whether a server is attempting to lease conflicting IP addresses. By default, conflict detection is turned off, but you can enable it on the Advanced tab of a server's Properties dialog box in the DHCP console by setting the Conflict Detection Attempts value to anything greater than 0. The value indicates the number of times the DHCP service will test a new IP address before it is assigned to a client. Testing is done by pinging the address to see whether it is already assigned.

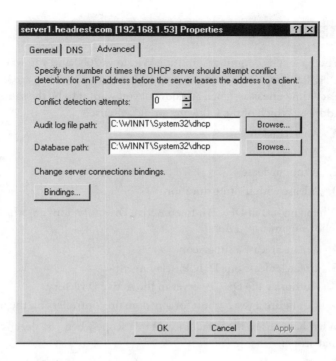

Exam Tip

You should turn on conflict resolution for a server only when actively testing for the assignment of conflicting IP addresses, as pinging each address can add considerably to your network traffic. Be sure to turn conflict detection off when you have finished troubleshooting a problem.

CHECKPOINT

✔**Objective 4.01: Configure, Administer, and Troubleshoot DHCP on Servers and Client Computers** This objective provided an overview of how DHCP clients and servers communicate. It also looked at how to install the DHCP service on a Windows 2000 computer, how to create and manage DHCP scopes, and issues regarding using multiple DHCP servers.

REVIEW QUESTIONS

1. You have four computers running Windows 2000 and you want to use DHCP to give them each a unique address whenever they are started. Each time one is assigned an address, you want it to be the same address. Which of the following would you use?

   A. An exclusion

   B. A reservation

   C. A unique lease

   D. A lease with infinite duration

2. When you install DHCP into an Active Directory domain, which of the following must you do?

   A. Create at least a superscope.

   B. Create at least one DHCP Relay Agent.

   C. Authorize the DHCP server in the Active Directory.

   D. Configure a reservation for any domain controllers on the network.

3. What happens to the current leases in a scope when you deactivate that scope?

   A. Nothing. Clients continue to use those leases until the lease expires.

   B. Clients are given new leases from another scope.

   C. Current leases are revoked immediately.

   D. You cannot deactivate a scope with current leases.

4. Which of the following messages is used to deliver a new IP address, subnet mask, and other information to a prospective DHCP client?

   A. DHCPDISCOVERY

   B. DHCPOFFER

   C. DHCPREQUEST

   D. DHCPACK

5. What type of message does a prospective DHCP client use to test an offered IP address to see if it has already been assigned to another client?

   A. ARP

   B. DHCPTEST

   C. PING

   D. DHCPREQUEST

6. A computer is configured with a lease of ten days. At what point will that computer first try to renew that lease, assuming the default settings?

   A. Three days
   B. Five days
   C. Seven days
   D. Eight days

7. Which of the following must you do in order to use a DHCP scope?

   A. Create the scope.
   B. Authorize the scope.
   C. Activate the scope.
   D. Register the scope.

8. What is the default lease duration used by a Windows 2000 DHCP server?

   A. Three days
   B. Five days
   C. Eight days
   D. Ten days

9. You have a small network with two subnets. You have configured a DHCP server for each subnet (named DHCP1 and DHCP2) and have made sure that the router between the subnets can pass DHCP requests. What would be the most effective way to configure the scopes on these servers?

   A. Create one scope on each server that includes all the assignable IP addresses for each server's own subnet.
   B. Create one scope on each server that includes all the assignable IP addresses for each server's own subnet. Then, create a superscope on each server that includes the scopes of both servers.
   C. Create two scopes on each server: one that includes 75 percent of the IP addresses to be assigned to the local subnet and one that includes 25 percent of the addresses for the remote subnet.
   D. Create two scopes on each server: one that includes 50 percent of the IP addresses to be assigned to the local subnet and one that includes 50 percent of the addresses for the remote subnet.

10. A computer with a lease of eight days tried to renew its lease at four days, when 50 percent of the lease had expired. The leasing DHCP server has not responded. At what point will the computer begin

broadcasting DHCPREQUEST messages in an attempt to renew its lease from other servers?

A. At 50 percent of the remaining time since the T1 value, or six days

B. At 75 percent of the original lease duration, or six days

C. At 87.5 percent of the original lease duration, or seven days

D. When the original lease expires, or eight days

REVIEW ANSWERS

1.   **B**   A reservation is an IP address within the pool that is leased out to a specific client according to that client's hardware address. The lease is permanent and does not need to be renewed. Reservations are typically used for computers such as notebooks that are moved and restarted often.

2.   **C**   DHCP servers on a Windows 2000 network using Active Directory must be authorized in Active Directory before they are allowed to assign IP addresses. This means that the DHCP service must be installed on a domain controller or a member server running Windows 2000.

3.   **A**   When you deactivate a scope, it prevents any new clients from receiving leases from that scope. Current leases are unaffected and clients can go on using leased IP addresses. Should a scope remain inactive until a client's lease expires, renewal of that lease will fail, and the client will begin the lease process again and obtain a lease from a different scope, if one is available.

4.   **B**   Any DHCP server that receives a DHCPDISCOVER message, and that has an available IP address in a scope appropriate for the subnet, returns a DHCPOFFER message. This message is broadcast to the local network segment and includes the hardware address of the client so that clients can determine which messages are meant for them.

5.   **A**   When a DHCP client receives a DHCPOFFER message, it tests the offered IP addresses by sending an Address Resolution Protocol (ARP) message to the IP address that is being offered. B is wrong because there is no such message. C and D are wrong because PING and DHCPREQUEST messages are not used by the client to test IP addresses. PING messages are used by a server to test IP addresses when conflict detection is turned on.

6. **B** The renewal time value (T1) for a client is set to 50 percent of the original lease duration. At this point, the client tries to renew its lease by sending a DHCPREQUEST message to the leasing server.

7. **A C** In order to use a scope, it only needs to be created and activated. B is wrong because scopes do not need to be authorized; only DHCP servers require authorization. D is wrong because there is no such thing as registering a scope.

8. **C** Windows 2000 DHCP servers provide eight-day leases by default, though you can change this value.

9. **C** A commonly recommended practice is that each DHCP server should be configured with one scope that includes 75 percent of the available IP addresses for the local subnet and one scope that includes 25 percent of the available IP addresses for one remote subnet. This way, a client can still retrieve an IP address even if the DHCP server on the local subnet is down. This practice requires that routers between the subnets be configured as DHCP relay agents.

10. **C** The rebinding time value (T2) is set to 87.5 percent of the original lease duration by default. If a client reaches this point in the lease (because the leasing server has not responded to the message sent at the T1 value), the client enters a rebinding state and begins to broadcast DHCPREQUEST messages looking for any server that can renew its lease.

Managing Windows Name Resolution

CHAPTER 5

	NEWBIE	SOME EXPERIENCE	EXPERT
ETA	3 hours	2 hours	1 hour

Name resolution is one of the more important processes on a network. As you learned in Chapter 3, the Internet Protocol in TCP/IP identifies computers on a network using IP addresses. In order to make identifying computers a bit friendlier to people, computers are given names. Because of this, some system needs to be in place to translate (or resolve) computer names into IP addresses. One of the two types of names a computer can be given is called a NetBIOS name, and there are a number of methods for providing NetBIOS name resolution. These methods are the focus of this chapter. The other type of computer name, a host name, is covered in Chapter 6.

Objective 5.01

Troubleshoot Name Resolution on Client Computers

In order to troubleshoot name resolution on a client computer, you must first understand the basic principles of the name resolution system in use on a network. Windows 2000 networks use two basic systems. The first, and widely preferred, method is the Domain Name System (DNS), a long-time Internet standard that has now become the standard on networks running Windows 2000. The second type of name is NetBIOS, a fast and simple naming system that has been used since the early days of Microsoft networking.

While Microsoft is clearly trying to push NetBIOS to the sidelines as a mainstream naming convention, it will continue to be used, particularly on networks with computers running earlier versions of Windows than Windows 2000. Even Windows 2000 computers still have NetBIOS names to be compatible with earlier versions, though these names now take second place in importance to computers' DNS names. And as an administrator, you will likely find some form of NetBIOS name resolution system in place on your network.

Resolving NetBIOS Names

Over the years that NetBIOS has been in use, there have been several methods for resolving NetBIOS names. These include simple broadcasts by clients looking for computers, static files named LMHOSTS files that contain name–to–IP address mappings, and dynamic databases of mappings managed by the Windows Internet Naming System (WINS). We'll talk about each of these resolution methods in the following sections.

Travel Advisory

Although we've been saying that a NetBIOS name is given to a computer, this is not quite accurate. A NetBIOS name is a unique 16-byte address that is used to identify a NetBIOS resource on a network. An example of such a resource might be the Server service on a Windows computer. A computer can actually have a number of different resources available, each of which is represented by a different NetBIOS name. The computer name given to a Windows computer can be up to 15 characters. Each service that runs on the computer is given a NetBIOS name that uses this 15-character name plus an extra sixteenth character that identifies the service. For example, the Messenger service running on a computer named server1 would be given the NetBIOS name server1<03>, where <03> is the special sixteenth byte character given to the name to indicate that service.

NetBIOS Name Cache

Whenever a Windows computer successfully resolves a NetBIOS name through whatever method, it stores that name and the resolved IP address in a special cache in its memory. Since this NetBIOS cache holds already-resolved names, the cache is the first place that a computer checks whenever it needs to resolve a name. If the name is already in the cache, the resolution is instant and there is no need to waste network bandwidth resolving the name by another method.

Unfortunately, since the cache is kept in memory, it is not permanent but is cleared whenever a computer is restarted. In addition to this, most entries in the NetBIOS cache are kept only a brief time anyway before they are expired. By default, Windows 2000 computers cache remote NetBIOS names for 600 seconds. This keeps the information in the cache up to date.

Exam Tip

You can view the contents of a NetBIOS name cache by typing **nbtstat -c** at the command prompt. The results show the NetBIOS names in the cache, the IP address to which the names are mapped, and the life of each entry (the time before it is expired).

NetBIOS Broadcasts

If a computer does not find a suitable entry in its NetBIOS name cache, it can send a broadcast message (called a NAME QUERY REQUEST message) to the local IP subnet to resolve the name. If a computer on the subnet receives the message and has the correct NetBIOS name, it responds by sending back a

POSITIVE NAME QUERY RESPONSE message containing its IP address. The sending computer then updates its NetBIOS cache and can begin communications with the resolved computer.

The problem with using the broadcast method is that broadcasts are normally confined to the local subnet. On a network with multiple subnets, computers are unable to resolve names of computers on remote subnets using a broadcast. This problem is solved by using either an LMHOSTS file or a WINS server, discussed in the upcoming sections.

LMHOSTS Files

An LMHOSTS file is a file with static (unchanging) mappings of NetBIOS names and IP addresses. Each entry on an LMHOSTS file consists of a NetBIOS name, its corresponding IP address, and one or more optional keywords that help define the entry. When using an LMHOSTS-based naming solution, each computer has its own LMHOSTS file and can use it to resolve NetBIOS names. Here is a sample of entries from an LMHOSTS file:

```
192.168.3.82      sales_DC        #PRE      #DOM:networking
192.168.3.168     Exchange01      #PRE      # source server
192.168.3.201     Jerry
192.168.3.205     server1         #PRE

#INCLUDE \\server1\naming\lmhosts
```

Table 5-1 lists the important keywords that you can use in an LMHOSTS file.

TABLE 5.1	Commonly Used Keywords in LMHOSTS Files
Keyword	**Description**
#PRE	Specifies that an entry should be preloaded into the NetBIOS name cache during initialization. This makes the name accessible immediately by the computer without having to parse the LMHOSTS file.
#DOM:domainname	Specifies that the entry is a domain controller.
#BEGIN_ALTERNATIVE #END_ALTERNATIVE	Begins and ends a section of the LMHOSTS file used to group multiple #INCLUDE statements, in case the location named in the main include entry is not available for some reason.
#INCLUDE	Loads the entries from a separate LMHOSTS file on another server. This allows you to, for example, keep a centralized LMHOSTS file that the LMHOSTS files on individual computers load during initialization. You should use this keyword along with the #PRE keyword to load the IP address of the computer where the file is stored.

TABLE 5.1	Commonly Used Keywords in LMHOSTS Files *(continued)*
Keyword	**Description**
#MH	MH stands for multihomed, a designation for a computer with interfaces on more than one network segment. This entry is used to specify multiple entries for a computer with more than one network interface and IP address.

WINS Servers

Letting computers resolve NetBIOS names through broadcast is okay on small networks using a single subnet, but on larger networks it just isn't feasible. Using LMHOSTS files will work, but it quickly becomes complicated, since you have to maintain LMHOSTS files on every computer or coordinate centralized LMHOSTS files. To address these limitations, the Windows Internet Naming Service (WINS) was introduced. WINS is a database-driven service that tracks NetBIOS names and IP addresses. Clients communicate directly with a WINS server to resolve names. This eliminates the problem with multiple subnets and is not as difficult to maintain as an elaborate LMHOSTS configuration.

WINS Name Resolution   WINS Name Resolution is a much more elegant solution than using either broadcasts or LMHOSTS files, because of the reduction in administrative overhead and because of its scalability to larger networks.

WINS clients are configured with the IP address of one or more WINS servers on a network. Because of this, they can initiate communication directly with a WINS server. When a WINS client needs to resolve a NetBIOS name, it first checks its NetBIOS name cache to see if the name has already been resolved. If the name is not present in the cache, the client sends a NAME QUERY REQUEST message to its primary WINS server asking for a resolution. If the WINS server has a mapping for the requested name, it transmits the IP address back to the WINS client using a POSITIVE NAME QUERY RESPONSE message. The client can then communicate directly with the resolved computer.

If the WINS server does not have a mapping in its database, it sends a NEGATIVE NAME QUERY RESPONSE message to the client. In this case, the client will use other WINS servers, if it has others configured. A client can use up to 12 WINS servers, but using multiple WINS servers can cause a significant delay in name resolution. If no WINS server is available, the client will resort to another method of resolution, such as a broadcast.

The exact method used for name resolution depends on how the client is configured. This configuration is referred to as the client's *node type*. There are six node types available; they are listed in Table 5-2.

TABLE 5.2	NetBIOS Node Types

Node Type	Description
B node	A B node client always tries broadcasts first for name registration and resolution if no match is found in its NetBIOS name cache. If the broadcast is unsuccessful, the client will try an LMHOSTS file, then a HOSTS file, and then a DNS server, if the client is configured to use any of those.
P node	A P node client always uses a name server such as WINS for registration and resolution if no match is found in its NetBIOS name cache. If no name server is found, it will then try a HOSTS file and a DNS server, if so configured.
M node	M node clients use only broadcasts for name registration, if no match is found in the NetBIOS name cache. For resolution, M node clients attempt to use broadcasts first and then use a name server for resolution if the broadcast fails.
Modified B node	Modified B node clients use only broadcast for name registration. For resolution, they try a broadcast first and then switch to an LMHOSTS file if the broadcast fails. This is the default node type for a Windows computer that is not a WINS client. While the exam and product documentation make a distinction between B node and modified B node, there is no practical difference in day-to-day use.
H node	H node clients use only a WINS server for name registration, if no match is found in the NetBIOS name cache. For resolution, they first attempt to use a WINS server. If that fails, they will try a broadcast instead.
Microsoft enhanced H node	This type of client works just like the H node client. However, if both the WINS server and the broadcast fail to resolve a name, enhanced H node clients also try LMHOSTS files, DNS queries, and then a HOSTS file (discussed in Chapter 6), in that order.

WINS Name Registration and Renewal   Perhaps the best part of using WINS is that client computers register their own names and IP addresses directly with the WINS server automatically, eliminating the need for you to enter them manually. Whenever a client computer starts up, it registers its name and IP address with a WINS server by sending a NAME REGISTRATION REQUEST message. The WINS server checks its database to see whether the computer name or IP address has already been registered. If neither have, the server sends a POSITIVE NAME REGISTRATION RESPONSE message to the client and all is done.

If the name or IP address has been registered, the server sends a series of test messages to the registered client. If the target computer returns an acknowledgment message, the WINS server then sends a NEGATIVE NAME REGISTRATION RESPONSE to the client that attempted to register the name, preventing the client's information from being added to the WINS database. If the test messages that the WINS server sends out are not answered, the WINS server deletes the erroneous information from its database and goes on to assign the name and IP address to the client that attempted to register the name.

Whenever names and IP addresses are registered with a WINS server, the entry is assigned a Time to Live (TTL) value that specifies the duration for which the entry is valid. By default, this value is six days. If the client remains connected to the network for half the TTL value (three days, by default), it begins trying to renew its registration in the WINS database. If the client does not receive a response from the server that the renewal is successful, the client will repeat its attempt every two minutes until half the remaining TTL (4.5 days, by default) remains, and will then try to renew its registration using a secondary WINS server, if it has one configured. The client will proceed in this manner until renewal is successful or until the TTL value expires.

WINS Proxy Agents   You can also enable non-WINS clients to use a WINS server to resolve NetBIOS names by installing a WINS proxy agent. By definition, a non-WINS client cannot directly communicate with a WINS server to resolve a name. A WINS proxy agent works by receiving the NetBIOS broadcasts created by non-WINS clients. If the queried name is in the proxy agent's name cache, it responds to the request. If not, the proxy agent adds the name to the cache with a status of pending and performs the resolution using the WINS server. The resolution is used to update the name cache so that when the non-WINS client sends its next query, the name is in cache and the WINS proxy can respond. WINS proxies act as a sort of intermediary between WINS servers and non-WINS clients. Since non-WINS clients communicate with broadcasts, a WINS proxy agent must exist on every subnet where non-WINS clients need to resolve NetBIOS names.

To configure a computer running Windows 2000 to act as a WINS proxy, you must change the value in the Windows Registry to 1: HKEY_ LOCAL_MACHINE\SYSTEM\CurrentControlSet\Services\NetBT\Parameters\ EnableProxy.

Using WINS

Managing WINS on a network is not terribly difficult. This section covers the installation of the WINS service on a computer running Windows 2000, basic WINS configuration, and setting up a Windows 2000 computer to be a WINS client.

Installing the WINS Service

WINS runs as a service in Windows 2000; you can include it during the installation of the operating system or add it later much as you can other services. Once it is installed, it begins running immediately.

Use the following steps to install the WINS service on a computer running Windows 2000 Server:

1. Click Start | Settings | Control Panel and then double-click the Add/Remove Programs icon in the Control Panel window.

2. In the Add/Remove Programs window, click Add/Remove Windows Components. This starts the Windows Components wizard.

3. Select the Networking Services item from the list of components and click Details.

4. From the list of subcomponents that appears, select the Windows Internet Name Service (WINS) item and then click OK.

5. Click Next to begin installing the WINS service.

6. When installation is complete, click Finish.

Once the WINS service is installed, it begins running and accepting client communications immediately. There is little configuration you need to do, unless you want to change how the WINS database is handled or you need to replicate database information to other WINS servers. If you do need to perform advanced WINS management, click Start | Programs | Administrative Tools | WINS to open the WINS console shown in Figure 5-1.

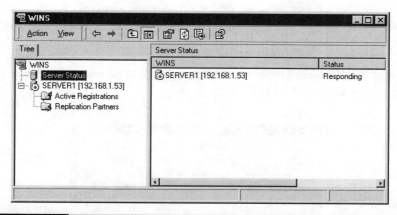

Use the WINS console to configure advanced properties for your WINS server.

Travel Assistance

This chapter includes only introductory information on configuring a WINS server, mostly because it is not required information on the exam. For detailed information on planning and managing a WINS environment, check out the Microsoft Windows 2000 Resource Kit, from Microsoft Press.

Configuring a WINS Client

On computers that use the Dynamic Host Configuration Protocol (DHCP) to automatically assign TCP/IP information to client computers, you will probably not need to configure WINS clients manually; information about WINS servers is most likely included in the DHCP information (see Chapter 4 for more on DHCP). If you are not using DHCP or you need to configure a client's WINS information manually anyway, it's quite easy.

The following procedure shows how to configure a computer running Windows 2000 with WINS information. The procedure will be much the same for other types of clients.

1. Click Start | Settings | Network and Dial-Up Connections.

2. Right-click the connection for which you want to configure WINS and choose Properties from the shortcut menu. For most computers, this will be the connection named Local Area Connection.

3. In the Properties dialog box for the connection, select Internet Protocol (TCP/IP) and click Properties. This opens the Internet Protocol (TCP/IP) Properties dialog box.

4. Click Advanced to open the Advanced TCP/IP Settings dialog box and switch to the WINS tab.

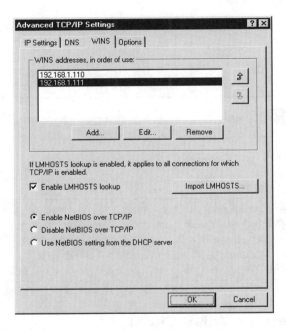

5. Click Add to open the TCP/IP WINS Server dialog box.

6. Click Add to open a dialog box that lets you add the IP address of a WINS server to be used by the client. Keep adding WINS servers in this manner until you have finished and then click Cancel to return to the Advanced TCP/IP Settings dialog box. Keep in mind that using more than one or two WINS servers can dramatically increase the time it takes to perform a successful resolution.

7. Use the arrows to the right of the listed WINS servers to adjust the order in which WINS servers are used by the client. The primary WINS server should be at the top of the list.

8. Use the Enable LMHOSTS Lookup option to allow the client to use an LMHOSTS file for name resolution and click Import LMHOSTS to specify the file's location. A client configured with

addresses for a WINS server will attempt to use those servers first and then fall back on the LMHOSTS file. If no servers are configured, the client simply uses the LMHOSTS file.

9. Use the options at the bottom of the dialog box to specify one of three options. Enabling NetBIOS over TCP/IP allows NetBIOS name resolution by the client using the options configured in the dialog box. Disabling it prevents NetBIOS name resolution. Using settings from the DHCP server lets the client obtain WINS servers, LMHOSTS file information, and node type from a DHCP server.

10. Click OK when you have finished, and then exit the remaining dialog boxes that are still open.

When you return to Windows, the WINS server information for the client takes effect immediately and the client should be able to resolve NetBIOS names. For clients other than Windows 2000 or Windows XP, you may need to restart the computer first.

Troubleshooting Name Resolution Clients

Since the WINS service is relatively simple, most of the problems that arise when using WINS are on the client side and usually come about when a client can't connect to a network resource. The simplest way to determine whether it is a client or WINS server problem is to see whether more than one client is affected. If only one client is affected, you can be pretty sure it is the client with the problem. Otherwise, you may need to do some investigation on the server end.

When a client cannot resolve a NetBIOS name, there's usually not a nice message that lets you know this is the case. Instead, the client usually just can't get to a network resource. To help troubleshoot client problems, you should check the following:

- Can you ping the IP address of the client? If you can't, then the problem may not be with WINS, but with TCP/IP instead. See Chapter 3 for information on using the ping utility and on troubleshooting TCP/IP.

- Can you ping the name of the client? If you can, then the name is being resolved successfully and you can look elsewhere for the source of the problem, such as the server the client was trying to connect to.

- If name resolution is the problem, the next thing you should check is whether WINS is correctly configured on the client. Use the information in the section "Configuring a WINS Client," earlier in the chapter, to make sure the right WINS servers are specified. If the client uses

DHCP to determine its WINS information, make sure the DHCP server is correctly configured. Use the ipconfig /all command to display WINS and DHCP information for the client. This command is covered in detail in Chapter 3.

- If WINS is configured correctly, ping the IP address of the WINS server to make sure that the client and server can communicate. If they cannot, you'll need to troubleshoot the network connectivity or the WINS server.

CHECKPOINT

✔ **Objective 5.01: Troubleshoot Name Resolution on Client Computers** This objective looked at several NetBIOS name resolution methods, including broadcasting, LMHOSTS files, and WINS. It also examined the installation of the WINS service, configuration of a WINS client, and basic troubleshooting techniques for WINS clients.

REVIEW QUESTIONS

1. You have a small network with only two subnets, A and B. You have configured a WINS server on subnet A. Both subnets contain WINS clients, but there are also a number of non-WINS clients on subnet B. Which of the following should you do to make sure that non-WINS clients can resolve WINS clients?

   A. Configure a WINS proxy agent on subnet A.
   B. Configure a WINS proxy agent on subnet B.
   C. Create static mapping for all non-WINS clients on the WINS server.
   D. Nothing.

2. You have just installed the WINS service on a computer running Windows 2000. What must you do before the WINS service can accept client requests?

   A. Use the WINS console to activate the WINS service.
   B. Authorize the WINS service in Active Directory.
   C. Create a WINS database.
   D. Nothing.

3. Which of the following keywords is used in an LMHOSTS file to automatically copy an entry into a computer's NetBIOS name cache?

    A. #DOM

    B. #PRE

    C. #LOAD

    D. #INCLUDE

4. Which of the following NetBIOS node types ensures that a client will attempt to use a broadcast for name resolution first and then attempt to use a WINS server?

    A. B node

    B. P node

    C. M node

    D. H node

5. What is the first message sent by a WINS client when it tries to resolve a NetBIOS name by broadcast?

    A. NAME QUERY REQUEST

    B. NAME RESOLUTION REQUEST

    C. ADDRESS MAP REQUEST

    D. ADDRESS RESOLUTION REQUEST

6. After how much time does a WINS client initially try to renew its registration, by default?

    A. 25 percent of the TTL value

    B. 50 percent of the TTL value

    C. 75 percent of the TTL value

    D. 87.5 percent of the TTL value

7. You recently installed a new computer for one of your users. The user complains that he cannot access a number of resources on the network. You test the network connectivity by pinging the IP addresses of those resources and find that the resources reply to the ping message. What should your next step be?

    A. Ping the primary WINS server's IP address.

    B. Ping the primary WINS server's NetBIOS name.

    C. Ping the NetBIOS name of the network resources.

    D. Check the WINS configuration on the client.

8. When a client cannot resolve a NetBIOS name, what is the first thing you should check?

   A. You should check for a corrupt database on the WINS server.

   B. You should check the status of the WINS server.

   C. You should check the configuration of the WINS client.

   D. You should check to see if there is a static mapping on the WINS server for the client.

9. A WINS client is configured as a P node. Assuming the name is not found in the client's NetBIOS name cache, what resolution method will that client always try first?

   A. Broadcast

   B. WINS server

   C. LMHOSTS file

   D. DNS query

REVIEW ANSWERS

1. **B**   Non-WINS clients broadcast their resolution requests. For this reason, the messages of non-WINS clients on subnet B would not be intercepted by the WINS server on subnet A. You must configure a WINS proxy agent on subnet B to intercept these broadcasts and forward them to the WINS server. C is wrong because, while you do need to create static mappings for non-WINS clients, this is done so that the WINS clients can resolve the non-WINS clients.

2. **D**   Once the WINS service is installed, it goes to work immediately. The WINS service does not need to be activated or authorized.

3. **B**   #PRE specifies that an entry should be preloaded into the NetBIOS name cache during initialization. A is wrong because #DOM specifies that an entry is for a domain controller. C is wrong because the keyword #LOAD does not exist. D is wrong because #INCLUDE is used to attach the contents of another LMHOSTS file.

4. **C**   M node clients use only broadcasts for name registration. For resolution, M node clients attempt to use broadcasts first and then use a WINS server for resolution if the broadcast fails.

5. **A**   If a computer does not find a suitable entry in its NetBIOS name cache, it can send a broadcast message (called a NAME QUERY REQUEST message) to the local IP subnet to resolve the name.

6. **B** At half the TTL value (three days, by default), a WINS client tries to renew its registration in the WINS database. If it is not successful, the client repeats its attempt every two minutes until half the remaining TTL is left and then tries to renew its registration using a secondary WINS server, if it has one configured. It alternates between servers until it is successful or the TTL expires.

7. **C** Pinging the IP address of the network resources successfully means that TCP/IP is configured correctly on both the local and remote computers and that network connectivity is sound. Your next step should be to ping the NetBIOS names of the resources. If successful, name resolution is not the problem. If unsuccessful, you should proceed to check the client's WINS configuration.

8. **C** Unless multiple clients cannot resolve NetBIOS names all at once, the first thing you should check after determining that name resolution is the problem is whether WINS is configured correctly on the client.

9. **B** P node clients always use a name server such as WINS for registration and resolution. If this fails, they will try resolving the name using a HOSTS file or DNS server, if they are configured with information for using them.

Managing Domain Name System

	NEWBIE	SOME EXPERIENCE	EXPERT
ETA	4 hours	2 hours	1 hour

In the previous chapter, you learned about using WINS and other methods to provide resolution of NetBIOS names to IP addresses. Host names are another way to name a network device and have been used on the Internet since its beginning. The Domain Name System (DNS) is a service that resolves host names to IP addresses. This chapter provides an overview of DNS and shows the basic configuration of Windows 2000, both as a DNS server and as a client. You'll also learn some techniques for troubleshooting DNS name resolution problems.

Objective 6.01 Configure, Administer, and Troubleshoot DNS

In versions of Windows previous to Windows 2000, DNS and host names were second in importance to WINS and NetBIOS names on Microsoft networks. In fact, many administrators never bothered much with DNS because it was considered more a part of network design than network administration. This has all changed with Windows 2000, largely because Windows 2000 depends heavily on DNS for many of its basic services. To begin with, Active Directory and DNS are inextricably linked; DNS provides the structure for Active Directory. Many other system functions, such as Kerberos authentication and domain controller location, are also reliant on DNS. Because of this tight integration, it is essential that you understand and be able to manage a network built around DNS.

Travel Assistance

Obviously, no one chapter can make you an expert in DNS. The goal of this chapter is to give you enough of a grounding in DNS basics and its configuration in Windows 2000 to help you understand the administrative tasks associated with DNS and to help you pass the exam. You can learn more about the architecture of DNS and the Windows 2000 implementation in the Windows 2000 Resource Kit.

Understanding the Domain Name System

During the early days of the Internet, when it was known as NSANET and consisted of only a few hundred computers, it was relatively easy to keep track of all the host names and IP addresses on the network. All of these mappings were located in a file named HOSTS.TXT, which was on a central computer on the network. Whenever a computer needed to resolve a host name, it consulted that file (occasionally copying it to the local computer). As the network grew, however, it became impractical (and soon, impossible) to use a single file to hold all the mappings. There were three real problems:

- The file became too big to manage effectively and required administration many times per day.
- All name resolution traffic had to be routed through the computer that held the HOSTS file and the file could not be copied enough to be continually up to date.
- The file used a flat data structure, so every computer on the network had to have a unique host name.

DNS was created to solve these three problems. The database is distributed across many computers on the Internet, all these computers sharing the burden of name resolution. The DNS namespace is also hierarchical and broken down into different levels. A particular host name has to be unique only within its domain instead of within the whole network.

Domain Name Space
The DNS name space is organized as a hierarchy that works much like the folder structure on a computer. You cannot have two files named README in the same directory. However, there are probably dozens of files by this name scattered across different directories on your computer. That's how DNS works, too. You could not have two hosts named server1 within the same domain, but every different domain out there could have one host named server1. Figure 6-1 illustrates the hierarchical nature of domain name space.

The Root Domain   At the top of the DNS hierarchy, there is a single domain called the *root domain.* The root domain is represented by a single period, much

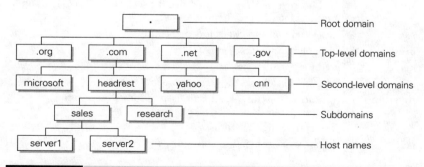

FIGURE 6.1   The DNS hierarchy

the same way that the root directory on a hard drive partition is represented by a single period.

Top-Level Domains   Top-level domains are controlled by the Internet Activities Board (IAB), an Internet authority controlling the assignment of domain names, among other things. Top-level domains have names like com (for business) and gov (for government). Table 6-1 lists all of the top-level domains currently being used.

Second-Level Domains   Beneath the top-level domains, there is a second level of domains that is registered to individual organizations. For example, microsoft.com and yahoo.com are second-level domains within the top-level domain com. Once a second-level domain is registered, control of the namespace for that domain is passed to the registering organization to manage. They can even further divide the namespace into another level of domains. For example, a company with the domain headrest.com might divide the domain into the subdomains sales.headrest.com and research.headrest.com.

TABLE 6.1   Top-Level Domain Names

Name	Type of Organization
com	Commercial organizations
edu	Educational institutions
org	Nonprofit organizations, though this is not strictly enforced
net	Network service providers, though this is not strictly enforced
gov	Government institutions
mil	Military institutions
num	Telephone numbers
arpa	Used for reverse DNS lookups. See the section "Reverse Lookup Queries," later in the chapter.
xx	Two-letter country codes for each country
info	Available for all uses
name	Used for personal sites
biz	Available for all uses, targeted at business sites
museum	Museums, museum organizations, and individuals in the museum profession
coop	Cooperative organizations
aero	Members of the aviation community

Fully Qualified Domain Names   A fully qualified domain name (FQDN) is the full description of a particular host's place in the DNS hierarchy. The following is an example of an FQDN:

> server1.sales.headrest.com

The name refers to a host named server1 in a subdomain named sales, which is in a second-level domain named headrest that is in the top-level domain com, which of course is in the root domain (.).

Zones and Name Servers

In addition to being segmented into domains, the DNS namespace is also broken up into portions called *zones*. Each zone is a file representing a contiguous portion of the namespace for which a particular name server (or group of servers) is responsible. A zone actually corresponds to a series of resource records stored on a DNS server that map IP addresses to various hosts and services in the zone. This database of records is considered authoritative for all the domains contained in that zone.

A zone encompasses at least one domain, which is referred to as the zone's *root domain*. The zone may also contain *subdomains* of that root domain but does not necessarily have to hold all the subdomains of the root domain. Consider the example shown in Figure 6-2, which shows a second-level domain named headrest.com that contains two subdomains, sales.headrest.com and research.headrest.com. In this case, headrest.com is the root domain of zone1 and sales.headrest.com is also contained in this zone. A separate zone, zone2, has been configured for the subdomain research.headrest.com.

Zones must contain contiguous domains within the namespace. This means that a single zone could contain a domain and its subdomains, but a zone could

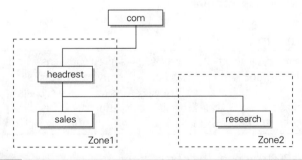

FIGURE 6.2   The domain name space is broken into nested zones of authority.

not contain two different subdomains without also containing the parent domain. Take a look at the example in Figure 6-2 again. Zones could be configured the way they are shown in the figure, or a single zone could be configured that contained headrest.com and its two subdomains. You could not, however, create a zone that contained the headrest.com domain and then create a separate zone that contained just the two subdomains.

Each zone has at least one name server responsible for knowing the address information for each device within that zone, and a single name server can be configured to manage more than one zone. Each name server also knows the address of at least one parent name server. If a particular name server cannot resolve a host name, it can pass the query on to another name server that may have the information. You'll learn more about this in the next section, "The Name Resolution Process."

You can also create multiple name servers for a single zone. One of these name servers contains a master copy of the zone database file, which is referred to as the primary zone file. Other name servers created for a zone act as secondary servers, and each contains a secondary zone file. When records in the zone are updated, they are updated on the primary server and then replicated to the secondary servers. Using multiple servers in a zone provides a number of important benefits:

- **Redundancy**   If a primary name server fails, secondary servers can provide DNS services to your network.
- **Load balancing**   On large networks, creating multiple servers distributes the load of client requests among the primary and secondary servers, decreasing response time.
- **Remote access**   Creating secondary servers on remote subnets prevents client requests from having to cross remote access links, decreasing response time.

Exam Tip

On the exam, pay close attention when you are given questions with a graphical depiction of networks. Putting secondary name servers on subnets is not required, but putting secondary name servers on remote subnets (those connected by a WAN link) can improve performance and reduce network traffic across the link.

Windows 2000 supports three types of zones:

- **Active Directory integrated**   In this type of zone, the DNS database is stored within Active Directory. All DNS servers in an Active Directory–

integrated zone are considered primary servers; any of them can be updated and any of them can resolve client requests. Active Directory is responsible for replicating zone information between DNS servers, often making replication quicker and making it a part of Active Directory management instead of a separate management practice.

- **Standard primary**   The master copy of the DNS database resides in a standard ASCII text file. Only this primary zone can be directly modified.

- **Standard secondary**   The zone information is a read-only replica of an existing standard primary zone and helps provide a backup to the primary zone. Zone information is updated on the primary DNS server and then transferred to any secondary servers.

The Name Resolution Process

Resolving a name means determining the IP address that is associated with that name. In DNS, the client that performs name resolution is called a *resolver*. In Microsoft operating systems, this resolver is named the DNS Client service. The resolver operates at the application layer of the TCP/IP model (see Chapter 3 for more on this) and is often built into different programs that may need to resolve host names. For example, when you type an address into your Web browser, the browser uses DNS to query the name server configured on the local host and re-solve the name.

There are two types of queries that a resolver can perform: a forward lookup query, which translates names to IP addresses; and a reverse lookup query, which translates IP addresses to names. Both types are services by DNS name servers.

Forward Lookup Queries   The most common type of query is the forward lookup query, where a host or domain name must be resolved to an IP address. In this type of query, a resolver sends a resolution request to its configured name server. If that name server has the information, it passes it back to the cli-ent. If it does not, it in turn sends queries to other name servers until it finds the information.

The following example shows this process at work as a resolver on the Internet attempts to resolve the name www.yahoo.com (see Figure 6-3):

1. The resolver sends a query to its local DNS server, asking for resolution of the domain name. The name server either returns the information to the resolver or does not. The name server cannot refer the resolver to another name server. This type of query is a recursive query—the server must either respond with the mapping or reply that the name/IP was not found.

2. The local name server that receives the request from the resolver checks the zone(s) under its authority. If the requested host name or domain is in one of its zones, it returns the information to the client. If not, as in this case, it checks its local name cache to see if the name has been recently resolved. If it has not, it sends a query for www.yahoo.com to a root name server.

3. The root name server has authority for the root domain and replies to the local server with the IP address of a name server that has authority for the com top-level domain.

4. The local name server sends out another query for www.yahoo.com to the IP address supplied by the root name server. These types of queries are called *iterative* queries, since the same query is sent to multiple servers until resolved.

5. The com authoritative server replies with the IP address of a name server that has authority over the yahoo.com second-level domain.

6. The local name server sends another query for www.yahoo.com to the IP address of the yahoo.com name server.

7. The yahoo.com name server replies to the query with the IP address for www.yahoo.com.

8. The local name server returns the IP address of www.yahoo.com to the original resolver.

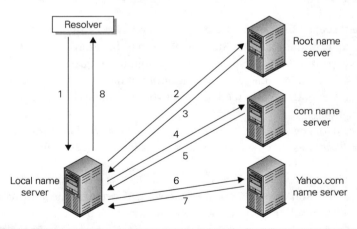

FIGURE 6.3 A number of name servers can be involved in a single forward lookup query.

Exam Tip

Most name servers use a cache to store recently resolved names. If a query comes in for a name that is contained in a name server's cache, the server can return the IP address directly without referring the query to another name server. Entries in a cache have a Time to Live (TTL) value; when that time expires, the entries are removed. On a Microsoft DNS server, the default TTL for an entry in a name server cache is 60 minutes.

Reverse Lookup Queries   A *reverse lookup* query is one in which an IP address is resolved to a host or domain name. Some utilities, such as nslookup (which you'll learn about later in the chapter), ping, and netstat, use reverse lookups. Reverse lookups can also be useful if you are trying to keep track of network usage, if you are trying to track down a host that is causing issues on the network, or even if you are trying to verify the identity of a host.

Since DNS databases are indexed using names and not IP addresses, searching for a name on the basis of an IP address within a regular DNS database structure would be a slow process. To solve this problem, a special domain was developed named in-addr.arpa, which stands for Inverse Address—Advanced Research Projects Agency. In-addr.arpa uses the IP address as an index to the host's resource record information. When the proper resource record is located, the host name can be extracted.

Nodes in the in-addr.arpa domain are named after the numbers in the dotted decimal representation of an IP address. However, because IP addresses get more specific from left to right and domain names get more specific from right to left, the order of the IP address octets is reversed when building the corresponding name in the in-addr.arpa domain. For example, a host name with the IP address 172.124.201.35 would be a PTR record in the 124.172.in-addr.arpa zone file. The entry in that file would take the form 201.35 IN PTR *host_name*.

The in-addr-arpa domain is built using a hierarchy just like a standard DNS domain. As the in-addr-arpa domain is built, special resource records called pointer (PTR) records are added to the domain's database to map IP addresses to host names. You'll learn more about resource records in the next section.

Resource Records

The zone files contain the *resource records* used to resolve names. The resource records contain the IP addressing information for various types of resources on the network. Table 6-2 shows many of the types of resource records supported by the Windows 2000 DNS service.

TABLE 6.2	Resource Records Used by the Windows 2000 DNS Service

Resource Record	Description
A	An *address record*, which maps a host name to an IP address using the IP version 4 format (the standard 32-bit format used today).
AAAA	Also an address record, this one uses the 128-bit format of the next generation of the IP protocol, IPv6.
CNAME	A *canonical name* record establishes an alias, a synonym for a host name. Using CNAME records, you can have more than one name resolve to a single IP address.
MX	A *mail exchanger* record identifies the mail server for a specified DNS domain.
NS	A *name server* record identifies a name server for a specified DNS domain.
PTR	A *pointer* record associates an IP address with a host in a DNS reverse-naming zone.
SOA	A *start of authority* record specifies the domain for which a DNS server is responsible. It also specifies a variety of parameters that regulate operation of the DNS server.
SRV	The SRV record allows you to use multiple servers for a single domain, to move services between hosts easily, and to designate hosts as primary servers for a particular service. The SRV record is required in order for Active Directory to be used.
WINS	A *Windows Internet Name Server* record identifies a WINS server that can be consulted to obtain names that are not recorded in the DNS name space. See Chapter 5 for more on WINS.
WINS_R	A *reverse WINS* record causes Microsoft DNS to use the nbstat command to resolve reverse-lookup (address-to-name) client queries.
WKS	A *well-known service* record describes services provided by a specific protocol on a specific adapter. Any protocol specified in the %systemroot%\system32\drivers\etc\protocols file can be specified in this record type.

Exam Tip

You will not be required to know all the different types of resource records on the exam, though it is important to know the types of records that exist. For the exam, be sure you know what the following records are used for: A, CNAME, MX, NS, PTR, SOA, SRV, and WINS.

Configuring and Administering DNS in Windows 2000

DNS runs under Windows 2000 as a service, and it should come as no surprise that the service is fairly easy to install and configure. Most of the work with DNS comes in the form of understanding DNS and planning its implementation. Now that you understand some of the basics of DNS, it's time to look at installation and configuration.

Installing the DNS service

There are three ways you can install the DNS service on a computer running Windows 2000:

- **During Windows installation**   By default, the service is not included during a standard installation of Windows 2000, but you can include it if you want.
- **Using Add/Remove Programs**   If DNS was not installed during the installation of Windows 2000, you can install the service later using the Add/Remove Programs utility in the Control Panel. We'll go over the steps for this method later in this section.
- **Using the Active Directory wizard**   Installation of Active Directory Services requires the presence of a DNS server. If no DNS server is available on a network when Active Directory is installed, the Active Directory wizard will offer to install the DNS service for you. If you are using Active Directory–integrated zones and know that a particular domain controller will be a DNS server, this is the best method to use for installing DNS, since the wizard automatically configures much of the zone information for you.

Exam Tip

Computers running the DNS service (and any other servers on your network, for that matter) should be given a static IP address, and not use a dynamic IP address assigned by DHCP. When configuring TCP/IP on a DNS server, you should also configure the computer to use itself as a DNS server.

Use the following procedure to install the DNS service on a computer running Windows 2000:

1. Log on to the computer using an account with administrator privileges.

2. Click Start | Settings | Control Panel and then double-click Add/Remove Programs in the Control Panel window.

3. Click Add/Remove Windows Components to start the Windows Components wizard.

4. From the list of components, highlight the Networking Services component and click Details.

5. From the list of subcomponents (shown next), select the check box next to the Domain Name System (DNS) component and click OK.

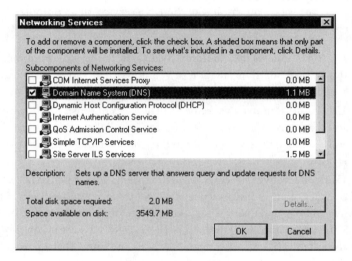

6. Click Next to begin the installation of the DNS service. You may be prompted to supply the location of the Windows 2000 installation files during this process.

7. Once the files have finished copying, click Finish.

Configuring DNS

You'll handle configuration of DNS through a snap-in for the Microsoft Management Console, which becomes available once DNS is installed. You can use this same snap-in to manage all the DNS servers on a network.

If you let the Active Directory wizard install DNS automatically prior to installing Active Directory Services, the wizard automates much of the process of configuration for you, including the initial creation of a root zone. This root zone is given a name identical to the Active Directory forest root name (see Chapter 10 for more on this). The wizard also activates Dynamic DNS, a feature discussed later in the section "Configuring Dynamic DNS."

If you installed the service manually, then the first time you start the DNS snap-in, you should be prompted to run the Configure DNS Server wizard. This wizard lets you specify a root server (or configure the new server as one if there is not a root server already), and then steps you through the creation of forward and reverse lookup zones. If you are not prompted, you will need to run the wizard manually by selecting Action | Configure The Server before you can do anything else.

The DNS snap-in is shown in Figure 6-4. The left-hand pane shows the DNS servers available on the network and zones configured on those servers. The right-hand pane shows the resource records defined for a selected zone.

Creating a New Zone   Like many operations throughout Windows, creating a new zone, whether it's a forward or reverse lookup zone, is a wizard-driven process. Following is the procedure for creating a new forward lookup zone:

1. Click Start | Programs | Administrative Tools | DNS to open the DNS snap-in.

2. Expand the server container and select the Forward Lookup Zones folder. Right-click the folder and choose New Zone from the shortcut menu. On the opening page of the wizard, click Next.

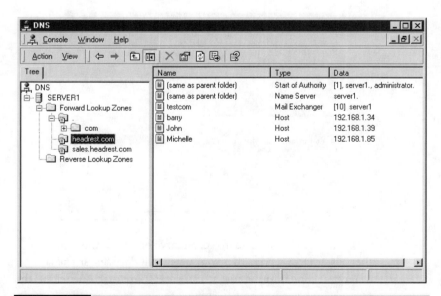

FIGURE 6.4   Using the DNS snap-in

3. Choose the type of zone you want to create. Choices include Active Directory integrated (if you are using Active Directory), standard primary, or standard secondary. See the earlier section "Zones and Name Servers" for a description of these zone types.

4. Enter a name for the new zone and click Next. It is standard practice to name a zone after the highest-level domain that it will service—the zone's root domain. For example, if a zone services both headrest.com and sales.headrest.com, you should name the zone headrest.com.

5. What happens at this point depends on the type of zone you are creating:

   • If you are creating an Active Directory–integrated zone, the wizard ends now and you can click Finish.

   • If you are creating a standard primary zone, you must specify a name for the new zone database. The wizard suggests a name for you based on the name of the zone (with .dns tacked on to the end). You can modify it as you want, but be careful to use a name that helps identify the zone. You can also use an existing file, but the file must be located in the %systemroot%\system32\dns folder.

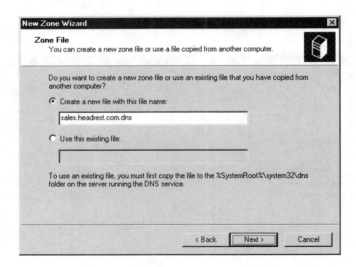

   • If you are creating a standard secondary zone, you must specify the master DNS servers that your new secondary server will contact to request zone information. If you enter more than one server, the secondary server attempts to contact the master servers in the order specified.

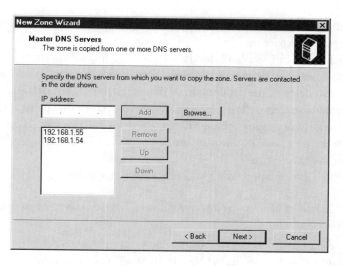

Creating a reverse lookup zone is a little different from creating a forward lookup zone, but it is still pretty simple. Right-click the Reverse Lookup Zones folder in the DNS snap-in and choose New Zone. Click Next to skip the opening page of the wizard, and then choose the type of zone you want to create; the same types are available as for a forward lookup zone.

Whichever zone type you choose, the next step is to identify the zone, shown next. You can either enter the network ID portion of the network the zone covers (the easy way) or fill in the actual name of the reverse lookup zone (which is the network ID in reverse plus the in-addr.arpa domain). Both methods achieve equivalent results, but entering the network ID does not work in all circumstances.

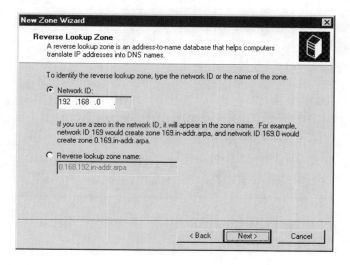

Delegating Zones As you learned previously, DNS provides the ability to break up a namespace into zones. A zone always begins as a storage database for a single domain, but you can extend the zone by adding subdomains of that domain. You can also create separate zones to hold subdomains; in this case, you will need to delegate the subdomain to that new zone. When delegating zones within a namespace, you must create name server records that point at the servers in charge of managing the zone file for the delegated domain. These records indicate the new zone's authority and are necessary for referring DNS server requests to the new zone.

Use the following procedure to create a zone delegation:

1. Click Start | Programs | Administrative Tools | DNS to open the DNS snap-in.

2. Select the subdomain for which you want to create a delegation, right-click it, and choose New Delegation. This opens the New Delegation wizard; click Next to skip the opening page.

3. Enter the name of the delegated domain. This is the domain for which you want to delegate authority to another zone file. It should be a subdomain of the main domain. Click Next to go on.

4. Click Add to add the names and IP addresses of any servers that will host the newly delegated zone. Click Next when you are done.

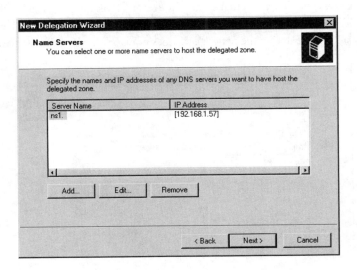

5. Click Finish to exit the wizard.

Configuring Dynamic DNS   Dynamic DNS (DDNS) allows Windows 2000 DNS clients to register and dynamically update their own resource records with a DNS server. This dramatically reduces the need for manual administration of records. You can enable and disable DDNS on a per-zone basis.

Windows 2000 clients with static IP addresses attempt to register their IP addresses with the DNS server whenever the IP address changes or whenever the client boots up. Windows 2000 DHCP clients attempt to update the DNS records whenever an IP lease changes, such as at the original issuance or upon renewal. By default, the Windows 2000 client updates its own A record and the DHCP server will update the PTR record for the client.

Exam Tip

Only Windows 2000 (or Windows XP) DNS clients can directly update their own DNS records. Other types of clients that use DHCP can use their DHCP server as a DNS proxy that can perform updates for them, but this requires configuration on the DHCP server.

To configure a zone for dynamic updates, select and then right-click the zone in the DNS snap-in and choose Properties. On the General tab of the zone's Properties dialog box (shown in Figure 6-5), set the Allow Dynamic Updates option to one of the following:

- **No**   Dynamic updates are not allowed for the zone.
- **Yes**   Dynamic updates are allowed for the zone.
- **Only Secure Updates**   This option is available only for Active Directory–integrated zones. When it is selected, only DNS requests using the Secure DNS (DNSSEC) specification are honored. This means the computer must authenticate itself using its account before it can update its record, preventing malicious updates.

Viewing and Creating Resource Records   You may occasionally find it necessary to manually add or update resource records on a Windows 2000 DNS server. While Dynamic DNS frees you from having to deal with the most common types of records (notably A and PTR records), there are other types of records that are required on most networks. Mail exchanger (MX) records, for example, are used to designate a mail server within a zone and are required for the proper flow of e-mail. You can find a description of various record types in the earlier section "Resource Records."

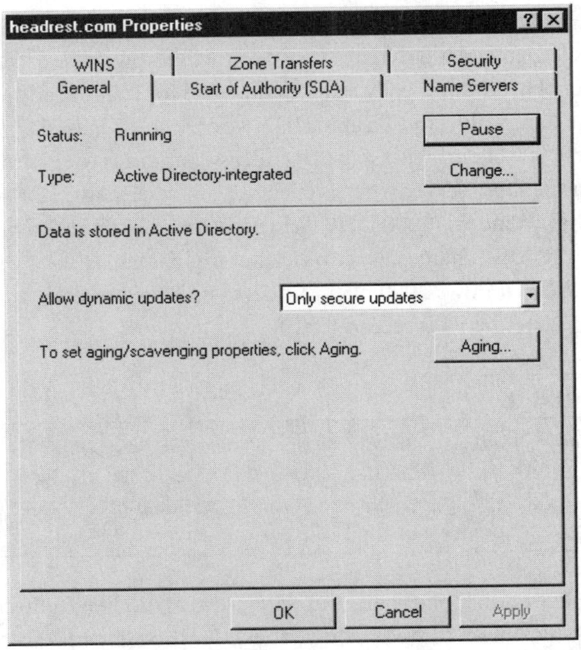

FIGURE 6.5 Use a zone's Properties dialog to configure options for the zone, such as whether DDNS is enabled.

Resource records are shown in the right-hand pane of the DNS snap-in whenever a zone is selected. You can view the contents of a record by right-clicking it and choosing Properties. A sample A record is shown in Figure 6-6. This particular record type shows the parent domain, the host name, and the current IP address. You can update the IP address by simply entering a new value and also update the associated pointer (PTR) record.

Creating Records

Creating new resource records is also easy. The process differs a bit depending on the type of record you are creating, mostly because the information you need to know to create the record varies. You can create any supported type of record by right-clicking the zone in which you want to create the record and choosing Other New Records from the shortcut menu. This opens a dialog box listing available record types for you to choose from. Select the record type and click Create Record to open a blank dialog box to be filled in for the new record.

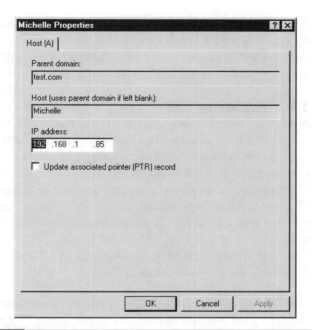

FIGURE 6.6   You can view and update a record by opening its Properties dialog box.

There are also commands available on the shortcut menu for quickly creating the more common types of records (all of which are also available using the Other New Records command). These common types include

- **Host**   This command is used to quickly create new host (A) records that map a host name to an IP address. You'll need to know the host name and the IP address of the host to create a record of this type. You can also specify during creation that a PTR record for the host be created.
- **Alias**   This command is used to create a new alias (CNAME) record, which is essentially a pointer to a host or other alias record. To create an alias, you'll need to provide an alias name and the name of a target host or other alias. You can browse the directory to find the target host.
- **Mail Exchanger**   This command is used to create a new mail exchanger (MX) record, which identifies a mail server associated with a domain. You'll need to provide a host or domain name and the name or IP address of a mail server. Any messages sent to the host or domain name are directed to the mail server. You can also specify a priority for

the mail server, which is a number from 0 to 65,535 that ranks the mail server's priority related to other configured mail servers. If multiple mail servers are configured for the same domain, servers with lower priority numbers are used before servers with higher priority numbers.

Using SRV Records

On a Windows 2000 network, a Service Locator (SRV) record is used by a client to locate a server that provides a particular service, such as authenticating the user or searching Active Directory. SRV records map a service to a server's host name, as identified in that server's host record. SRV records are crucial on a Windows 2000 network, as they are required for services like Active Directory to even start. When a Windows 2000 domain controller starts up, its NetLogon service uses dynamic updates to register its SRV records with the DNS database automatically.

You can use one of three methods to verify that an SRV locator record has been successfully registered with the DNS database:

- Use the DNS console to verify that the appropriate records have been created for each DNS zone. Active Directory creates its SRV records in the _msdcs/dc/_sites/default-first-site-name/_tcp folder and in the _msdcs/dc/_tcp folder. In these locations, you'll see an SRV record displayed for both the _kerberos and _ldap services.

- Open the Netlogon.dns file in the %SystemRoot%\System32\Config folder using a standard text editor, such as Notepad. The first record displayed is the domain controller's LDAP SRV record and will look something like this: _ldap._tcp.*domain_name*. This method is useful if you use non-Microsoft DNS servers to support Active Directory.

- Use nslookup to verify the record. At the command prompt, type **nslookup**. At the nslookup prompt, type **set type=all** and press ENTER. Type **_ldap._tcp.dc._msdcs.** *domainname* and press ENTER. Nslookup should return one or more SRV records.

Managing DNS Network Traffic

Whenever a client requests a DNS resolution, network traffic is generated. In large organizations, this traffic can become considerable. In addition to planning a good DNS structure, there are three methods you can use to help alleviate DNS traffic: secondary DNS servers, caching-only servers, and zone transfers.

Using Secondary DNS Servers

As you learned previously, a secondary DNS server functions something like a backup server that is used to service client requests. Secondary servers contain zone files that are not directly updated but must be replicated from the primary DNS server for the zone. Placing secondary servers close to users (i.e., placing a secondary server on the same subnet as users) helps reduce the potential amount of DNS traffic across a network. Placing secondary servers close to users also decreases the perceived response time experienced by users when their computer needs to resolve a name.

Using Caching-Only Servers

Caching-only servers are DNS servers that do not host a zone database at all. Rather, they perform name resolution on behalf of clients and cache the results. In this respect, caching-only servers are identical to DNS servers that are used to host a zone database. If a requested resolution is found in a server's cache, the resolution is handled and returned to the client immediately, without having to query other DNS servers.

Caching-only servers are great solutions for remote offices connected via WAN links. Because the server caches frequently resolved names and does not generate any zone transfer traffic, traffic across the WAN link is minimized.

To configure a caching-only server, you simply install DNS on a computer running Windows 2000, but do not create any forward or reverse lookup zones. Instead, you configure the caching-only server to use a forwarder, which is an authoritative DNS server that can resolve queries. To enable the use of forwarders, open the Properties dialog box for the caching-only server, switch to the Forwarders tab, and enter the IP addresses of servers to use as forwarders.

Exam Tip

Forwarders can also be configured on DNS servers that host a zone file. This is a way to designate a specific DNS server to which you want queries forwarded and provides another way to direct network traffic.

Using Zone Transfers

When changes to a zone (new, changed, or deleted records) are made in a zone that is not Active Directory integrated, they are made on the master server for the zone. When these changes are made, they are replicated to any secondary servers in the zone using a process called a *zone transfer*. In the original DNS specifications, only one type of zone transfer was available: a full zone transfer in which the entire zone database is replicated. New specifications have added another type of zone transfer: an incremental zone transfer in which only record changes are replicated instead of the entire zone database. In this section, we'll look at both of those types of zone transfers. We'll also look at another feature, named DNS Notify—a mechanism that lets master servers notify secondary servers that changes are available, and at how zone transfers work in Active Directory–integrated zones.

Full Zone Transfers   In a full zone transfer (AFXR), a full copy of the zone database is replicated from the master server to secondary servers. AFXRs are initiated by secondary servers using the following process:

1.   A secondary server begins the process when the amount of time in the Refresh field of the zone's SOA record expires. When this occurs, the secondary server polls the master server for its copy of the SOA.

2.   The master server responds with the SOA record. If the master server does not respond, the secondary server continues to try at regular intervals (specified by the Retry field in the SOA). If there is no response from the master server by the interval specified in the Expire field of the SOA, the secondary server discards its zone.

3.   The secondary server compares the serial number of the SOA sent by the master server to the serial number in its own SOA record. If the serial number in the master server's SOA is higher, the secondary server assumes its own SOA is out of date and sends a request for a full zone transfer (an AFXR request).

4.   The master server sends the full zone database to the secondary server.

Incremental Zone Transfers   Obviously, full zone transfers can generate a good bit of network traffic, especially in large organizations. To address this problem, the incremental zone transfer (IFXR) was introduced. IFXRs work in much the same way that AFXRs work. The secondary server still polls the master server, and the master server still responds with the SOA record. The difference comes when the secondary server determines that it requires a zone transfer. The secondary server sends an incremental zone transfer message (an IFXR message) to the master server.

The master server maintains a recent version history of the zone, which tracks any changes to records that occurred in recent version updates. If the master server has a newer version of the zone database than the secondary server, the master server can send only the changes that have occurred between the version that the secondary server has and the current version that the master server has. The master server sends the updates to the secondary server starting with the oldest changes and working toward the most current changes.

When the secondary server receives an incremental zone transfer, it creates a new version of the zone and begins replacing records with updates received from the master. When all updates have been made, the secondary server replaces its old version of the zone with the new version.

DNS Notify DNS Notify is yet another revision to the original DNS specifications. DNS Notify provides a way for the master server in a zone to notify secondary servers of changes, instead of making the secondary servers responsible for polling. The master server maintains a notify list that contains the IP addresses of secondary servers it should notify when changes to the zone are made. The process works as follows:

1. When the zone is modified on the master server, the master server updates the Serial Number field in the SOA record to indicate that a new version of the zone has been written.

2. The master server then sends a notify message to all secondary servers on its notify list.

3. Secondary servers that receive the notify message initiate an SOA query back to the notifying master server to determine whether the master actually has a later version of the zone.

4. If a secondary server determines that the master has a later version (i.e., the serial number of the master server's version is higher than that of the secondary server), the secondary server requests an AXFR or IXFR zone transfer.

Zone Transfers in Active Directory–Integrated Zones In an Active Directory–integrated zone, the zone database is replicated to all domain controllers and does not rely on master/secondary server roles. All domain controllers are considered authoritative for the zone, and records can be updated on any domain controller. Replication within Active Directory is performed on a per-property basis, meaning that only relevant changes to an object within Active Directory need to be replicated. You can learn more about the Active Directory replication process, including how conflict resolution takes place when objects are updated on more than one server at the same time, in Chapter 12.

Troubleshooting DNS

As with most services, especially complex ones, you'll experience your share of problems even on a carefully planned and configured DNS setup. This section describes some of the tools available to you for troubleshooting DNS.

Using the DNS Snap-in

The DNS snap-in offers some basic testing and monitoring features, including the ability to send DNS queries to a server to test its functionality and to log DNS events. Both are useful for monitoring your DNS servers.

Querying the DNS Server   In the DNS snap-in, select and then right-click any DNS server and choose Properties from the shortcut menu. Switch to the Monitoring tab of the server's Properties dialog box, shown in Figure 6-7. You can use this tab to perform two types of queries against the server:

- **Simple Query**   This query performs a test of the DNS server by using the local DNS resolver to send a simple iterative name resolution query. This test is useful in determining whether a server is responding to DNS requests at all and helps isolate DNS server problems from network problems.
- **Recursive Query**   This query performs a recursive test by having the local DNS resolver ask the server to resolve a query for the root of the DNS domain namespace. This type of query is useful in determining not only whether a server is responding to requests, but whether zone delegations and SOA records are correctly configured.

Using DNS Logging   By default, events concerning the DNS service are logged in the Windows 2000 System log, as are events for all services. You can view these events using Event Viewer. You can also use Event Viewer to help track down problems on DNS clients.

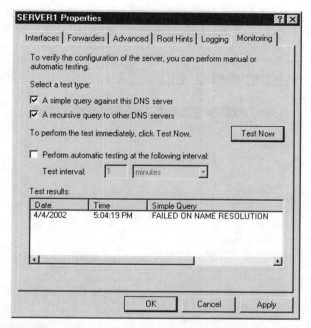

FIGURE 6.7   Use the DNS snap-in to perform basic tests of a DNS server.

In addition to this, you can use the DNS snap-in to direct Windows 2000 to log many specific DNS events to a separate DNS log file. You do this using the Logging tab of a server's Properties dialog box in the DNS snap-in, as shown in Figure 6-8. Information logged in this manner is stored in a file named Dns.log in the %systemroot32%/System32/dns folder. Logging is useful for tracking down specific problems, but you should turn it on only for this purpose and you should limit the logging options to only those related to the problem, when possible. Otherwise, you'll find yourself with a very large log file. Table 6-3 lists the available logging options.

Using Nslookup

Nslookup is a command-line tool that lets you perform query testing of a DNS server and view detailed responses to your queries. This tool is extremely handy in diagnosing DNS problems and for verifying resource records. You can use nslookup in two modes: noninteractive and interactive.

Using Nslookup in Noninteractive Mode   Using nslookup in noninteractive mode enables you to look up a single piece of information in a zone database.

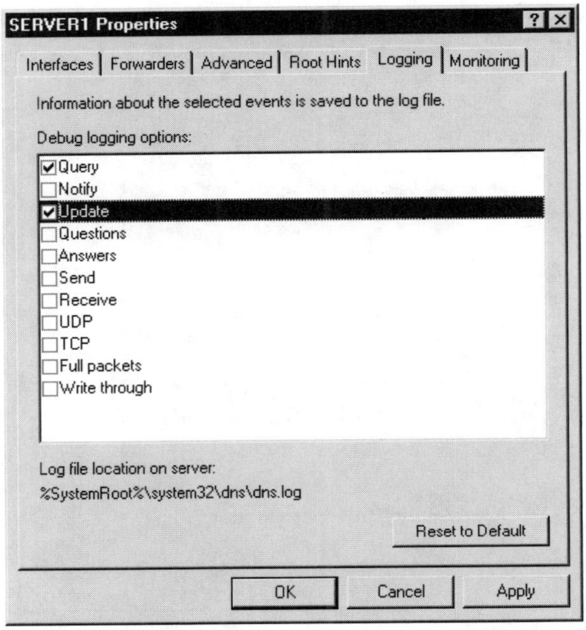

FIGURE 6.8 Enable logging when you need to troubleshoot specific DNS problems.

TABLE 6.3 Logging Options for the DNS Service

Logging Option	Description
Query	Logs queries received by the DNS service from clients.
Notify	Logs notification messages received by the DNS service from other services.
Update	Logs dynamic updates received by the DNS service from other computers.
Questions	Logs the contents of the question section for each DNS query message processed by the DNS service.
Answers	Logs the contents of the answer section for each DNS query message processed by the DNS service.
Send	Logs the number of DNS query messages sent by the DNS service.
Receive	Logs the number of DNS query messages received by the DNS service.
UDP	Logs the number of requests received over a UDP port.
TCP	Logs the number of requests received over a TCP port.

TABLE 6.3	Logging Options for the DNS Service *(continued)*

Logging Option	Description
Full Packets	Logs the number of full packets written and sent by the DNS service.
Write Through	Logs the number of packets written through by the DNS service.

For this, you will use the command with the following syntax, which specifies the DNS name you want to resolve and the server you want to query:

```
nslookup <name> <server>
```

The information returned shows basic information about the name you look up, such as the IP addresses it is associated with.

Using Nslookup in Interactive Mode   Interactive mode is a much more useful way of using nslookup than in noninteractive mode. Interactive mode starts a special command prompt session with tools for looking up names and records, performing zone transfers, and more. You can enter interactive mode by simply typing **nslookup** at the command prompt. To leave interactive mode, just type **exit** at the prompt and press ENTER.

Once you have entered interactive mode, you will use the set command with various options to tell nslookup how to resolve queries. These options are listed in Table 6-4.

TABLE 6.4	Options for the Set Command in Nslookup Interactive Mode

Option	Description
set all	Shows all the options available with the set command.
set d2	Puts nslookup in debug mode so you can examine the query and response packets between the resolver and the server.
set domain=*domain_name*	Tells the resolver what domain name to append for unqualified queries (i.e., those where you don't specify a fully qualified domain name).
set timeout=*time-out*	Specifies a time-out value for the resolver to use. This option is useful where slow network links often cause the query to time out and you need to increase the allowed time for testing purposes.
set type=*record-type*	Tells the resolver which type of resource record to search for, such as A, PTR, or MX. To resolve all queries (the default setting), use set type=all.

TABLE 6.5 Options for Using the ls Command in nslookup Interactive Mode

Option	Description
-t *querytype*	Lists all records of the specified type. Query types include all available types of resource records. Using the -t command by itself (without specifying a query type) along with a domain name lists all hosts in the domain.
-a	Lists aliases of hosts in the domain. This is the same as using the command ls -t CNAME.
-d	Lists all records for the domain. This is the same as using the command ls -t ANY.
-h	Lists CPU and operating system information for the domain. This is the same as using the command -t HINFO.
-s	Lists well-known services of hosts in the domain. This is the same as using the command -t WKS.

Once you have configured any options you want to use, you can begin performing queries. To perform a query, just type *name server*, using the name you want to resolve and the server you want to use for the resolution. A successful query will return information on the record; an unsuccessful query will return a time-out message.

You can also use the command ls *name* in interactive mode to perform a variety of functions. These are listed in Table 6-5.

Using Ipconfig on DNS Clients You can use the ipconfig command on DNS clients to view DNS information configured for the client, and to view and reset locally cached information used for resolving DNS names. Check out Chapter 3 for detailed information on using the ipconfig command. Table 6-6 shows the ipconfig command options specific to DNS.

TABLE 6.6 Options for Using the ipconfig Command on DNS Clients

Command	Description
Ipconfig /all	Displays DNS configuration information for the client, including the FQDN and DNS suffix search list.
Ipconfig /flushdns	Purges and resets the DNS resolver cache.
Ipconfig /displaydns	Displays the contents of the DNS resolver cache.
Ipconfig /registerdns	Refreshes all DHCP leases and registers any related DNS names.

CHECKPOINT

✔**Objective 6.01: Configure, Administer, and Troubleshoot DNS**   This objective looked at the basics of the Domain Name System (DNS) architecture, including how the DNS namespace is segmented into domains and how name servers are used to store resource records and resolve DNS queries. This objective also looked at how to install and configure the DNS service on a computer running Windows 2000 and some of the tools available to you for troubleshooting DNS.

REVIEW QUESTIONS

1. You have three DNS name servers on your network. Which features of Windows 2000 DNS might you use to improve fault tolerance?

    A. Service resource location records

    B. Zone delegation

    C. Primary and secondary zones

    D. Per-property zone replication

2. When using Dynamic DNS with DHCP, which of the following records for a Windows 2000 client is the DHCP server responsible for updating by default?

    A. Only the A record

    B. Only the PTR record

    C. Both A and PTR

    D. The DHCP server does not update records

3. Which of the following commands would you use to purge a DNS client's local DNS cache?

    A. Ipconfig /flush

    B. Ipconfig /flushdns

    C. Ipconfig /clear

    D. Ipconfig /cleardns

4. What two types of queries can you perform using the Monitoring tab of a server's Properties dialog box in the DNS snap-in?

   A. Simple

   B. Lookup

   C. Domain

   D. Recursive

5. Which of the following resource record types are used to establish an alias for an existing host name?

   A. A

   B. FORWARD

   C. CNAME

   D. HINFO

6. You want to enable Dynamic DNS for a specific zone and configure the server to allow only secure updates. What is required for you to do this?

   A. The zone must be a root zone.

   B. The zone must be Active Directory integrated.

   C. The zone must have an SRV record.

   D. You cannot enable DDNS for a specific zone—only for an entire server.

7. Which of the following commands would you use in nslookup interactive mode to list all of the hosts in the domain headrest.com?

   A. ls headrest.com

   B. ls -t ALL

   C. ls -t ANY

   D. ls -t HOSTS

8. You suspect that one of your DNS servers is having trouble with dynamic updates. Which of the following logging options would you enable to track all dynamic updates received by the server?

   A. query

   B. update

   C. ddns

   D. questions

9. You have recently created a new standard primary zone, and then find that your Windows 2000 DHCP clients are not registering their IP addresses. Which of the following could be the problem?

    A. You have not enabled dynamic updates for the zone.

    B. Only Active Directory–integrated zones allow dynamic updates.

    C. Only standard secondary zones allow dynamic updates.

    D. Standard zones require the DHCP server to update the client records.

10. Which of the following commands would you use to force a client to reregister itself with a Dynamic DNS server?

    A. Ipconfig /renew

    B. Ipconfig /register

    C. Ipconfig /registerdns

    D. Ipconfig /flushdns

REVIEW ANSWERS

1. **C** By configuring primary and secondary zones, you enable multiple servers to service client queries. This would increase the fault tolerance of the zone, as a failure of one server would not stop client queries from being processed.

2. **B** The DHCP server is, by default, responsible for updating PTR records with DDNS. Windows 2000 clients update their own A records. The DHCP server can be made to update A records for non-Windows 2000 clients.

3. **B** Ipconfig can be used to display DNS information on a DNS client and to display, flush, and refresh the information in a client's local resolver cache. The ipconfig /flushdns command is used to flush the cache.

4. **A D** A simple lookup performs an iterative query from the local resolver and is used to test basic functionality. A recursive query forwards a resolution request to another server and forces a more exhaustive query of the server.

5. **C** A canonical name (CNAME) record establishes an alias, a synonym for a host name. A is wrong because an A record is a basic host record. B is wrong because there is no such record type as FORWARD. D is wrong because an HINFO record is used to record information about the name, operating system, and CPU type of a host.

6. **B**   You can enable DDNS on a per-zone basis. In order to configure DDNS to allow only secure updates, a zone must be an Active Directory–integrated zone. If it is not, you can accept only unauthorized updates.

7. **A**   The command ls headrest.com would list all the hosts in the domain headrest.com. C is wrong because this command would list all records of any type in the domain. B and D are wrong because ALL and HOSTS are invalid command options.

8. **B**   The update option logs dynamic updates received by the DNS service from other computers. A is wrong because the query option logs queries received by the server. C is wrong because DDNS is not a valid option. D is wrong because the questions option logs the contents of the question section for each DNS query message processed by the DNS service.

9. **A**   All zone types (standard primary, standard secondary, and Active Directory integrated) allow dynamic updating by Windows 2000 clients, so the only valid answer here is that you haven't enabled dynamic updating. D is wrong because the DHCP server does not have to update host records for Windows 2000 clients, though it does update PTR records.

10. **C**   Use ipconfig /registerdns to refresh all DHCP leases and register any related DNS names.

P A R T

III

Creating, Configuring, Managing, Securing, and Troubleshooting File, Print, and Web Resources

Sharing and Publishing Network Resources

CHAPTER 7

	NEWBIE	SOME EXPERIENCE	EXPERT
ETA	5 hours	4 hours	2 hours

One of the key features of Active Directory is the ability it affords you to structure your organization into more manageable pieces and to delegate authority over those pieces. But how does that benefit the end user? One benefit is that users now have a central repository for company information. If a user needs to call the sales representative located in the Fiji branch, all that user has to do is search the Active Directory, which responds with all the details that the system knows.

This chapter covers sharing printers and folders with the network. It also covers many printer management issues. It then examines the Windows 2000 Distributed File System (Dfs), a system used to organize shared folders in disparate network locations, and how resources are published in Active Directory.

Create Shared Resources and Configure Access Rights

Objective 7.01

Sharing resources is pretty much the point of having a network, so, as you might imagine, it is a pretty important topic on the exam. This section covers three aspects of sharing resources on a network: printer sharing, file and folder sharing, and the Distributed File System (Dfs).

Configuring, Managing, and Sharing Printers

Configuring printing for a network is one of the more common tasks you'll deal with as an administrator. There are scenarios that you might face in the real world or on the exam that you might never think of. This section concentrates on installing, managing, and sharing printers.

Before we get into the actual procedures, though, you should ensure that you understand the terminology that Microsoft uses when they talk about printing:

- **Print device**   The literal physical hardware device that produces printed material. It is the heavy thing in the box that you come back from the store with.

- **Printer**   The link that is established between the print device and the operating system itself. Printers are logical representations of underlying print devices and are represented by icons in a computer's

Printers folder. You can arrange multiple printers that link to one print device, or establish one printer for multiple print devices. We'll talk about both of these configurations a bit later.

- **Printer driver**   The software that tells the hardware what to do. It converts the documents or graphics into a language the printer understands. Some printer drivers are provided within Windows; often, you must supply drivers from the manufacturer during installation of the printer.

- **Printer queue**   Documents that are waiting to be printed. When a document is sent to a printer, it enters a queue for that printer. The queue is actually a directory on the hard drive in which documents are stored until they can be spooled to the printer.

- **Print spooler**   Tracks the print job through the printing process, ensuring that jobs go to the proper ports and that priorities are enforced. Print jobs are saved to the hard drive of the print server in a spool file. It's different from a queue, though: "queue" is the word used to describe the collection of files waiting to be printed, but the spooler is an actual service and an actual location for the spool directory.

Configure a Local or Network Printer

When you set up a printer on a computer, that printer can be either local (attached to the local computer) or remote (attached to another computer on the network and shared, or attached directly to the network). The setup for a local or remote printer begins the same way, using the Add Printer wizard. You can start this by double-clicking the Add Printer icon in the Printers folder (accessible through the Control Panel folder). Keep in mind that the printer you set up (be it local or network) is a logical object that allows you to manage an actual print device. You can configure a printer that links to one device, to multiple devices, or to no device at all.

There are a few points you might want to keep in mind when setting up your printer:

- To create a printer on a DC, you need to be a member of the Administrators Server Operators or Print Operators local group. Members of the Domain Admins and Enterprise Admins groups are automatically members of the Administrators local group.

- If creating a printer on a Member server, you need to be either a member of the Administrators or Power Users local group on the server or a member of the Domain Admins or Enterprise Admins global group.

- Make sure you have the correct Windows 2000 printer drivers for your printer. Just because it ran under NT 4 doesn't mean it will work under 2000.

- You can configure a printer on a Windows 2000 Professional or Server system. If on a Professional system, then you can have only ten simultaneous connections to add print jobs to the spool.

Exam Tip

If you put a printer on a Windows 2000 Professional system that is part of a domain and want it to be searchable for others in Active Directory, all you need to do is share it. Because it is in the domain, Windows 2000 automatically publishes the printer to Active Directory.

Travel Assistance

This exam does not expect you to know many details about the actual installation process, so we have not covered it in detail here. You can learn more about the printing process in *Mike Meyers' MCSE Windows (R) 2000 Server Certification Passport (Exam 70-215)*, by Dan Newland and Rob Scrimger (Berkeley: Osborne/McGraw-Hill, 2001).

Setting Printer Properties

Once a printer is installed, you can make changes to the configuration using the Printer's Properties dialog. There are at least six tabs to choose from (some printer drivers add extras) with many options to help you set the printer up the way you prefer. Let's briefly review the important features of each tab:

- **General**   Allows you to specify Name, Location, Comments. In addition, you can establish some Printing Preferences, including page layout (portrait or landscape) and some deeper preference settings. You can also choose to Print Test Page to ensure that your printer is working properly. This dialog box can be accessed and used on the server itself, on the administrator's workstation, and on any workstation that uses the printer. Anyone who has the correct permission settings (which we will discuss shortly) can change these settings.

- **Sharing**   Allows you to share the printer and configure the share name you'd like to use. You can also install additional drivers for the printer, which provides support for non-Windows 2000 computers trying to connect to the printer, such as Windows 95/98/ME or Windows NT 4.0 systems.

- **Ports**   Shows you the port that the printer is using (LPT1, LPT2, and so on). You can add other ports, including support for a TCP/IP network–connected printer. You can also enable printer pooling on this tab, something we will discuss shortly.

- **Advanced**   This tab, shown next, has many options. You can configure Availability, which specifies the times the printer is available. If a job is sent to the printer while it is unavailable, the job is held in the spooler and printed later. You can also configure Priority, which is covered a bit later, and change the print driver. The Spool Print Documents So Program Finishes Printing Faster option configures the spooler to store print jobs on a hard drive before or during printing. The Hold Mismatched Documents option is good for jobs that use different paper sizes or layouts (letter and legal, for instance), because it will continue to print jobs that use one size of paper and wait until you change the paper before it prints the jobs using the missing paper size (which prevents wasted printing). There is also a Separator Page button that allows you to configure a page that will print between jobs, helping to distinguish between and identify different print jobs.

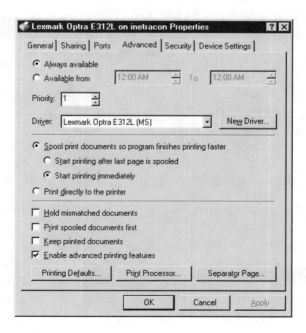

- **Security**   Allows you to configure several printer permissions, including Print, Manage Printers, and Manage Documents. These are covered a bit later in the chapter. The Device Settings tab gives you the ability to change all sorts of settings, including paper size and such.

Printer Pools

You can configure a single printer to point to multiple print devices—a configuration known as a *printer pool*, illustrated in Figure 7-1. In order to set up a printer pool, identical print devices must be used (or at least print devices that use an identical driver). Printer pools free users from having to figure out which printer is available for them to fire off a quick print job. They simply print to the printer, and the first available print device handles the job. Needless to say, it is also a good idea to locate all the print devices together so that users do not have to search for their documents in different locations.

Travel Advisory

The Windows Messenger Service sends a message back to users to tell them the actual name of the print device they've printed to, so you might think that it doesn't matter how you place the print devices in your pool. However, users often dismiss the message, so it really is best to keep print devices close together.

So, what happens if one device jams or runs out of paper while processing a print job? That one job is held in place until the printer is fixed or until paper is added. Other jobs are routed to available print devices in the pool.

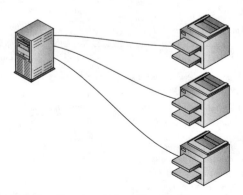

FIGURE 7.1   The Printer pool

To configure a printer pool, use the following steps:

1. Click Start | Settings | Printers.
2. Right-click the printer you want to work with and select Properties.
3. Click the Ports tab.
4. Select the check boxes next to the ports that have print devices connected to them.
5. Select the Enable Printer Pooling option.
6. Click OK.

Setting Printer Priorities

Here is a scenario for you. You have two groups, the Managers group and the Users group. The Managers are tired of having their print jobs waiting in line with the Users. They want their jobs to be bumped to the top of the printing list. Can you do that? Yes, using printer priorities.

Basically, setting up priorities involves taking the same print device and establishing two or more separate logical printers for that device. Continuing the previous example, you would set up permissions so that only the Managers group can print to the first one and only the Users group can print to the second. You would assign a higher priority to the printer used by the Managers than to the one used by the Users group. Do this by entering a number between 1 and 99 in the Priority box on the Advanced tab of a printer's Properties dialog box. Higher numbers are given priority over lower numbers.

When a user from the Managers group prints, as illustrated in Figure 7-2, that printer is given priority over print jobs printed by members of the Users group, because the Managers' printer is assigned a priority of 99 and the Users' printer is assigned a priority of 1 (1 is the default priority for all new printers). If ten jobs from members of the Users group are waiting in the queue and a member of the Managers group prints a job, the Managers' job goes straight to the top of the queue and will print after the currently printing job.

Exam Tip

For the exam, it is important to remember that 99 is highest priority and 1 is lowest. Higher numbers print first.

Configuring Printer Availability

There are times when you might have a printer that is getting hit with both small and large print jobs. Having a 3-page document sitting in the print queue behind

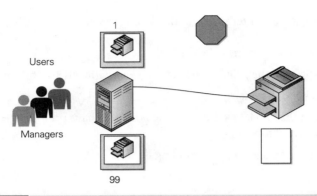

Users

Managers

1

99

FIGURE 7.2   Print priority settings

a 500-page document is not good for productivity and can actually get users a little upset with you. So, what are your options? Well, you could get another print device for the large jobs. However, another solution is to configure the availability features we talked about previously. These are found on the Advanced tab of a printer's Properties dialog box.

Here's an example of using printer availability to solve the problem we mentioned before. You could create two logical printers (let's call them LargeJobs and SmallJobs) that point to the same print device. You could then set the availability times for SmallJobs to be during the regular workday and for LargeJobs to be from only 6 P.M. to 6 A.M. Instruct users that they should print only large jobs (over 50 pages, maybe) to the LargeJobs printer, as long as it is not an urgent print job.

Configuring Permissions for a Printer

Windows 2000 lets you control printer use and administration through the use of permissions. You can configure permissions for a printer using the Security tab of a printer's Properties dialog box, shown next. The list at the top of this tab shows users and groups for which permissions on the printer are configured. Click Add to add a user or group to the list. Select a user and click Remove to take that user off the list.

To set permissions for a user on the list, select the user and use the check boxes in the Permissions window. There are three different permissions you can configure: Print, Manage Printers, and Manage Documents. For each, you can allow a user the permission or explicitly deny it. Denied permissions always override granted permissions. For example, suppose a user was a member of two groups. One group was allowed permission to manage documents and one group was denied that permission. The user would be denied permission.

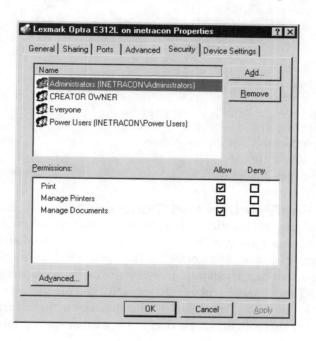

Exam Tip

Even though you can explicitly deny a permission on a printer (and other resources, for that matter), you should exercise this ability only when absolutely necessary. Denying permissions is often used as just a lazy method of getting around an improperly planned permissions structure. Occasionally, denying a permission can be a valid way to remove a permission from one user who would otherwise have that permission due to group membership.

Table 7-1 describes the functions that each permission allows a user.

TABLE 7.1	Printer Permission Settings			
Function		**Print**	**Manage Documents**	**Manage Printers**
Print documents using the printer.		Yes	Yes	Yes
Make a connection to the printer (i.e., install the printer on the user's computer).		Yes	Yes	Yes
Cancel, pause, and resume your personal documents in that printer's print queue.		Yes	Yes	Yes
Cancel, pause, and resume all documents in that printer's print queue.			Yes	Yes
Configure job settings on all documents in that printer's print queue.			Yes	Yes
Change permissions and properties on the printer.				Yes
Share or delete the printer.				Yes
Take ownership of the printer.				Yes

Managing Printers and Documents

You can manage a printer and the documents waiting in that printer's queue (depending on your assigned permissions for the printer) by double-clicking the printer's icon in the Printers folder. This opens a window for the printer, shown next, that displays all the documents waiting in the printer queue and provides access to a number of useful commands. You can also access this window by double-clicking the printer icon that shows up in the System Tray (the area of the taskbar with the system clock) while a document is printing.

AGFA-AccuSet v52.3 - Paused						
Printer Document View Help					
Document Name	Status	Owner	Pages	Size	Submitted
msoe - Notepad		Administrator	8	83.8 KB	3:50:15 PM 4/24/2002
setuplog - Notepad		Administrator	67	813 KB	3:50:20 PM 4/24/2002
eula - Notepad		Administrator	9	103 KB	3:50:27 PM 4/24/2002
3 document(s) in queue					

This window lets you manage aspects of the printer itself and the documents waiting in the queue. The Printer menu contains many of the same commands that are available on the shortcut menu you get when you right-click a printer in the Printers folder. Using this menu, you can do the following:

- Make the printer the default printer on the computer that you are using.
- Change printing preferences, which are the same options found on the Layout and Paper/Quality tabs of a printer's Properties dialog box.

Anyone with the Manage Documents permission can change the printing preferences, which affect all users using the printer. These settings are not reset automatically.

- Pause printing for all documents in the queue. This option is useful when troubleshooting a printer or changing its configuration. Print jobs can still be added to the queue, but no jobs are printed until the printer is unpaused.
- Cancel all documents, which deletes all print jobs from the printer. This command should be used as a last resort for a malfunctioning printer.
- Configure sharing and printer properties. These commands provide shortcuts to the various tabs of the printer's Properties dialog box.

The Document menu in a printer's window provides a number of additional commands for working with individual documents in the queue. You can select a document and then use any of the commands on the menu to manipulate it. These commands are also available by right-clicking the document in the window and include

- **Pause**   Temporarily suspends a job already waiting in the queue. Other unpaused documents continue printing and will jump ahead of the paused document in the queue.
- **Resume**   Resume a paused job.
- **Restart**   Start printing a job over from the beginning.
- **Cancel**   Delete a job from the queue.
- **Properties**   Open a Properties dialog box for the print job that shows advanced information, and lets you adjust the priority for the job and set scheduling restrictions (one-time adjustments that affect only that job).

Optimization and Troubleshooting of Your Printers

Troubleshooting printers and print jobs can be frustrating and is a pretty big topic. Here are a number of common problems you may run into and their corresponding solutions:

- What if you cannot cancel a print job that is stuck in the queue? You will have to Stop and Restart the Spooler service. You find this service in the Services applet from within the Control Panel.

- What if you have a problem with printing on a system where the print spooler is on a drive that is running out of room? You may need to change the location of the spool file. The default directory for the print spooler is \\winnt\system32\spool. One way to change this easily is listed in the following steps:
  1. Click Start | Settings | Printers.
  2. In the Printers window, select File | Server Properties.
  3. Click the Advanced tab.
  4. Enter the path to the new spool directory in the Spool Folder text box.
  5. Click OK.
- What if the print device malfunctions and there are jobs in the queue? One option is to have users re-print to a working print device. Another option is to redirect their print jobs. You must have Manage Printers permissions on both printers to do this. Use the following steps:
  1. Click Start | Settings | Printers.
  2. Right-click the printer that holds the documents you want to redirect and select Properties.
  3. Click the Ports tab.
  4. To send documents to another printer on the same printer server, click the port the other printer is assigned and then click OK. To send documents to another printer on a different print server, click Add Port, select Local Port, and then click New Port. Type the name of the print server and the share name of the printer.

Travel Advisory

The term "port" is used to define a connection point on a computer where data is passed in and out of the system. So even though you are choosing a "Local Port," you are providing a UNC path for another shared printer. Transmissions to the local port are redirected to the UNC path, which allows use of the printer by applications that can print only to a local port.

  5. Click OK. All documents in the queue, with the exception of the document that was printing, will print on the other print server. Sometimes, restarting that document or the printer will preserve the document that was printing.

Shared Folders and Web Folders

Sharing is the key to networking. After all, what good would a file server be if you couldn't share the folders on that server? The actual process of sharing is one of the easiest things you can do in Windows.

By default, only members of the Administrators, Server Operators, and Power Users groups can share folders. Administrators can share folders on any system they choose. Server Operators can share folders on domain controllers. Power Users can share folders on Member Servers and computers they are assigned accounts on.

To share a folder, simply right-click the folder and then choose Sharing. This brings you to the Sharing tab, shown in Figure 7-3.

On the Sharing tab, you have a few important options. Foremost, you can enable and disable sharing. You can also assign a share name, the name that users see when they access the resource over the network. A share name does not have to be the same as the name of the folder. Shared folders become visible on the network as soon as they are shared. Note that visible does not mean accessible; you will configure accessibility through permissions. To prevent a folder

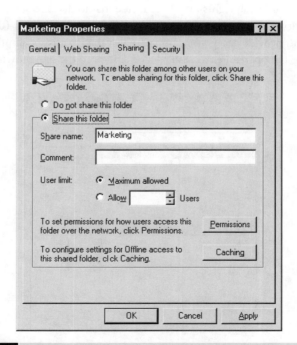

FIGURE 7.3   The Sharing tab

from being visible on the network, though, you can add a $ to the end of the share name. In this case, the folder is still shared but is not visible by other users browsing the network; in order to access the share, you have to know the share exists and know the exact name of the share.

Some hidden shares are created by default and are used to provide remote administrative access to hard drives and system folders. Using the dollar sign suffix makes these shares hidden to users but allows the administrator access to the system.

Exam Tip

Keep these share options in mind, especially the hidden share potential. Remember, too, that if you plan to map to a hidden share or publish a hidden share, you need to indicate the $ in the UNC. A proper UNC for this example would be *server_name**share_name*$.

Configuring Share Permissions

Another option you have on the Sharing tab for a folder is to configure permissions. Share permissions are one of the deciding factors in what users can access a shared folder and what rights they have inside that folder once they gain access. Share permissions work in conjunction with NTFS permissions (discussed in Chapter 8) to provide access to resources. Click the Permissions button (shown in Figure 7-3) to open a Permissions dialog similar to the one shown next.

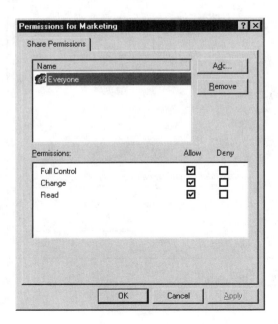

At the top of the dialog, you'll find a list box listing all of the users and groups that have been assigned share permissions on the folder. Remove a user or group by selecting it and clicking Remove. Click Add to add a user or group. Select any user or group and use the check boxes in the Permissions list box to allow or deny individual permissions.

There are three share permissions available:

- **Read**   With this permission, a user can access the folder through the share and can open documents and read them (without making changes). Users can also execute applications in the folder. Finally, the read permission permits readers to copy files to other folders (where they will be able to make changes on their own copy). This permission includes both Read (R) and Execute (X) rights.

- **Change**   Provides users the ability to open documents, execute files, copy files, and make changes on open documents. Change permission also lets users delete files. So this includes Read (R) and Execute (X) rights, along with Write (W) and Delete (D).

- **Full Control**   Includes all the abilities of the Change permission, but also allows users to change permissions on the folder itself and even take ownership of the folder. So this includes Read (R), Execute (X), Write (W), and Delete (D) rights, along with Permissions (P) and Take Ownership (O).

Travel Advisory

By default, the Everyone group is given Full Control permission on new shares. Some administrators change this as soon as they share a folder by removing the Everyone group from the list and assigning permissions to more appropriate groups. Most administrators leave the Everyone group with Full Control for shared permissions and rely on NTFS permissions (discussed in Chapter 8) to provide security. Both are valid methods.

When creating shares, you need to be aware of two very important aspects of the sharing process. The first is that you can share out only entire partitions (by right-clicking the partition and configuring Sharing) or folders; you cannot share individual files.

The second thing to be aware of is that you can share out folders that are located on either FAT/FAT32 or NTFS partitions. On FAT/FAT32 partitions, share security is the only security you will have. On NTFS partitions, the share permissions will interact with local NTFS permissions to form a more sophisticated security context. Partitions, file system formats (FAT/FAT32 and NTFS), and NTFS permissions are all covered in detail in Chapter 8.

Using Multiple Share Permissions

It is possible for a single user to have different sets of share permissions on a single shared folder. For example, suppose a user is a member of two different groups. That user might have one set of permissions assigned to one group, one set assigned to another group, and yet another set assigned directly to the user account.

When a user has multiple permissions on a single share, those permissions are combined to create the user's *effective permissions*. For example, if a user is a member of one group that has read permission on a shared folder and another group that has change permission, the user will have read and change permissions.

The exception to this rule is that if a permission is specifically denied to a user from any source, that denial overrides everything else. For example, if a user is a member of a group that has change permissions on a shared folder and a member of a group that has been denied change permissions, the user is denied the permission.

In practice, it is best to assign permissions to groups instead of to individuals and to allow permissions rather than deny them. In fact, denying permissions should be avoided altogether, as the practice can lead to complex problems on large networks. This practice will help keep permissions easier to understand and apply. One time that you may need to deny a permission is when you want to prevent access to a share by a particular user that has been granted access through group membership.

Manage a Domain-Based Distributed File System (Dfs)

The Distributed File System (Dfs) provides a way for files located on multiple servers to appear to users as though they were all located in a single place. In fact, you can think of Dfs as a "share of other shares." Dfs was first introduced in Windows NT 4.0 Service Pack 3, although it was never really used under Windows NT.

Dfs organizes shared folders on different computers into a single logical directory structure, as illustrated in Figure 7-4. The root of this hierarchy is called the *Dfs share*. When a user connects to the Dfs share using Windows Explorer or another application, it appears as though the DFS share were one simple share that contains a number of folders. Only when you connect to the share using the Dfs Console (the tool used to administer Dfs) will you see that the hierarchy is only a logical representation of different shared file resources. Dfs provides some really nice features. Rather than users having to know where shared folders are located and which servers hold those folders, the Dfs server maintains this information. If anything changes and folders are moved to other servers, you simply change the path on the Dfs server and users are none the wiser.

To create a Dfs share, you must first create the Dfs root, which is essentially a container in which to store Dfs links that point to other shares on the network. There are two types of Dfs roots: stand-alone and domain based. A stand-alone Dfs root displays the file system from one single computer; it is not a part of Active Directory. The drawback of a stand-alone Dfs is that there is no fault tolerance built into the root node of the structure (subnodes can be fault tolerant, depending on where they are stored).

A domain-based Dfs root can include shares from more than one computer within the domain, and it is stored and automatically published in Active Directory. The advantage to a domain Dfs is that it does provide fault tolerance for the Dfs root, because the Dfs topology is replicated to other domain controllers. Table 7-2 lists the differences in stand-alone and domain Dfs roots.

Creating a Dfs Root

The first step in creating a Dfs structure is to create a Dfs root. To do this, use the following procedure:

1. Log on as an administrator and click Start | Programs | Administrative Tools | Distributed File System. This opens the Distributed File System Console.

2. Select Action | New Dfs Root to start the New Dfs Root wizard.

3. Click Next to skip the opening page of the wizard.

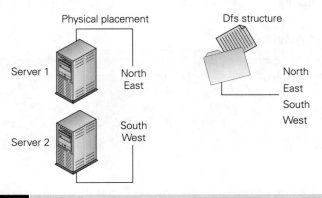

Physical placement

Dfs structure

Server 1   North
East

South
West

Server 2

North
East
South
West

FIGURE 7.4   The physical structure and logical Dfs structure

TABLE 7.2	Domain-Based Versus Stand-Alone Roots

Domain-Based Dfs Root	Stand-Alone Dfs Root
Uses AD to store the tree and synchronize changes.	No AD integration. Dfs information is stored in the local registry.
Allows for multiple levels of links.	Can have only a single-level hierarchy.
Supports file replication through FRS.	Does not support file replication services.
You can have only one domain-based Dfs root (with 32 replicas).	You can have as many stand-alone Dfs roots as you would like.

4. Choose whether to create a domain Dfs root or a stand-alone Dfs root and click Next. Creating a domain Dfs root requires that Active Directory be available.

5. If you chose to create a domain Dfs root, you will see a page asking you to select a domain. From the list of domains, select the domain that will host the Dfs root and click Next.

6. Enter the name of the server that will host the Dfs root and click Next.

7. The Dfs root must be a shared folder. Specify whether you want to use an existing share or create a new one, and click Next.

8. Enter a name for the Dfs root (the share name users will see) and an optional comment to help identify the share. Click Next.

9. Click Finish to close the wizard and create the new Dfs root.

Once you have created the Dfs root, you can begin creating links in the root by right-clicking the root in the Dfs console and selecting New Dfs Link.

Travel Advisory

Obviously, there is more to using Dfs than we can cover here, and honestly, Dfs is not featured heavily on the exam. To learn more about using and managing Dfs, check out Microsoft's step-by-step guide to configuring Dfs at http://www.microsoft.com/technet/treeview/ default.asp?url=/TechNet/prodtechnol/windows2000serv/deploy/ confeat/dfsguide.asp.

Client Access to Dfs

As you might guess, any client running Windows 2000 can access a Dfs structure with no problem. For other types of clients, Dfs support varies:

- **DOS, Windows for Workgroups, Windows 3.*x*** No Dfs client capabilities.
- **NetWare** No Dfs client capabilities.
- **Windows 95** Windows 95 clients can use Dfs by downloading a special client for Dfs versions 4.*x* or 5.0. This client is available at http://microsoft.com/ntserver/nts/downloads/winfeatures/ NTSDistrFile/default.asp.
- **Windows 98** Windows 98 includes a client for accessing a stand-alone Dfs structure, but you must download the Dfs 5.0 client to access domain-based Dfs structures.
- **Windows NT 4.0 (SP3)** Windows NT 4.0 clients updated with Service Pack 3 include a fully functional Dfs client.

> **Exam Tip**
>
> Keep these requirements in mind when confronted with Dfs client scenarios.

Objective 7.02 Publish Resources in Active Directory

The term "Publish" is defined as "to make known, to circulate, to make public, or to distribute." When an object is published in Active Directory, it can be easily searched for. Just as you might call telephone information for the number of a person, you can use Active Directory to locate information about users, computers, printers, folders, and any other resource. However, if a phone number is not listed (or is "unpublished"), it is difficult to locate the person you're looking for. The first part of this chapter explains the resources that are already published in Active Directory, which additional resources you should publish, how to publish those resources, and how to search for resources within Active Directory.

Introduction to Published Resources

Most common resources are published automatically within Active Directory. You don't have to do a thing. These resources include user accounts, computers, and printers on Windows 2000 servers that are members of the domain. This means that users can search for those objects and can immediately take advantage of the benefits of Active Directory.

There are resources, though, that are not published automatically to Active Directory. One important example would be printers on non-Windows 2000 servers and on Windows 2000 servers that are not part of the domain. Another resource that is not published automatically is shared folders (regardless of what type of computer they are on). For these resources to be available within Active Directory, you must publish them yourself.

> **Exam Tip**
>
> Printers installed on non-Windows 2000 servers (or on any servers that are not part of a domain) and shared folders are not published automatically to Active Directory. If presented with a scenario where you need to provide easy search access to these resources (where a user doesn't need to know the entire UNC path to the resource), you must publish them.

Publishing a Resource

You publish resources in Active Directory using the Active Directory Users and Computers tool. To publish a resource, you must first make sure it is set up properly. For printers, this means the printer should be installed and shared. Folders just need to be shared. You must also know the Universal Naming Convention (UNC) path of the object being published. The UNC path follows the convention *server_name**share_name*. For example, if you have shared a printer named Picard on a server named Trek, the UNC path to the share would be \\Trek\Picard.

The following steps show how to publish a shared printer in Active Directory:

1. Log on as an administrator and click Start | Programs | Administrative Tools | Active Directory Users and Computers.

2. In the console tree, expand the domain node and locate the container in which you want to create the shared printer object.

3. Right-click the container and select New | Printer. This opens the New Object – Printer dialog box shown in Figure 7-5.

4. Enter the UNC path of the shared printer and click OK to publish the printer to Active Directory.

Travel Advisory

If the printer is not accessible at this point (for example, if it hasn't been installed or shared), the publishing process will fail.

Publishing a shared folder follows almost exactly the same steps as publishing a printer. Once you select the Organizational Unit in which you want to publish the folder, choose the New | Shared Folder command instead of the New | Shared Printer command. The only difference in the process is that, in addition to providing a UNC path for the shared folder, you also provide a name by which that resource will be known in Active Directory. You do not provide a name for a published printer.

Helping Users Find Published Resources

Once you have published these resources, they are much easier for users and administrators to locate and work with. A user can search for a printer by selecting

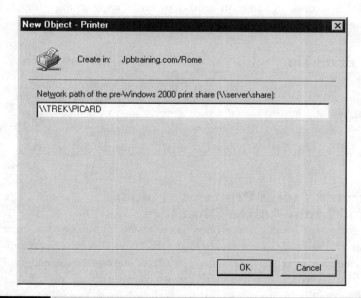

FIGURE 7.5 Entering the UNC path for a published printer

Start | Search and then selecting the For Printers option in the Search dialog box. The normal information requested is name, location, and model. Of course, there are other tabs available that provide users the ability to really narrow their searches according to advanced criteria.

Travel Advisory

One of the nice features about publishing printers within Active Directory is the ability to indicate a printer's location, which helps users find appropriate remote printers. Consider the user that has to print a document to the Hong Kong branch. He isn't sure which printer to search for, but he knows he is looking for one in Hong Kong, the Second Floor office. You can structure all of this through the use of printer locations.

Travel Assistance

For additional information on this subject, go to Start | Help; on the Index tab, type **Printer Location Tracking**. Here, you will be offered several good selections, such as enabling location tracking, naming conventions, and troubleshooting.

The same descriptions and keywords can be given to folders that you've published. Try to think of common words that would apply to the folder in question—and remember, the simpler, the better.

Exam Tip

One of the best features of published resources is that you can change the physical location of the shared folder (i.e., move it to a different server) without your users ever having to know about it. You would simply have to update the UNC path on the published object. This makes life easier for everyone involved.

Searching for a Printer or Folder from Within Active Directory

In addition to providing users an easy way to search for published resources, administrators can search for resources using the Active Directory Users and Computers tool. Just select Action | Find to open the dialog box shown in Figure 7-6.

Use the Find drop-down list to specify what type of object you're looking for, and then use the In drop-down list to specify where to look. You can narrow

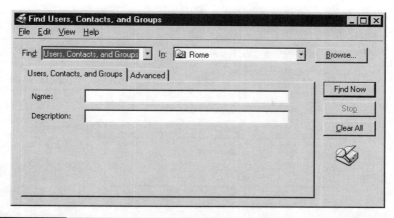

FIGURE 7.6   Searching for items in Active Directory

your search by including other information, too, like Name and Description; or you can leave these fields blank to find all objects of the type and in the location you choose. The Advanced tab provides some even stronger options for narrowing a search. As an example, say you have to search for user in the Rome OU. You know his name starts with James and his phone number begins with 555. Using the Advanced tab, shown in Figure 7-7, you can fine-tune your search to include this information and much more.

Travel Advisory

For users to search Active Directory, they can use the Search command on their Start menu. Using the Search tool, they can choose to search for people and then either indicate specific information about the person or use the Advanced tab to indicate partial information that AD might be holding.

Publishing Network Services

You can also publish certain network services (for example, Windows 2000 Certificate Services) in Active Directory to make it easier for administrators to find and manage the services and to allow delegation of administrative tasks. Publishing a service also provides a way for administrators to manage the service without having to worry about which computer provides the service or where that computer is located.

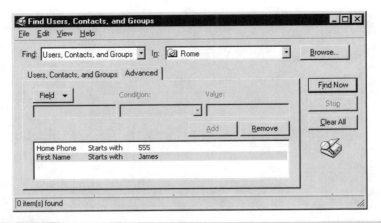

FIGURE 7.7 Fine-tuning your search through the Advanced options

Two types of information are typically published to Active Directory:

- **Binding information** Binding information lets clients connect to services that do not have well-known bindings. Publishing the bindings for these kinds of services allows Windows 2000 to automatically establish connections with these services.

- **Configuration information** Certain configuration information can be common across client applications. For example, company information entered into particular programs should be the same for all programs used in a company. By publishing configuration information, you can reduce the amount of configuration required on a client computer.

CHECKPOINT

✔**Objective 7.01: Create Shared Resources and Configure Access Rights**
This objective looked at the configuration and management needed to set up and share printers on a network. It also looked at the process of sharing of folders and discussed Web sharing. Finally, it provided an overview of Dfs.

✔**Objective 7.02: Publish Resources in Active Directory** This objective looked at the different reasons for publishing non–Windows 2000 shared printers and shared folders in Active Directory and the methods for doing so.

REVIEW QUESTIONS

1. You have a Windows 2000 Professional system that is a member of the Corp domain. It has a printer connected to it that is shared out. How do you ensure that this printer is published in Active Directory?

    A. Go to the OU that you want the printer to be managed from, right-click and choose New – Printer. Then enter the UNC path of the printer.

    B. Go to the Properties dialog box of the printer and select the Publish To Active Directory check box on the General tab.

    C. From within the systems printer settings, under File – Server Options, enable the printer to be published.

    D. Do nothing.

2. If you wanted to set up a printer with the highest priority, which of the following options would you choose for the priority of that printer?

    A. 0

    B. 1

    C. 99

    D. 100

3. You have domain-based Dfs set up for your network. You would like all of your clients to access your Dfs. You have 100 Windows 2000 systems, 150 Windows 98 systems, 20 Windows for Workgroups systems, and 5 NetWare clients. Which of the following can you perform?

    A. Install the Dfs client on the Windows for Workgroups systems.

    B. Install the Dfs client on the NetWare systems.

    C. Install the Dfs client on the Windows 2000 systems.

    D. Install the Dfs client on the Windows 98 systems.

4. From within what tool does an Administrator search for Active Directory objects such as published folders?

    A. Active Directory Users and Computers

    B. Active Directory Domains and Trusts

    C. Active Directory Sites and Services

    D. Active Directory Object Searches

5. You are running out of disk space on your C drive. Your printer is having difficulty printing, and you think the problems are related. You have another drive installed. How would you rectify the problem? (Choose all that apply.)

   A. Stop and Restart the Spooler service.

   B. Change the location of the spool file to the other disk.

   C. Delete stuff from your C drive and move it to your D drive.

   D. Cut the spool file from within System32 and paste it to your D drive.

6. Consider the following scenario. Bill (a member of both the Sales and the Managers group) is attempting to access a file that is in a shared-out folder. No NTFS permissions have been established. What are Bill's share permissions for the folder?

User/Group	Share
Managers	Change
Sales	Full Control

   A. Read

   B. Change

   C. Full Control

   D. No Access

7. You have a folder named Research that is shared out as a hidden folder on the network from a server named FileServe. Sebastian has permission and wants to map a drive to it. What does he need to type?

   A. \\FileServe\Research

   B. \\FileServe\$Research

   C. http://fileserve/research

   D. \\FileServe\Research$

8. You want to share folders. Which of the following file systems could you use? (Choose all that apply.)

   A. HPFS

   B. FAT

   C. NTFS

   D. FAT32

9. Jenny wants to have the ability to pause or cancel her own print jobs from the printer queue. What permission level does Jenny need to have on the logical printer?

   A. Print

   B. Manage documents

   C. Manage printers

   D. Full Control

10. When you share out a folder, what are the default share permissions?

   A. Administrators: Full Control

   B. Everyone: Full Control

   C. Users: Full Control

   D. Everyone: Read

REVIEW ANSWERS

1. **D** Printers that are hosted on Windows 2000 systems in a domain are automatically published to Active Directory. Answer A is unnecessary because it already is published. Answers B and C are fictitious; you cannot publish a printer in this way.

2. **C** The value 99 is the highest priority; 1 is the lowest. Answer A is incorrect because there is no 0 value available. Answer D is also incorrect because there is no 100 value available.

3. **D** The only thing you can do is install the client on the Windows 98 machines. The Windows 98 system has the stand-alone client, but not the domain client. The Windows systems have the client automatically. The Windows for Workgroups systems and the NetWare systems don't have a Dfs client.

4. **A** Administrators can use the Active Directory Users and Computers tool to search for objects. They can select Action and then Find to search. Answers B and C are incorrect because these tools perform other tasks. Answer D is fictitious.

5. **B C** The real answer is "move the spool file," but you might just delete stuff from C if that is possible, so either one is acceptable. Answer A is incorrect, although this will often correct other printing problems when printers stop functioning normally. Answer D is

incorrect because it will actually cause more problems. Moving the spool file is not a cut-and-paste operation. You have to let your server know where it is through properties in the Server Properties of the Printers applet.

6. **C**   Because Bill is in both groups, the permissions combine; however, they do not conflict with each other. They combine to allow the least amount of restriction, and so give Bill the Full Control level of permissions.

7. **D**   To share out a folder as a hidden share, you need to put the dollar sign at the end of the share name and then use that dollar sign in your UNC path. The correct UNC path is *server_name\share_name*. Answer A is incorrect because it doesn't use the dollar sign. Answer B is incorrect because it puts the dollar sign in the wrong place. Answer C is incorrect because it uses a Web sharing connection and doesn't consider the dollar sign.

8. **B C D**   Sharing is possible for both FAT/FAT32 and NTFS file systems. Only NTFS, however, supports local security settings, but sharing works on both. Answer A is incorrect because Windows 2000 doesn't even support HPFS.

9. **A**   This question is somewhat deceptive. You think you need higher permissions than you really do. If a user can print to a printer, that user can pause or cancel her own jobs. Answer B is incorrect because this is the next level of permissions up and would allow Jenny to manage other people's jobs, not just her own. Answer C is incorrect because this would allow Jenny to manage all jobs and configure permissions on the printer. Answer D is incorrect because no such setting exists.

10. **B**   By default, the dynamic group Everyone gets Full Control. It is not recommended that you deny these permissions, because it will affect all your users' access. Microsoft actually recommends that you leave the default and then use NTFS permissions.

Managing Data Storage and NTFS Permissions

	NEWBIE	SOME EXPERIENCE	EXPERT
ETA	7 hours	5 hours	3 hours

This chapter focuses on the different file systems that Windows 2000 supports and how permissions work with those file systems. We'll also look at the new Disk Management tool used to configure hard disks for both performance and fault tolerance. Finally, we will look at some of the additional features that NTFS provides over other file systems, including the Encrypting File System (EFS), disk quotas, and compression.

Objective 8.01 Manage Data Storage

W indows 2000 Server provides new tools for handling storage solutions. Additional drivers have been added to the operating system to ensure operability with more devices, and important storage solutions such as Removable Storage Manager (RSM) and Remote Storage Service (RSS) have been added to enhance storage abilities.

Choosing a File System

A file system is used by an operating system to organize and track the files on a disk. Windows 2000 supports three different file systems:

- **File Allocation Table (FAT)**   FAT was first introduced in DOS. Partitions formatted using FAT are limited to 4GB but are readable by all versions of Windows. It is a relatively slow file system that does not do a very good job of handling the way files are stored on large disks, resulting in a good bit of wasted disk space. FAT can be used to dual-boot between Windows 2000 and other operating systems. So, essentially, FAT is a fast file system the works fine on smaller drives.

- **File Allocation Table 32 bit (FAT32)**   FAT32, a 32-bit version of FAT, was introduced with the second release of Windows 95. Partitions using FAT32 may be up to 32GB in size and are recognized by all versions of Windows beginning with Windows 95 Service Release 2 and Windows NT 4.0. Neither FAT nor FAT32 provide any file-level security. FAT32 can be used to dual-boot between Windows 98 and 2000/XP (not NT) operating systems.

- **NT File System (NTFS)**   NTFS was introduced with Windows NT. Windows 2000 uses NTFS version 5. Partitions using NTFS may be up to 2 terabytes (although you can extend a partition beyond this limit using alternate techniques) and are recognized by all versions of Windows NT, Windows 2000, and Windows XP. NTFS provides such features as file-level security, compression, and encryption. NTFS also makes more efficient use of disk space than FAT or FAT32. One other notable difference is that, while FAT and FAT32 can be used to format a floppy disk, NTFS cannot be, due to the size of the index. NTFS cannot be used to dual-boot with operating systems that do not recognize the NTFS file system (like Windows 95, 98, and Me). You can dual-boot with other versions of NT, such as NT 4.0 or XP/.NET.

Exam Tip

Windows 95, 98, and Me cannot recognize NTFS partitions. You can create a dual-boot situation in which Windows 2000 and Windows 98 (for example) are installed on the same computer and in which some partitions are formatted with FAT32 and some with NTFS. Any partitions that are formatted using NTFS will not be accessible to the Windows 98 operating system.

Windows 2000 provides a way to convert a disk partition from FAT/FAT32 to the NTFS file system. This is a one-way conversion; Windows 2000 has no built-in method to convert in the other direction. Conversion is done using the CONVERT command at the command prompt using the following syntax:

```
Convert volume /FS:NTFS [/V] [/CvtArea:filename] [/NoSecurity] [/X]
```

- *Volume*   Refers to the drive letter or volume name of the partition to be converted. If you use a drive letter, be sure to include the colon after the letter (e.g., C:).

- **/FS:NTFS**   Specifies the conversion to NTFS.

- **/V**   Switches the conversion to verbose mode, where more detailed information is displayed during the process. This switch is optional.

- **/CvtArea:***filename*   Specifies a contiguous file in the root directory of the drive that will be used as a placeholder for the system files. This switch is optional.

- **/NoSecurity**   Configures security settings on all files and folders on the converted partition at the default level. This makes all files available to the Everyone group. This switch is optional.

- **/X**   Forces the volume to dismount if any files are currently opened. This switch is optional.

Using Disk Quotas

Disk quotas allow administrators to set restrictions on the space that users take up on a partition, providing a great way to control the use of storage space on servers. However, quotas can be used only on drives formatted with NTFS. Once quota limits are established, the system keeps track of the disk usage and calculates the amount of space used by each user. Often, users attempt to work around quota settings by compressing files, but quotas are calculated using the uncompressed value of the users' files and folders. Also, the calculation is based on the ownership of the file or folder (which simply means a user's disk space is calculated from the files that he or she owns). Quotas are also established on a volume-by-volume basis, and the settings are not shared with other volumes. This is reasonable because you might establish a quota for the server that retains a user's home directory, but you wouldn't establish the same quota limit on the file server that the user works with.

Exam Tip
Remember how quotas are calculated, especially that they are calculated using an uncompressed value. If a user receives a "disk is full" error and you aren't certain why, make sure that the user has stored less than their quota without compression.

Configuring Disk Quotas

Quota implementation is quick and easy to do (assuming you have an NTFS partition). Once you institute the use of quotas on a partition, you can then configure additional options. Quotas are not enabled by default, but you can enable a quota for a partition using the following steps:

1. Log on as an administrator and double-click the My Computer icon.
2. Right-click the drive on which you want to set quotas and select Properties from the shortcut menu.
3. Click the Quota tab, shown in Figure 8-1.
4. Select the Enable Quota Management option.

Most of the options on the Quota tab are relatively easy to figure out. You can establish a maximum level of disk usage for users and elect whether to deny additional disk space to users exceeding the limit. Without this option enabled, the system only notes the infraction but does nothing to stop it. If this option is

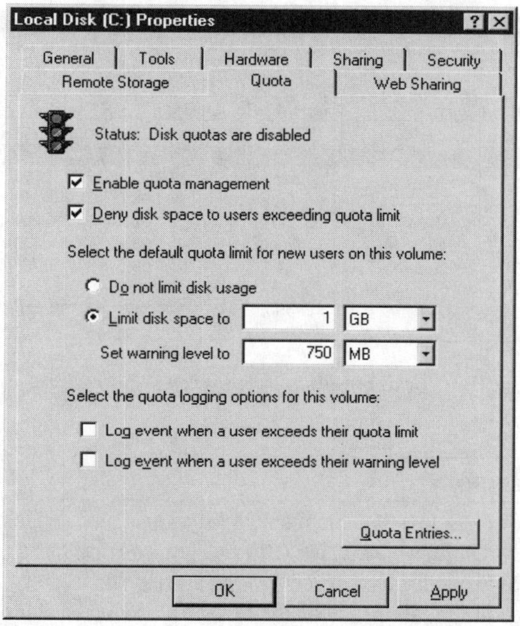

FIGURE 8.1   The Quota tab from the disk Properties dialog box

selected, the user is cut off at the threshold, even though that user may be on a drive with plenty of free space.

Clicking Quota Entries opens the window shown in Figure 8-2, which provides you with the ability to view, edit, and create quota entries. If you have quotas set on a volume that you would prefer not apply to certain individuals, you can create specific quota entries and choose the option Do Not Limit Disk Usage for a particular user. This prevents the disk quota from affecting the user. You can also use this dialog box to apply quotas only to specific users.

Exam Tip

If you want the Quota to affect only one set of folders (for example, a user's home folders), you can place those folders on the user's own partition to ensure that the quota affects only those home folders and doesn't affect the user's access to other disk space.

Status	Name	Logon Name	Amount Used	Quota Limit	Warning Level	Percent Used
⚠ War...	Tim Duggan	tduggan@Jp...	299.99 MB	300 MB	200 MB	99
OK		BUILTIN\Ad...	3.61 GB	No Limit	No Limit	N/A
OK	steve	steve@Jpbtr...	0 bytes	300 MB	200 MB	0
OK	[Retrieving ...	S-1-5-21-120...	0 bytes	1 GB	750 MB	0
OK		NT AUTHO...	20.21 MB	1 GB	750 MB	1
OK	Internet Gue...	JPBTRAININ...	0 bytes	1 GB	750 MB	0
OK	Launch IIS ...	JPBTRAININ...	1.64 KB	1 GB	750 MB	0

Quota Entries for Local Disk (C:)
Quota   Edit   View   Help

7 total item(s), 1 selected.

FIGURE 8.2   The Quota Entries management window

Travel Advisory

You can quickly determine the quota status for a partition by opening the partition's Properties dialog box. A traffic light icon displays a red light if quotas are disabled, a yellow light if Windows is rebuilding quota information, and a green light if the quota system is functioning.

Using the Encrypting File System (EFS)

The Encrypting File System (EFS) uses public-key encryption to secure files and folders on an NTFS-formatted volume. Only the user who encrypts the file or folder and a special account designated as a Recovery Agent can access it. The user's certificate is used to decrypt the file key, which is stored in the DDR. The file key is then used to decrypt the actual file. The entire process is transparent to the user; EFS works by encrypting files as they are stored and decrypting them as they are accessed.

Encrypted files remain encrypted whether they are moved, copied, or renamed. Information even remains encrypted if pieces of encrypted data are stored in temporary files or in the paging file. If a user other than the one who encrypted the file or folder attempts to access the document, the system returns a No Access message box, regardless of the permission settings on the document. This means a person could have Full Control over the folder, and even Take Control over the folder, but if it was encrypted by another user, it is still inaccessible. The only person who can access the encrypted information is the user and a designated Recovery Agent.

Encrypting a Folder or File

Encrypting a file or folder is a relatively simple process. You can configure a folder (and its contents) to be encrypted using the following steps:

1. Right-click the file or folder and select Properties from the shortcut menu.

2. On the General tab, click Advanced. This opens the Advanced Attributes dialog box, shown in Figure 8-3.

3. Select the Encrypt Contents To Secure Data option and click OK.

4. Choose whether you want changes applied to only the selected folder or to the contents of the folder, as well, and click OK.

Once an object is encrypted, you can remove encryption by following the same procedure and disabling the Encrypt Contents To Secure Data option.

Exam Tip

Files and folders can be either encrypted or compressed; they cannot be encrypted and compressed simultaneously. Another key point to remember is that encrypted files should not be shared, which makes sense because the only user that can normally decrypt the file is the one that encrypted it.

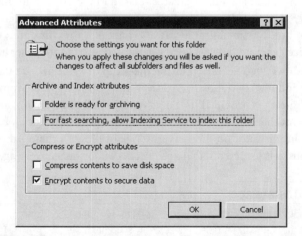

FIGURE 8.3   Use the Advanced Attributes dialog box for a folder to set encryption.

EFS Recovery Agent

The biggest question about encryption is always, "What do you do when a user can no longer access files that they encrypted?" For example, what happens if the user's file encryption certificate and associated private key are lost or damaged (through a disk failure without backup or some other type of mishap)? This is where the Recovery Agent comes to the rescue.

The EFS Recovery Agent is an important safeguard to ensure that there isn't a single point of failure on accessing encrypted data. By default, the Domain Administrator account is the EFS Recovery Agent for the domain and the local Administrator account is the EFS Recovery Agent for stand-alone systems. Additional Recovery Agents can be configured through Active Directory and Microsoft's Certificate Server, a capability that can prove to be helpful so that the workload doesn't fall completely into the administrator's hands.

A default local recovery policy is automatically created when an administrator account logs on to the computer for the first time. When this process occurs, that administrator becomes the default recovery agent. In many situations, this is the local Administrator account. In some situations, however, the first account used to log on to Windows 2000 is not the local Administrator account:

- **Windows 2000 Professional** When Windows 2000 Professional completes setup and restarts, the Network Identification wizard prompts the user to select either an automatic logon account or a username and password for logon purposes. When a username is specified, that account is created, placed in the Local Administrators group, and then logged on to the computer. Because the newly created account is the first administrator to log on to the computer, the EFS service generates a self-signed certificate issued to that user account.

- **Windows 2000 Server** During the setup of Windows 2000 Server or Windows 2000 Advanced Server, the option to join a domain or workgroup is provided. If the server is joined to a domain, any user account that is a member of the Domain Administrator global group is an administrator on that server. If one of these Domain Administrator accounts is logged on, that account becomes the recovery agent.

Travel Assistance

For a complete guide to using EFS and working with Recovery Agents, check out the following article on Microsoft's TechNet site:
http://www.microsoft.com/technet/treeview/default.asp?url=/
TechNet/prodtechnol/windows2000serv/deploy/confeat/efsguide.asp.

Managing NTFS Compression

NTFS compression, as its name implies, is available only on partitions formatted with the NTFS file system. As with file encryption, a file or folder is set to either a compressed or uncompressed state. The actual compression and uncompression are handled transparently as files are accessed. Compressed files are fully accessible by Windows Explorer, as well as by Windows- and DOS-based applications. There is no need to uncompress files manually before use.

> **Exam Tip**
>
> You cannot encrypt and compress an object at the same time.

Configuring Compression

You can configure compression on drives, as well as on folders and files; however, the procedure for compressing a drive is slightly different than for compressing a folder or file. To compress a drive, open the Properties dialog box of the drive, and, on the General tab, enable the Compress Drive To Save Disk Space option shown in Figure 8-4. You can select this option to compress the drive.

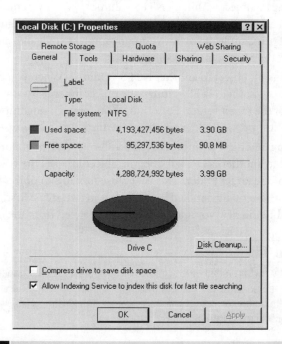

FIGURE 8.4   Compressing an NTFS partition

To compress a folder or a file, use the Properties dialog box for the object. Click Advanced on the General tab and use the dialog box that opens to enable the compression option (refer to Figure 8-3). When you click OK, you will be asked whether you want to compress just the current folder (assuming the object was a folder) or all the objects in the folder as well.

At this point, you may be wondering how you can tell the difference between a compressed object (folder/file) and an uncompressed one. From any open folder, choose Tools | Folder Options (you can also get there through the Control Panel), switch to the View tab of the dialog box that opens, and scroll through the list for the Show Encrypted or Compressed NTFS Files in Color option.

Compression Inheritance

When it comes to moving or copying objects that have compression set on them, there are some basic rules that apply:

- **Copying an object within an NTFS volume** When you copy an object within an NTFS volume, the file inherits the compression state of the target folder. For example, moving an uncompressed file into a compressed folder results in the file being compressed.

- **Moving an object within an NTFS volume** When you move an object within an NTFS volume, the object retains its original compression state. For example, if you move an uncompressed file into a compressed folder, the file remains uncompressed.

- **Copying an object to another NTFS volume** When you copy an object to another NTFS volume, the object inherits the compression state of the target folder. For example, moving an uncompressed file into a compressed folder results in the file being compressed.

- **Moving an object to another NTFS volume** When you move an object to another NTFS volume, the object inherits the compression state of the target folder. This is because moving an object to another volume is actually handled by Windows in two steps: first, the object is copied to the new volume, and then it is deleted from the old volume.

Exam Tip

The easiest way to remember the methods of compression inheritance is to know that the only time an object retains its original setting is when it is moved to a new location within the same partition. Otherwise, the object inherits the target folder's settings.

Managing Storage

Windows 2000 uses two different types of storage: basic and dynamic. Basic storage uses the traditional method of partitioning and formatting. Microsoft has introduced (and is encouraging the use of) dynamic disks as a means of providing added functionality that isn't available using basic disks. A disk can be basic or dynamic, but you cannot use both storage types on a single disk. This section looks at the difference between basic and dynamic disks and also examines some of the basics of storage management.

Basic Storage

Basic storage is the traditional method of handling disks, and all versions of Windows and DOS support it. A basic disk (i.e., one formatted for basic storage) makes use of disk partitioning. A partition is a logical section of a hard disk on which data may be written, and partitions allow you to segment the storage on a drive. For example, you could use one partition for storing system files, one for storing a Web site, and one for storing user files. Every hard disk must be partitioned before it can be used. Often, a disk is set up as one big partition, but you may also divide a disk into several partitions. When you partition a disk, you decide how much disk space to allocate to each partition.

Basic disks use the standard partition table to record disk information. This is stored in the Master Boot Record (MBR), which is a single sector at track 0, side 0, sector 0. The MBR (discussed more in Chapter 2) is 512 bytes in length and contains information about the physical layout of the disk and the partition table. There are four spaces available in the partition table, which can contain up to four primary (bootable) partitions or up to three primaries and one extended (that can be broken down to logical drives). In order to help prevent head contention, the drives should normally be configured as a single partition.

Partitions come in three forms:

- **Primary**   A *primary* partition can be set as the bootable partition. A computer running a Windows operating system can use up to four primary drives (three if you also use an extended partition), any one of which may be set as the active, or bootable, drive.

- **Extended**   An *extended* partition provides a way to get around the four-primary-partition limit. Extended partitions cannot themselves be formatted and used, but serve rather as a shell in which you can create logical partitions.

- **Logical**   Any number of *logical* partitions may be created inside an extended partition. Logical partitions may not be set as the active partition, and thus cannot be used to hold operating systems. Instead, logical partitions are normally used for organizing files. All logical partitions are visible, no matter what operating system is booted.

Disadvantages of using basic disks within Windows 2000 include the fact that you cannot make disk changes without rebooting your system. Also, you cannot set up new volumes, mirrored volumes, or striped volumes under Windows 2000 with basic disks. In essence, you are forced to use dynamic volumes if you want to enable fault tolerance in Windows 2000.

Creating and Deleting Partitions   Working with partitions and drive letters in Windows 2000 is done using a tool named Computer Management, which is available in the Administrative Tools folder. The Computer Management tool is used to access several different system tools and to manage the storage devices on your computer. To work with partitions, you must open the Storage container and select Disk Management, as shown in Figure 8-5.

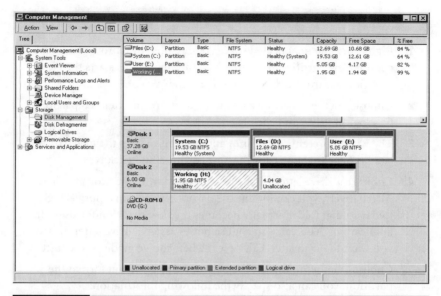

Volume	Layout	Type	File System	Status	Capacity	Free Space	% Free
Files (D:)	Partition	Basic	NTFS	Healthy	12.69 GB	10.68 GB	84 %
System (C:)	Partition	Basic	NTFS	Healthy (System)	19.53 GB	12.61 GB	64 %
User (E:)	Partition	Basic	NTFS	Healthy	5.05 GB	4.17 GB	82 %
Working (...	Partition	Basic	NTFS	Healthy	1.95 GB	1.94 GB	99 %

FIGURE 8.5   Managing storage with the Computer Management console

Travel Advisory

You can also manage storage on systems in your domain by using Active Directory Users and Computers, right-clicking the computer you want to manage, and then choosing Manage from the shortcut menu.

The right pane displays current disk information. The top half shows all formatted partitions (logical drives) on your computer. The bottom half shows each physical disk drive on the computer (including removable disks) and the allotment of partitions on those disks. The computer represented in Figure 8-5 is set up as follows:

- Disk 1 is a 40GB drive (manufacturer specifications vary from drive to drive, so it actually has 37.28GB available) with three partitions. These partitions have the drive letters C, D, and E. The C partition is a primary partition, indicated in dark blue. D and E are logical partitions, indicated in light blue and surrounded by a green frame that represents the extended partition that contains them.

- Disk 2 is a 6GB drive that has one 2GB partition and 4GB of unallocated space that may be partitioned.

You can create a new partition using the following steps:

1. Right-click the unallocated space (represented by a brown bar) and choose New Partition from the shortcut menu. This starts the New Partition wizard. Click Next to go past the Welcome page.

2. Choose whether to create a primary partition, an extended partition, or a logical drive, and click Next.

3. The wizard presents minimum and maximum sizes the new partition can be. Specify the size for the new partition and click Next.

4. Choose the drive letter for the new partition from the drop-down menu. Alternatively, you can mount the partition inside an empty NTFS folder so that folder actually becomes the new partition for users and applications. You can also choose not to assign a drive letter or path if you want to do so later. Click Next when you've made your choice.

5. Choose whether to format the partition or not. If you format the partition, you can also specify the following information:

   - **File system**   Choose NTFS or FAT32.

   - **Allocation unit size**   This represents the size of the clusters or allocation units, which is the number of sectors that will be combined together to make up a cluster or allocation unit used in the partition. A file will always use an even multiple of this size: a file of 8.2KB will use 16KB even if the cluster size is 8KB. For this reason, it is almost always better to leave this at the default. The one advantage to choosing a larger size is that larger files can be written more quickly to disk, as an entire cluster is written at once and there is less overhead managing 65,000 things than there is managing 16.7 million.

   - **Volume label**   The name of the drive as it appears in Windows explorer.

   - **Perform a quick format**   A quick format rewrites the master file table and skips testing for bad blocks on a disk. If you have already performed a full format on a disk (or have used a utility like chkdsk.exe to scan for bad blocks), a quick format will save you a lot of time.

   - **Enable file and folder compression**   Enables compression on the drive. You can also do this later by going into the drive's Properties dialog box.

6. Click Finish to create the new partition and begin formatting if you
    chose to format the disk. Note that, while the partition is being
    formatted, you cannot perform other activities that involve the new
    partition, but you can continue to work with other partitions.

Formatting Partitions   Unformatted partitions in the Computer Management
window look just like formatted partitions but are not labeled with a file system
(you can see in Figure 8-5 that formatted partitions are all labeled NTFS). You
can format any partition, whether it is already formatted or not, using the Computer Management window. Note that all data on a partition is lost when it is formatted. To format a partition, right-click a partition and choose Format. A dialog
opens enabling you to specify the volume label, file system, allocation unit size,
and other options. Choose your options and click OK to begin formatting. Windows warns you that all data on the drive will be overwritten.

Dynamic Storage

Dynamic disks allow for added functionality in Windows 2000 over basic disks.
The primary difference between a basic disk and a dynamic disk is that a small
space is reserved at the end of the latter to record more information about the
use of the disk.

With dynamic disks, you can create striped volumes, mirrored volumes, and
RAID 5 volumes (or stripe sets with parity), all of which are discussed later in
the chapter. The primary benefits of using dynamic disks are that you aren't
limited in the types of volumes you can create and that volumes can have
recoverability, since information is stored about what parts of what volumes is
stored on the disk. You can also extend volumes to encompass space from other
hard disks or create volumes that use space on multiple drives (as long as the
other hard disks are also dynamic disks). The goal of dynamic storage is to make
it easier to recover the more advanced forms of volumes.

Windows 2000 supports several types of volumes when using dynamic disks.
Some of those volume types are considered non-fault tolerant, in that they can-
not survive the failure of a disk. Some of these volume types are fault tolerant.
These volume types are discussed in the next two sections.

Non-Fault-Tolerant Volumes   Volumes that are not fault tolerant have no
built-in method of assuring the safety of data on the volume in the event of
a disk failure. Windows 2000 supports two types of volumes that are not
fault tolerant:

- **Simple volumes**   Consist of the space used from one dynamic disk
  and are the same as partitions on a basic drive. A disk can contain one

or multiple simple volumes (which may remind you somewhat of partitions under basic disks). Simple volumes are not fault tolerant, in that a disk failure wipes out the entire volume.

- **Spanned volumes** Consist of space from at least 2 dynamic disks, and as many as 32 dynamic disks (which is the Windows 2000 name for the volume sets used by NT 4.0). A spanned volume writes data to one disk in the volume until that disk is full. Then the space on the next disk is used. If the data in any of the disks is lost, the entire volume is lost.

- **Striped volumes** Consist of space on between 2 and 32 hard drives on which blocks of each file of data are written across the multiple disks. Disk striping provides increased speed and maximization of disk space (because all of it is used for data). However, if one drive fails, all of the data is lost. Striped volumes are also referred to as RAID 0 volumes.

Fault-Tolerant Disk Structures Windows 2000 supports three levels of fault tolerance, using a system known as a Redundant Array of Independent Disks (RAID). These levels are termed RAID 1 and RAID 5.

- RAID 1, also referred to as *mirrored volumes,* uses the technique of writing the same data to two physical disks (hence the "term mirror"). RAID 1 requires two hard drives: one for the original data and the other to hold a copy of the original data. With RAID 1, 50 percent of the disk space is used for redundancy because one drive holds a copy of information on the other drive. If one disk in a mirror fails, a copy of the data is available on the other disk in the mirror. Problems can occur during a reboot if the drive that fails happens to be the one that was your bootable system, but it's not a big deal; you can use a boot floppy to access the second drive and resolve the situation. The positive side to a mirrored volume is fault tolerance; the negative side is loss of half of your disk space. If you have two drives with 10GB each, only 10GB worth of data can be written.

  Mirrored volumes are really intended to be used for the system and boot partitions and are, in fact, the only solution available. If you are mirroring the system and boot partitions, you should use drives with the same disk geometry and the same partitioning (voluming) scheme to ensure the descriptions of the physical disk layouts are the same.

Travel Advisory

A variation of RAID 1 called *duplexing* may increase your speed and fault tolerance. This is a mirrored solution that uses two disk controllers. The benefit here is additional fault tolerance in the case of the controller going bad. It also provides a little faster speed (depending on the controllers in use) because the single controller doesn't have to ensure the write between both drives.

- RAID 5, also referred to as *disk striping with parity,* is the process of data being written evenly across each of the drives in the array. RAID 5 is similar to a striped volume, but parity information is stored for fault tolerance. Parity is a calculation that can be used to reconstruct the data in case of a failure. RAID 5 requires at least three hard drives and has an overhead proportional to the number of hard drives used; the parity information uses the equivalent space of one member of the set. If three drives are used, there is a one-third disk overhead for the parity information.

Defragmenting Disks

When you delete a file on your computer, Windows doesn't really remove it. It just marks that space as available for new information to be written. When a new file is written to disk, part of the file might be written to one available section of disk space, part might be written to another, and part to another. This piecemeal writing of a file is called *fragmentation.* It is a normal process, and Windows keeps track of files just fine. The problem is that when a drive has a lot of fragmentation, it can take longer getting the read/write head to the right location and waiting for the correct sector(s) to pass under the read/write head. You can speed up drive access significantly by periodically defragmenting your drive.

Windows 2000 includes a utility, Disk Defragmenter, that you can use to defragment a drive. You can access Disk Defragmenter through the Computer Management window (shown in Figure 8-6) by clicking Defragment Now on the Tools tab of a drive's Properties dialog box, or by running Disk Defragmenter from the System Tools folder on the Start menu.

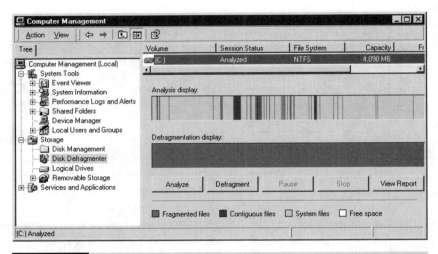

FIGURE 8.6 The Disk Defragmenter

The top part of Disk Defragmenter shows all partitions available on your computer. The Session Status column indicates whether a partition has been analyzed for fragmentation. To analyze a partition, select it and click Analyze. When the analysis is done, Windows lets you know whether it thinks the partition should be defragmented. A graphical representation (just below the disk partitions) shows the estimated disk usage before defragmenting, indicating fragmented, contiguous, and unmovable files. A second graphical representation shows the progress during the defrag and the estimated disk usage after defragmenting a partition. Click View Report to see a detailed analysis of disk space and a list of many of the fragmented files on the disk.

To defragment a partition, click Defragment. You can pause or stop a defragmentation at any time without damaging the data on your disk and restart it later.

Exam Tip

Defragmenting a disk is great for speeding up access to files when users report that the server is not retrieving files as fast as perhaps it did in the past. Keep in mind, however, that there is a proper time to do this. It can take hours to defragment a drive (especially with today's sizes), so choose a time when no work is going to be done.

Mounting Volumes

Another disk management feature that Microsoft has provided with Windows 2000 is mounted volumes. *Mounted volumes* look like folders but actually refer to other disk locations. This can be very helpful in expanding your disk space (or presenting the impression that you've expanded your disk space) without adding another drive letter or drive mapping to your disk structure.

For example, let's say you have a folder called Files on your server. All your users are automatically mapped to that folder when they log on. However, the disk is running low on space. You can create a mount volume folder on the server that actually refers to another disk location, and users would then place new documentation in the new area.

So, essentially, you can create a single drive letter that holds disk space from multiple disks. This allows users to access all of that disk space without having to be involved in where that space is coming from on the server. Another great use for mounting volumes relates to CD-ROM drives, which can be mounted into a single drive, making a series of CD-ROMs easily available.

> ### Exam Tip
> You can use mount volumes on both basic and dynamic disk structures that are formatted with NTFS. These volumes may give you the added space you need on a disk structure that seems limited in expandability. Keep in mind that you have to create an empty folder that will be the target (or mounting point) for the drive.

Managing NTFS Permissions

NTFS permissions are rules applied to a file system object (a file or folder, for example) that govern which users can access the object and what they can do once they access it. Given the name, it should be evident that NTFS permissions are available only on volumes formatted with NTFS. NTFS security is in effect no matter whether a user accesses an object locally (i.e., by sitting down at the local computer) or over the network. If a user is accessing a network share that has NTFS permissions applied to it, the NTFS permissions are combined with the share permissions to determine the user's effective access to the object. We'll get to this a bit later.

Travel Advisory

NTFS stores an access control list (ACL) for every system object on a volume. This ACL contains a list of users and groups that have been granted or denied access through NTFS permissions and the level of access specified.

Standard NTFS Permissions   NTFS folder permissions control the access that users have to folders and to all the subfolders and files inside the folders on which the permissions are applied. For this reason, you are much more likely to configure NTFS permissions on folders than on individual files. Table 8-1 lists the standard NTFS folder permissions available to you. You can allow or deny each type of access for a user or group.

While it is more effective to assign permissions to folders, you can certainly apply permissions directly to files, as well. Table 8-2 lists the standard NTFS permissions available for assigning to files.

Advanced Permissions   The standard NTFS permissions will be suitable for most circumstances. However, Windows also provides a number of advanced permissions that allow you to exert finer control over object access. In fact, the standard permissions listed in Tables 8-1 and 8-2 are really just preconfigured combinations of special permissions. Table 8-3 lists the advanced permissions and shows how they are associated with standard permissions.

TABLE 8.1   Standard NTFS Folder Permissions

Permission	Definition
Full Control	Allows all possible abilities, including read, write, change, delete, take ownership, and change permission abilities.
Modify	Allows the abilities to read, write, change, and delete.
Read and Execute	Allows the user the ability to read the contents of the folder and the files in the folder. Also allows the user to execute applications in the folder, or the specific application file.
List Folder Contents	Allows the user to see inside the folder and see the other subfolders and files.
Read	Allows the ability to see files, subfolders, permissions, attributes, and ownership.
Write	Allows the ability to change files, subfolders, permissions, attributes, and ownership.

TABLE 8.2	Standard NTFS File Permissions
Permission	**Definition**
Full Control	Allows all possible abilities, including read, write, change, delete, take ownership, and change permission abilities.
Modify	Allows the abilities to modify and delete the file, plus perform all the actions permitted by the Write and Read & Execute permissions.
Read & Execute	Allows the user the ability to read or execute the file.
Read	Allows the ability to read the file, permissions attributes, and ownership.
Write	Allows the ability to change the file permissions, attributes, and ownership.

While you won't need to know most of these advanced permissions for the exam, you should be aware of the following two advanced permissions:

- **Change Permission** You can use this permission to allow users the ability to change permissions on files and folders without giving them the Full Control permission.

- **Take Ownership** This permission allows a user to take ownership of a file or folder. Every file and folder on an NTFS volume has an owner,

TABLE 8.3	Advanced NTFS File Permissions

Advanced Permission	Full Control	Modify	Read & Execute	Read	Write
Traverse Folder/Execute File	✓	✓	✓		
List Folder/Read Data	✓	✓	✓	✓	
Read Attributes	✓	✓	✓	✓	
Read Extended Attributes	✓	✓	✓	✓	
Create Files/Write Data	✓	✓			✓
Create Folders/Append Data	✓	✓			✓
Write Attributes	✓	✓			✓
Write Extended Attributes	✓	✓			✓
Delete Subfolders and Files	✓				
Delete	✓	✓			
Read Permissions	✓	✓	✓	✓	✓
Change Permissions	✓				
Take Ownership	✓				
Synchronize	✓	✓	✓	✓	✓

usually the account that created the object. However, there are times you may need to change the ownership of an object, such as when a user's responsibilities change or there is a change in membership in a group that has ownership. In Windows 2000, you cannot assign ownership of an object. Ownership is granted to the creator of the object and can be changed only when someone else takes ownership. When an administrator takes ownership of a file, the Administrators group becomes the owner of the file. To take ownership of an object (if you have permission to do so), open the object's Properties dialog box, click Advanced on the Security tab, and switch to the Owner tab of the Advanced Control Settings dialog box that opens.

Travel Assistance
Since you won't need to know all the special permissions for the exam, a full description of each is not listed here. However, you can find a good description of every advanced permission in the Windows help files.

Managing Multiple NTFS Permissions

Since a user can be a member of multiple groups, a single user can receive multiple permissions on an object. For example, suppose a user is a member of a group named Sales and a group named Executives. A single object may be configured with one set of permissions for the Sales group, one set of permissions for the Executives group, and even another set of permissions for the individual user. As an administrator, you must understand how multiple sets of permissions are resolved.

This resolution can be boiled down to three basic rules:

- *Permissions are cumulative.* This means that a user's effective permissions on an object are the sum of all permissions from all sources added together. For example, assume that a user has both the Read permission and the Write permission on the same folder because the user is a member of two different groups. This user's effective permissions on the object are Read *and* Write.

- *File permissions override folder permissions.* File permissions always override folder permissions. If a user has permission to read a file but does not have permission to access the folder that holds the file, the user can still read the file.

- *Deny overrides other permissions.*   You can specifically deny access to an object. If a user or group has been denied access to an object from any source, then that user or group will not be able to access the object, regardless of permissions from other sources.

Let's look at an example of effective permissions. Assume that a user named Joe attempts to access a folder named Marketing. Joe is a member of three groups (Marketing, Engineers, and Executives), and the following permissions have been assigned on the Marketing folder:

- Joe has Write permission on the folder.
- The Marketing group has Full Control permission on the folder.
- The Engineers group has been Denied Full Control permission on the folder.
- The Executives group has Read permission on the folder.

Here's how it breaks down. The Executives group has Read permission, Joe's user account has Write permission, and the Marketing group has Full Control permission. Combining just these three sources would give Joe Full Control permissions. However, the Engineers group has been explicitly denied Full Control Permission. This has the effect of denying all the rights that the Full Control permission entails and, since denied permissions override granted permissions, Joe is denied Full Control of the resource. This effectively denies Joe access of any kind.

Combining NTFS and Share Permissions

In Chapter 7, we talked about how to configure share permissions on a file or folder. Share permissions work in conjunction with NTFS permissions to provide an extra layer of security when users access an object over the network. Share permissions apply only to users that access an object remotely; NTFS permissions apply to everyone that accesses an object, whether locally or remotely.

When a user accesses an object remotely, local NTFS permissions and share permissions are combined to determine the user's effective permissions on the object. In order to figure out the effective overall permission a user is given, use the following steps:

1. Determine the effective NTFS permissions. Remember that the least restrictive combination of permissions from multiple sources defines the effective permissions. For example, Full Control permission from one source combined with Read permission from another source yields Full Control permission for the user.

2. Determine the effective share permissions. As with NTFS permissions, the least restrictive combination becomes the effective permission.

3. Determine the effective overall permission. When you combine the effective share permission with the effective NTFS permission, the *most* restrictive combination wins. For example, if a user has Full Control on the NTFS side and Read on the share side, the user ends up with Read permission when accessing the object remotely.

Consider the following simple example. You have created a folder named Brochures. Its share permissions are set at the default, which provides the Everyone group the Full Control permission. The Marketing group are given the NTFS Modify permission. Any member of the Marketing group is given rights granted by the Modify permission.

As when you are combining NTFS permissions from multiple sources, denied permissions override granted permissions. Let's look at another example. Table 8-4 describes a set of permissions.

In this example, share permissions are left at the default (Everyone group has Full Control). No user or group has any other share permissions explicitly defined. This means that, at the network level, Joe has Full Control permission on the folder. However, NTFS permissions have not yet been applied. As a member of the Sales group, Joe would be given the Modify permission. As a member of the Marketing group, though, Joe is denied Full Control of the folder. Denied permissions always override granted permissions. Since Joe is denied every right associated with the Full Control permission, Joe has no access to the folder at all.

Let's try one more example, a bit more complicated this time. Consider the situation shown in Table 8-5.

First, let's figure out Joe's effective share permissions. This is simple. As a member of the Sales group, he is given the Read permission. No other group is assigned a share permission. Next, we figure out his effective NTFS permissions.

TABLE 8.4	An Example of a Permissions Combination		
User/Group	**Share**	**NTFS**	**Member Of**
Joe			Everyone group Sales group Marketing group
Everyone group	Full Control		
Sales group		Modify	
Marketing group		Denied Full Control	

TABLE 8.5		Another Example of a Permissions Combination	
User/Group	**Share**	**NTFS**	**Member Of**
Joe		Denied the Write permission	Everyone group
			Sales group
			Marketing group
Everyone group			
Sales group	Read	Modify	
Marketing group		Modify	

Both the Sales and Marketing groups give Joe the Modify permission, but his user account denied him the Write permission. This basically leaves Joe with the ability to read and delete files, but not change them (see Table 8-3 for a description of the advanced permissions Joe ends up with; just remove the advanced permissions granted by the Write permission from the list granted by the Modify permission).

Now, we combine the NTFS and share permissions. Joe has Read permission at the share level and read permission plus some others at the NTFS level. The most restrictive combination is applied and Joe is left with Read permissions.

Travel Advisory

While this section presents the way permissions actually work in Windows 2000 and you should understand the system for the exam, things are never really done this way in the real world (at least not on properly planned networks). By and large, administrators leave share permissions at the default setting (Everyone group gets Full Control) and manage security using only NTFS permissions. It makes things a lot easier to manage. Also, explicitly denying a permission should be done rarely, if at all. This was mentioned earlier in the chapter.

Setting Permissions

To set NTFS permissions for an object, right-click the object and select Properties from the shortcut menu. In the Properties dialog box that opens, switch to the Security tab. Figure 8-7 shows an example of this tab for a folder.

The list at the top of the tab shows the users or groups that have been assigned permissions on the object. Select a name and click Remove to remove the permissions for that user or group. Click Add to add a new user or group to the list. Highlight any name on the list and use the Allow or Deny option beside each permission to configure access. Click the Advanced button to bring up the list of special permissions that you can assign.

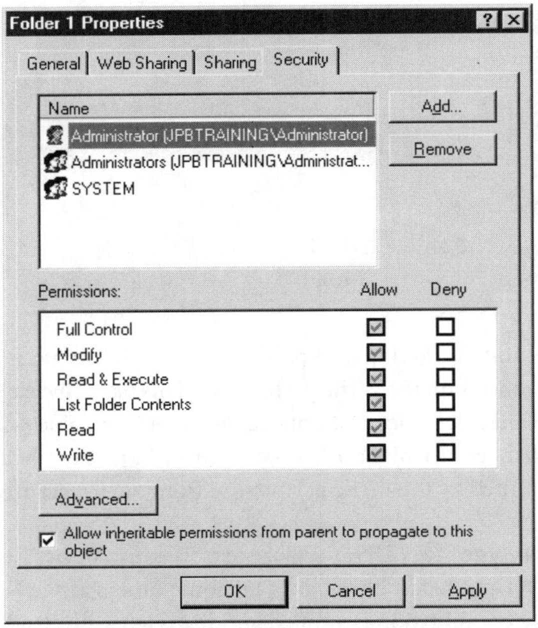

FIGURE 8.7   Setting NTFS permissions on a folder

Travel Advisory

As noted previously, deny permissions only when it is absolutely necessary to deny access to a particular user when that user has been granted permissions by group membership. Otherwise, denying permissions is not a recommended practice, as it can cause serious complications in the permissions structure on large networks.

Permissions Inheritance

By default, the permissions you assign to a folder propagate down to the folders and files inside that folder. This is called *inheritance*; the child objects inherit permissions from their parent objects. This means that when you apply a permission on an folder for a user or group, you are also applying that permission to all the items inside that folder.

However, you can prevent inheritance from occurring on a per-object basis. When you configure permissions for a folder (discussed in the preceding section;

see Figure 8-7 for details), you can disable the option that allows the object to inherit permissions from its parent object. If you do this for a folder, the current folder becomes the top-level parent and all objects inside that folder inherit permissions from the current folder.

When you disable this option, a separate dialog box opens that provides three options:

- **Copy** Copies the permissions from the parent folder to the current folder and then prevents any future permissions from being inherited from the parent.

- **Remove** Removes permissions that are assigned to the current folder and then prevents any future permissions from being inherited from the parent.

- **Cancel** Cancels the dialog box and reenables inheritance.

Moving and Copying Objects with Permissions

Obviously, there are times when you will need to copy or move objects that are assigned NTFS permissions. For a user to be able to copy objects to NTFS volumes, the user must have permission to write to the destination folder. For a user to move objects to NTFS volumes, the user must have write permission on the destination folder and delete permission on the original folder. This is because when a file is moved, Windows actually copies the file and then deletes the original. The user moving or copying the file becomes the owner of the file in its new location.

Permissions are affected in different ways when you perform the following actions:

- **Copying an object** If you copy an object to another location on the same partition, the copied folder inherits the NTFS permissions of the target location (i.e., the folder you copy it into). This is also true if you copy an object to another partition that is formatted with NTFS. If you copy an object to a FAT/FAT32 partition, all permissions are removed (since FAT/FAT32 doesn't support permissions).

- **Moving an object within the same partition** If you move an object to another location on the same partition, the copied object retains its current permissions, regardless of the permissions assigned to the folder it is copied into.

- **Moving an object to a different partition** If you move an object to a different partition that is formatted with NTFS, the moved object inherits the permissions of the target folder it is copied into. If you move an object to a different partition that is formatted with FAT/FAT32, all permissions are lost.

> ### Exam Tip
> When you create a folder or file, Windows 2000 assigns the Full Control permission to the Everyone group. You should change this default permission and assign more appropriate permissions. If you want all users to have access, it is much better to assign only needed permissions to a group like Domain Users.

CHECKPOINT

✔**Objective 8.01: Manage Data Storage** This objective covered a lot of information regarding storage management. First, it examined the different types of file systems Windows 2000 supports and when to use each one. Then, it examined the ability of NTFS to manage disks through quotas and the ability to encrypt and compress data. It then covered the two types of disks—basic and dynamic—and considered the different volume sets allowed. The objective also examined the configuration and interactions of NTFS permissions.

REVIEW QUESTIONS

1. You need to allow for a dual-boot arrangement on a 12GB hard disk between Windows 98 and Windows 2000. You plan to create two partitions of 6GB each, and you want both operating systems to boot and see files on each others' partitions. Which file system should you choose?

   A. FAT

   B. FAT32

   C. NTFS

   D. CDFS

2. You have a file in a compressed folder named Archive. You move the file to an uncompressed folder named Productive on a different NTFS partition. What will happen to the compression attributes on the file?

   A. It will be retained from the parent folder.

   B. It will be inherited from the target folder.

   C. Neither—it will be nonexistent.

   D. The administrator will be asked at the time the file is moved.

3. Which of the following types of basic disk partitions serves only as a holder for other drives?

   A. Primary

   B. Extended

   C. Logical

   D. Dynamic

4. You have upgraded your NT 4.0 Server to Windows 2000. Your C drive is running low on disk space. You would like to extend the disk space on this drive. How could you accomplish this?

   A. Extend the volume to portions of other disks.

   B. Convert the disk to dynamic and then extend the volume.

   C. Use a mount volume to provide extra space on the drive.

   D. Create a striped volume to extend the drive.

5. Greg leaves the company and his files are encrypted on the server. His account was accidentally deleted prior to decrypting the files. What is needed to resolve the situation?

   A. A Recovery Agent

   B. Take Ownership of the files

   C. Secedit

   D. An emergency repair disk

6. A user named Joe is attempting to access an NTFS file. Joe is a member of the Sales group. What are Joe's effective permissions?

User/Group	Share	NTFS Folder
Joe	Change	Modify
Sales	Full Control	Special Permissions: Deny: Delete

   A. Modify (R,W,X,D)

   B. Read (R,X)

   C. Special Permissions (R,W,X)

   D. No Access

7. A user named Joe is attempting to access an NTFS file. Given the following example, what are Joe's effective permissions?

User/Group	Share	NTFS Folder	Member Of
Joe	Change	Modify	Sales Managers
Sales	Full Control	Modify	
Managers	Read	Full Control	

A. Modify

B. Read

C. Change

D. Full Control

8. You have a 40GB hard drive that you formatted as a single partition so that you can install Windows 2000. Which of the following file systems should you use?

A. FAT

B. FAT32

C. NTFS

D. CDFS

9. Bonnie has enabled disk quotas on her partitions and established thresholds for her users. However, users are still exceeding their thresholds. What should Bonnie try next?

A. Select the Deny Disk Space To Users Exceeding Quota Limit option.

B. Select the Do Not Limit Disk Usage option.

C. Ask users to log out and back in again.

D. Manually, from within the Quota Entries option, stop the users from adding more to their disk.

10. A user named Johnny is in the Document Processing group. He was recently promoted to a managerial position and made a member of the Managers group. When he attempts to access one of the managers' folders, he is denied access. What is the likely solution for this problem?

A. Add Johnny to the Administrators group.

B. Remove Johnny from the Document Processing group.

C. Change the permissions on the folder to give Johnny specific access to the folder.

D. Check for network connectivity problems.

REVIEW ANSWERS

1. **B**   FAT32 is accessible by both Windows 98 and 2000, and both can see files on FAT32. Answer A is incorrect because FAT doesn't support hard drive partitions of this size. Answer C is incorrect because NTFS will not work for the 98 machine. Answer D is incorrect because CDFS is the CD file system for reading from CD-ROMs, not used for hard disks.

2. **B**   Because the file is moved to a different partition, it will inherit the target partition's compression structure. This is because a move between partitions is actually two steps performed by Windows: a copy and a delete. If it were moved on the same partition, then it would have been retained, so answer A is incorrect. Answer C is incorrect because it is still on an NTFS partition. Answer D is incorrect because the admin isn't asked.

3. **B**   An extended partition provides a way to get around the four-primary-partition limit. Extended partitions cannot themselves be formatted and used, but serve rather as a shell in which you can create logical drives.

4. **C**   Because the disk is the boot and system disk, even converting the disk to dynamic will not allow it to be extended, so a mount volume is your only option here. Answers A and B are incorrect because, regardless of whether the disk is basic or dynamic, it cannot be extended. Answer D is incorrect because you cannot create a striped volume with the boot/system disk.

5. **A**   EFS is meant to allow for additional security on a user's files. It is not meant to cause too much excessive pain for the administrators. The admins are, by default, Recovery Agents that can open up the users' files. The other options are incorrect.

6. **C**   In the combination of permissions, Joe comes through the Share with Full Control; but the NTFS permissions deny him the ability to delete on the folder level and the file level is inherited from above, so his effective permissions are R,W,X.

7. **D**   Joe comes through the share permissions with Full Control, since share permissions are combined with the least restrictive combination winning. On NTFS permissions, Joe also gets the Full Control permission, since the least restrictive combination prevails. When combining the share and NTFS permissions, the most restrictive combination prevails. However, since Joe has Full Control on both the share and NTFS side of things, he comes through it all with Full Control permission.

8. **C** NTFS is the only file system that supports volume sizes larger than 32GB, so you have to use NTFS. The other file systems are not possible solutions.

9. **A** To prevent the users from going beyond their limits, you must select the option Deny Disk Space To Users Exceeding Quota Limit. Without this option being set, the system will only note the infraction but do nothing to stop it. If this is selected, then the user may be on a drive with tons of free space, but the quota will cut the user off at the set threshold. Answer B is incorrect because this will eliminate the quota thresholds.

10. **B** The problem is, most likely, that Johnny is still in the Processors group and needs to be removed.

Managing Internet Information Services

	NEWBIE	SOME EXPERIENCE	EXPERT
ETA	3 hours	2 hours	1 hour

Configure and Troubleshoot Internet Information Services

Microsoft Internet Information Services (IIS) is a component included with Windows 2000 that features a world-class Web server, FTP server, and NNTP server. Using IIS, you can provide reliable, secure, and scalable Internet services on the Internet or a local intranet. This chapter covers installing, configuring, and troubleshooting IIS.

Overview of Internet Information Services

Internet access, particularly e-mail and the Web, has become ubiquitous in the past several years. Even within the boundaries of a corporate network, Internet technologies are used to provide workers easy, reliable access to company and network resources. Whenever you point your browser to a Web address, the browser retrieves the proper information from a Web server and displays it to you. Web servers run the software that allows them to store, retrieve, and modify all the pages and graphics that make up a Web site.

Internet Information Services version 5 is the Web server that comes with Windows 2000. IIS provides a number of powerful functions, including acting as a

- **Web server**   IIS complies with the Hypertext Transport Protocol (HTTP) 1.1 standard and supports advanced features such as Active Server Pages, Common Gateway Interface (CGI), Internet Server Application Programming Interface (ISAPI), and FrontPage server extensions.
- **FTP server**   The File Transfer Protocol is used to transfer files over a TCP/IP network, such as the Internet. Files are transferred between an FTP client and an FTP server. IIS provides a robust and completely configurable FTP server.
- **SMTP server**   The Simple Mail Transfer Protocol (SMTP) is a TCP/IP protocol used to send e-mail messages between computers. IIS provides a basic SMTP service that you can use to set up mail services from your Web pages.

- **NNTP Server** The Network News Transport Protocol (NNTP) service is a standards-based server for hosting electronic discussion groups where users can post and read threaded messages.

Installing Internet Information Services

Windows 2000 offers IIS version 5, a significant upgrade from previous versions that includes support for new Windows 2000 features such as Active Directory. IIS is not installed by default during the Windows 2000 installation, but it is easy to add later.

> **Travel Advisory**
>
> If you are performing an upgrade from a previous version of Windows, the setup program detects whether you are using any version of IIS, Personal Web Server, or Microsoft Peer Web Services. If a previous version is found, setup automatically upgrades the installation to IIS 5; you do not get the choice of whether to upgrade.

If you have a server running Windows 2000 on which IIS has not yet been installed, you can add it using the following procedure:

1. Log on to Windows 2000 as an administrator and choose Start | Settings | Control Panel.

2. Double-click the Add/Remove Programs icon in the Control Panel window.

3. On the Add or Remove Programs dialog box, click Add/Remove Windows Components. This opens the Windows Components wizard.

4. From the list of components, select Internet Information Services (IIS) and click Details.

5. On the list of subcomponents in the Internet Information Services (IIS) dialog box (shown next), select the components you want to install and then click OK. The available components are detailed in

Table 9-1; this table also shows whether the component is included in a default installation of IIS.

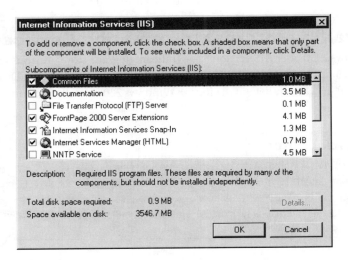

6. Click Next to proceed with the installation. If you are prompted for the Windows 2000 installation files, provide the installation CD or type the path where the files are located.

7. Once the required files are copied, click Finish to close the Windows Component wizard.

Travel Advisory

You can remove IIS from Windows 2000 using the same procedure as installation—just remove the check next to the option. The program files are removed and Registry entries are cleaned out, but any Web pages you have created remain. This makes it easy to save a Web site and even use it with other Web server software.

Creating and Managing Web Sites

Once IIS is installed, any services (such as WWW and FTP) that were included in the installation start automatically and users can immediately begin accessing those sites. Of course, this works only if there is content present, as might be the case if you upgraded from a previous version of IIS. You can open your site

TABLE 9.1	Components Included with IIS	

Component	Included by Default	Description
Common Files	Yes	Common files required for running other components of IIS.
Documentation	Yes	Help files and other documentation on using the Web server, the FTP server, and other components.
File Transfer Protocol (FTP) Server	No	Support for hosting an FTP site.
FrontPage 2002 Server Extensions	Yes	Components that allow users of FrontPage and Visual InterDev to author and administer Web sites.
Internet Information Services Snap-in	Yes	The main administrative tool used for managing IIS.
Internet Services Manager (HTML)	Yes	An HTML tool used to manage IIS from a Web browser. ISM (HTML) offers many, but not all, of the features offered by the IIS snap-in.
NNTP Service	No	Support for hosting Network News Transport Protocol (NNTP) sites and services.
SMTP Service	Yes	Support for the Simple Mail Transport Protocol (SMTP), which allows applications to send e-mail messages.
Visual InterDev RAD Remote Deployment Support	No	Visual InterDev Rapid Application Development (RAD) Remote Deployment Support enables the remote deployment of applications on the IIS Web server.
World Wide Web Server	Yes	Support for hosting and managing Web sites.

in a browser from your computer or from any computer connected to your local network by entering an address in one of the following formats:

- http://*computername*
- http://*ip_address*
- http://*fully_qualified_domain_name*

By default, the folder for your Web site is C:/Inetpub/wwwroot, and you can start creating Web pages right in this folder. Just name your home page

Default.htm or Default.asp and when someone browses to your site, that page loads automatically. Until you create your own home page, visitors to the site will get an "Under Construction" page; this page is automatically created during the installation of IIS. The names default.htm and default.asp are automatically set up as the pages defaulted to when a user visits a folder. You can set up others, if you like.

Using the Internet Services Manager

Once you have installed IIS, and whether or not you have created your Web site yet, all management takes place using a single tool—the Internet Services Manager (ISM). IIS includes two versions of this tool: one that is a snap-in for the Microsoft Management Console (MMC) and one that allows you to administer certain functions using a Web browser.

We're going to use the snap-in version in this chapter, and it is shown in Figure 9-1. Open it by selecting Start | Programs | Administrative Tools | Internet Services Manager. Notice that ISM uses a typical hierarchical view that is arranged first by computer and then by the types of sites available on that computer (Web, FTP, and SMTP).

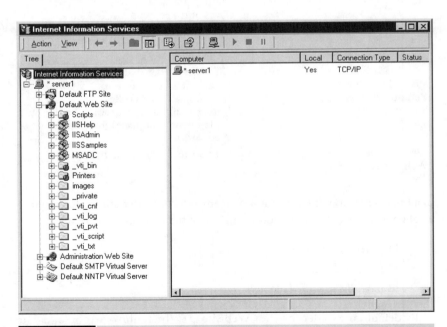

FIGURE 9.1   The Internet Services Manager

The default Web site created during IIS installation is simply named Default Web Site. You can rename this site by right-clicking it and choosing Rename from the shortcut menu. Under the Default Web Site object, each of the important folders configured for the site are displayed (these are all the folders in the C:\Inetpub\wwwroot folder).

Creating a New Web Site or Virtual Server

IIS provides the ability to host multiple Web sites on the same server, each site having its own structure and permissions. Web sites in IIS are often referred to as *virtual servers* because each site pretty much responds as if it were installed on a server all by itself. You can host multiple Web sites on a server in one of three ways:

- **Using a nonstandard port number with the IP address**   By default, port 80 is used for communications between Web browsers and servers. You can specify a different port number to be used for each Web site on a server. Using alternate port numbers also provides a limited form of security that is covered later in the section "Using Alternate Port Assignments."

- **Using multiple IP addresses**   You can configure each Web site on a server to use a separate IP address (and thus a separate name). You can configure the multiple IP addresses using the same network adapter or using different adapters.

- **Using host header names**   When browsers use HTTP 1.1, the HTTP header contains the actual fully qualified domain name of the server requested. You can have IIS direct web traffic based on the domain names in the headers, which lets you host more than a single domain name using a single folder structure.

Travel Advisory

The creation of multiple Web (or FTP) sites is supported only on computers running some edition of Windows 2000 Server. Computers running IIS on Windows 2000 (or XP) Professional support only the default sites.

You can create a new Web site using the following procedure:

1. Log on to Windows 2000 as an administrator and select Start | Programs | Administrative Tools | Internet Services Manager.

2. Right-click the server on which you want to create a new Web site and select New | Web Site from the shortcut menu. This starts the Web Site Creation wizard.

3. Click Next to skip the opening page of the wizard.

4. In the Description box, type a name for the new Web site and click Next.

5. On the IP Address And Port Settings page, shown next, select the IP address clients will use to connect to the Web site. By default, the (All Unassigned) option is selected. Unless you plan to use separate IP addresses to distinguish between Web sites, leave this setting alone.

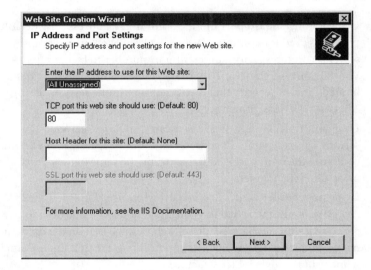

6. You can also specify an alternate port number to distinguish between Web sites (remember, the default port is 80). If you use alternate port numbers, you must also have users specify the port number in URLs they enter in their browser using the format http://*server_name:port_number*.

7. You can also distinguish between Web sites using host headers. To do this, type a name in the host Header box. Entering **Sales**, for example, would cause the URL http://Sales to specify the new site.

8. Once you have set any necessary options on the IP Address And Port Settings page, click Next.

9. Type the path for the home directory of the site. This can be either a regular path with drive letter or a path to a network resource using a Universal Naming Convention (UNC) path name. You can also use this page to specify whether anonymous access is allowed to the site. Click Next to go on.

10. Specify the permissions for the new site and click Next to go on. These permissions are detailed in the section "Web Home Directory" later in this chapter.

11. Click Finish to create the new Web site.

Starting and Stopping Sites

Once a new site is created, it is started automatically, and users can begin accessing it immediately. Sites also start automatically whenever the WWW service is loaded (which happens automatically when Windows starts, by default). Within ISM, you can manually start, stop, and pause sites whenever you need to using either a site's shortcut menu or the ISM toolbar. These functions work as follows:

- **Starting a site** When a site is started, it becomes fully functional and accessible to clients.

- **Stopping a site** When a site is stopped, clients can no longer connect to it and all current connections are immediately dropped.

- **Pausing a site** When a site is paused, the server no longer accepts new connections but current connections persist. Pausing a site before stopping it is the graceful way to bring a site down for management.

Exam Tip

In addition to letting you start, stop, and pause individual services, ISM also lets you restart IIS. This command stops and restarts all of the IIS services at once and is a great way to reset an IIS server without having to stop and start services individually or having to reboot the computer itself. Select a server in ISM and click Action | Restart IIS. A dialog box appears that lets you restart (stop and then start) all services, stop all services, start all services, or reboot the computer.

Managing Web Sites

As elsewhere in Windows, most of the management of sites in IIS happens using Properties dialog boxes. To manage a Web site, right-click the site and choose the Properties command. The most important tabs available on a Web site's dialog box. Properties are discussed over the next several sections.

Exam Tip

You can also manage the folders within a Web site by opening their Properties dialog boxes. The tabs available for an individual folder are a subset of those available for the Web site itself and work the same—except that settings made on a folder in a site override the same general settings made for the site. This chapter focuses on the management of the Web site, but the principles are the same for individual folders.

Web Site Properties   The Web Site tab, shown in Figure 9-2, is used for three purposes:

- **Web Site Identification**   Use this section of the tab to name the Web site (use the Description field), configure an IP address for the site if it's different from the computer's main IP address, and set the TCP port used to connect to the site. Unless you have special requirements, you should leave the TCP port set to 80, which is the default used by all Web browsers.

- **Connections**   Use this section of the tab to specify the time in seconds that a connection may remain idle before the Web server terminates it. The HTTP Keep-Alives option lets Web browsers maintain open connections with your server rather than having to reopen a new connection with each request. You should leave this option enabled to help increase server performance.

- **Enable Logging**   Use this section to have IIS keep a log of connections to your Web server and choose the format of those logs. Formats include WC3 Extended Log File Format (the default), Microsoft IIS Log File Format, and NCSA Common Log File Format. The Properties button opens a separate dialog for configuring the period a log file should cover, the naming convention for the file, the directory in which to store the log, and a number of extended options that you may include in the log.

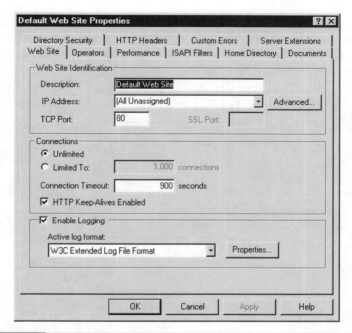

FIGURE 9.2   Managing Web Site properties

Web Home Directory   A *home directory* is the root directory of a Web site. By default, the Default Web Site uses the home directory c:\Inetpub\wwwroot, which is a directory located on the local computer. The Home Directory tab, shown in Figure 9-3, lets you modify this directory information. You can change the directory to any other directory on the computer by entering the path in the Local Path field. You can also make the home directory for your site point to a shared folder on another computer on the network or even point to another URL (if you want to redirect client requests to your Web site to another Web site).

If you choose a local or shared directory, you can set detailed access permissions on the directory. These permissions include

- **Script Source Access**   Allows a user to access source code for scripts in an ASP application. This permission is not enabled by default for a new site.
- **Read**   Allows a user to access a Web page in the directory. Since this permission is required for basic Web access, the Read permission is enabled by default.

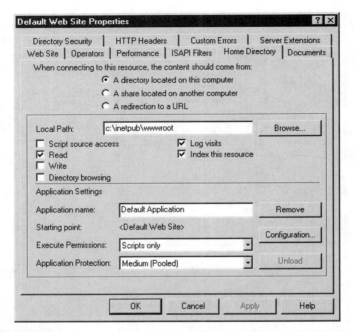

FIGURE 9.3 Configuring a home directory

- **Write**   Allows a user to upload files and their associated properties to a directory and change content in existing files. This permission is not enabled by default for a new site.

- **Directory Browsing**   Allows a Web browser to display a DOS-like listing of files in the directory if a default Web page cannot be found. This permission is not enabled by default for a new site.

- **Log Visits**   Records visits to the directory in the log file, if logging is enabled. See the section on the Web Site tab earlier in the chapter for information on enabling logging. This permission is enabled by default for a new site.

- **Index This Resource**   Allows Microsoft Indexing Service to include the directory when indexing a Web site. This permission is enabled by default for a new site.

In addition to setting permissions on a directory, you can also configure how Web-based applications are treated in the home directory, including what permissions and protection an application is given.

Documents   The Documents tab, shown in Figure 9-4, is used for two purposes. The first is to configure the names of the default documents for the Web site. A default document is one that loads automatically when no other document is specified in a browser. For example, if you typed **http://www.microsoft.com/windows** and did not include the name of a specific file on the end of the URL, the default document in the windows directory would be loaded. Four default document names may already be configured: Default.htm, Default.asp, index.htm, and iisstart.asp. Note that the iisstart.asp file is used only in the default Web site created by IIS and not in additional sites you create. These documents are used in the order shown on the list. For example, if both a Default.htm and a Default.asp document exist in a folder, the Default.htm document is used. Add a default document name by clicking Add and typing the name of the document. Order the documents on the list using the up and down buttons to the left.

The other use for the Documents tab is to enable a footer document to be included on all pages delivered from the Web site. The footer document should be a standard Web page and is included at the bottom of each page of the site when the page is displayed in a browser.

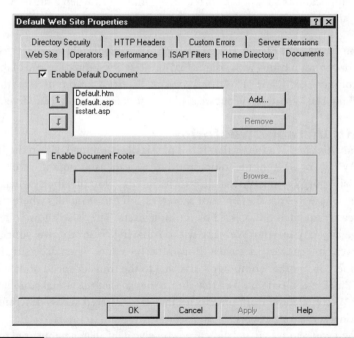

FIGURE 9.4   Configuring documents for a Web site

Directory Security   The Directory Security tab offers three different methods for configuring security: Anonymous Access and Authentication Control, IP Address and Domain Name Restrictions, and Secure Communications. These are covered in the section "Managing Security" later in this chapter.

HTTP Headers   *HTTP headers* are special code that is placed on all the Web pages in a site. These headers are not viewed by a typical browser but instead are used in the management of pages on a site. The HTTP Headers tab is used for four types of configuration:

- **Content Expiration**   Removes pages or entire folders from a site automatically on a certain date or after a specified period.
- **Custom HTTP Headers**   Special code you add to the pages in your site.
- **Content Rating**   Allows you to apply ratings to your site that are compatible with major content verification services.
- **Mime Mapping**   Multipurpose Internet Mail Extensions (MIME) Mapping allows you to associate certain types of files with certain applications so that the correct program is used when a file on your site is accessed.

Custom Errors   The Custom Errors tab lets you configure customized error messages for communicating with visitors to your site. For example, instead of the typical error message "404 HTTP Error," you could create a custom message that said something like "We're sorry, but we could not find that page on our server."

Using Virtual Directories

A *virtual directory* is a folder that is not physically contained within the IIS service (WWW or FTP) home folder but that appears as though it were to users who visit your Web site. Virtual directories increase your flexibility when determining where to store files on your server, as you can store files where they are most easily updated or accessed by multiple users. They also allow you to add storage capacity to your Web site without having to shut down your server. However, you may experience a drop in performance when accessing folders contained on another computer's disk due to the transfer speed of data over a LAN. Finally, you can set up virtual directories so that the actual contents for a single Web site come from directories that are scattered across different locations on a server or network.

   When you set up a virtual directory, you give it an alias, a name used to identify it in a Web browser. Using an alias provides several advantages. First, it is easier for a user to type in an alias as part of a URL (as in http://*alias_name*) than to type in a full directory name. Second, using alias names prevents users from knowing where an actual directory is located. Finally, using alias names makes it easier to move directories around in a site, as you can simply change the mapping between the alias and the actual directory.

You can create a virtual directory in ISM using the following procedure:

1. Log on to Windows 2000 as an administrator and select Start | Programs | Administrative Tools | Internet Services Manager.

2. Right-click a Web site (or FTP site) and select New | Virtual Directory. This opens the Virtual Directory Creation wizard. Click Next to skip the opening page.

3. Enter the alias you want to use for the new virtual directory and click Next.

4. Enter the location of the directory you want to use and click Next. You can enter a file path using a drive letter (for a local directory) or a full UNC (for a remote directory).

5. Select the permissions you want to assign to the virtual directory and click Next. These are identical to the permissions available for a Web site and are covered in the previous section "Web Home Directory."

6. Click Finish to exit the Virtual Directory Creation wizard.

Travel Advisory

If you are creating a virtual directory using a directory that is on the local computer running IIS, you can create the virtual directory without going into ISM. Right-click the folder and choose Properties from the shortcut menu. In the Properties dialog box for the folder, switch to the Web Sharing tab, select the Share This Folder option, and configure the alias and permissions in the dialog box that opens. If there are multiple sites, you must also select the site under which the new virtual directory should be created.

Creating and Managing FTP Sites

While Web servers can be used to transfer files, many people still prefer the ease and reliability of transferring files using File Transfer Protocol (FTP). The FTP service built into IIS is full-featured, and as with the Web server, you manage it using ISM. Compared to the management of a Web site, creating and managing an FTP site is pretty simple.

Travel Advisory

FTP relies exclusively on clear text communications, meaning that user authentication information (username and password) is not encrypted before being transmitted between client and server. For this reason, using FTP is discouraged on secure networks.

Creating a New FTP Site

When the FTP service is installed, a single FTP site named Default FTP Site is created and immediately made available. The default home directory for the site is C:\inetpub\ftproot, and you can start creating a directory structure and filling it with files as soon as the service is running. Users can log on to the site by typing the **ftp** command at the command prompt followed by the name of the server.

As with Web sites, you can create additional FTP sites on a server. Like creating a Web site, creating a new FTP site uses a wizard-driven interface:

1. Log on to Windows 2000 as an administrator and click Start | Programs | Administrative Tools | Internet Services Manager.

2. Right-click the server on which you want to create a new site and select New | FTP Site from the shortcut menu. This launches the FTP Site Creation wizard. Click Next to skip the opening page.

3. In the Description box, enter a name for the new FTP site and click Next.

4. In the IP Address And Port Settings page, choose the IP address to be associated with the new site (All Unassigned is chosen by default). You can also choose an alternate port number for the FTP service if you want. The default port number used by clients is 21. Click Next.

5. Type the path for the folder you want the site to use as its home directory. You can use either a full local path with a drive letter or a UNC. Click Next.

6. Specify the permissions (read and/or write) that you want to assign for the home directory and click Next.

7. Click Finish to exit the wizard and create the new site.

Managing FTP Sites

Once an FTP site is created, you can manage it in much the same way as you manage a Web site. Right-click an FTP site in ISM and choose Properties from the shortcut menu. The tabs involved in managing the FTP site are discussed in the next few sections.

FTP Site   The FTP Site tab, shown in Figure 9-5, lets you configure many basic settings for your FTP site. These settings include

- **Identification**   Use this section to name the FTP site, configure an IP address for the site if it's different from the computer's main IP address, and set the TCP port used to connect to the site. Unless you have special requirements, you should leave the TCP port set to 21, which is the default used by all FTP clients.

- **Connections**   Use this section of the tab to limit the number of simultaneous connections your site will support and to specify the time in seconds that a connection may remain idle before the Web server terminates it.

- **Enable Logging**   Use this section to have IIS keep a log of connections to your FTP site and choose the format of those logs. Formats include WC3 Extended Log File Format (the default) and Microsoft IIS Log File Format. The Properties button opens a separate dialog for configuring the period a log file should cover, the naming convention for the file, and a number of extended options you may include in the log.

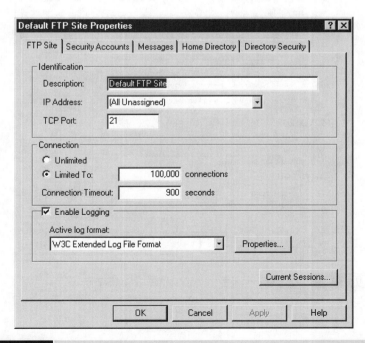

FIGURE 9.5   Configuring an FTP site

- **Current Sessions**   This button opens a dialog that shows all users currently connected to your FTP site.

Security Accounts   Use the Security Accounts tab, shown in Figure 9-6, to specify whether anonymous connections are allowed and to configure FTP site operators. If you do allow anonymous connections, you must select a specific Windows account that is used for anonymous connections. You can then configure permissions for this account on your FTP folders to provide security for your site. Use the FTP operators section of the tab to assign Windows user accounts that are able to administer your FTP site.

The Allow IIS To Control Password option is used to synchronize the Anonymous password used for the FTP site with the one used for the Anonymous user account in Windows. If this option is not selected, you can control the password using the Security Accounts tab.

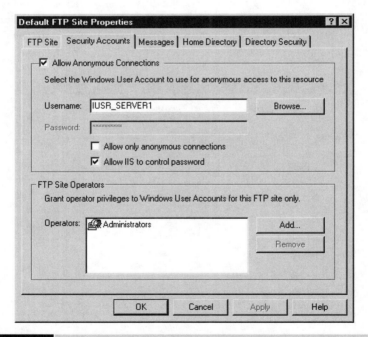

FIGURE 9.6   Configuring security accounts for an FTP site

Travel Advisory

In the real world, permissions on FTP and Web sites are almost always handled using NTFS permissions (discussed in Chapter 8) and not using the security features built into IIS.

Messages   The Messages tab lets you configure three different messages that are displayed automatically to FTP clients at different times. These messages include

- **Welcome**   A message that is displayed whenever a client logs on to the FTP server. This message is commonly used to welcome the user, display any rules for using the server, and display alert messages (such as when the server will be down for maintenance).
- **Exit**   A message that is displayed every time a client logs off the FTP server. This is a short message intended simply to let users know they have successfully logged off.
- **Maximum Connections**   A message that is displayed when a client is refused a connection to an FTP server because the maximum allowable number of connections had already been made. This is also a short message.

FTP Home Directory   A *home directory* is the root directory of an FTP site. By default, the Default FTP Site uses the home directory c:\Inetpub\ftproot, which is a directory located on the local computer. You can change this directory to any other directory on the computer by entering the path in the Local Path field. You can also make the home directory for your site point to a shared folder on another computer on the network. The Home Directory tab also lets you choose how file lists are displayed to clients: UNIX-style or MS-DOS-style. Finally, you can use the Home Directory tab to configure whether read and write access is allowed and whether visits are logged.

Managing Security

Windows 2000 and IIS provide a number of ways to prevent unauthorized users from accessing a Web or FTP site. Most of these are methods for blocking access to certain users or for restricting the way in which access to a site is gained. Some methods also protect data as it is being transferred over the network. We'll go over these methods in the next several sections.

Using Alternate Port Assignments

As you learned earlier, Web and FTP sites have a port number assigned to them that is used by clients to communicate with the sites. By default, Web clients use port 80, and FTP clients use port 21. These are standard ports that all Web and FTP client software is configured to use by default.

One way of hampering access to a site is to assign it a different port number. Assigning, say, port 9898 to a Web site would prevent any Web browser from making a connection to the site unless the user entered the correct port number as part of the URL. This would take the form http://*server_name:port_number* (http://sales:9898, for example).

I use the term "hampering" instead of "preventing" because using alternate port assignments is not really a strong security feature. There is nothing in place that prevents a user from trying different port numbers manually or even using a port scanner to find the open port. Essentially, using alternate port numbers will prevent casual users who don't know about port numbers from accessing a site.

You can change the port number used by a site either during the site's creation (see the earlier section, "Creating a New Web Site or Virtual Server") or using an existing site's Properties dialog box (see the earlier section, "Web Site Properties").

User Authentication

Requiring users' credentials to be validated in some way before they are allowed access to a resource is called *user authentication*. When a Windows 2000 user logs on to the network, for example, that user must supply a valid username and password. Windows 2000 must then authenticate the logon information, which it does using Kerberos V5 authentication. Once a user is validated, that user is assigned a ticket-granting ticket (TGT) that identifies the user whenever the user attempts to access resources during that logon session.

Each object on a Windows 2000 network maintains an access control list (ACL), a list of users and groups that are allowed access to the resource and the specific permissions they are assigned. In this same way, IIS lets you control the abilities that users have on a site through various methods of authentication. You can access the authentication controls for a site by switching to the Directory Security tab of a site's Properties dialog box and clicking the Edit button in the Anonymous access and authentication control section. Figure 9-7 shows the Authentication Methods dialog box for a Web site.

Available authentication methods include

- **Anonymous** Anonymous authentication allows any user to access the virtual server without providing a username or password. Most Web

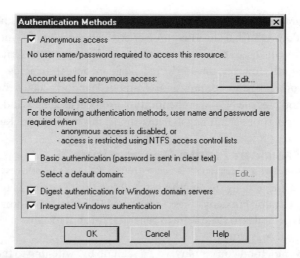

FIGURE 9.7   Controlling user authentication for a Web site

sites that you run into on the Internet provide anonymous access. When anonymous access is allowed and a user connects to a site, Windows 2000 uses an account with the default name IUSR_ *computername* (the NetBIOS name of the computer running IIS) to allow access to the site's resources. This account's password is randomly chosen to start with, but you can change it. You can also have IIS control the password, in which case, the password is synchronized with the Anonymous account in Windows 2000. You can assign permissions to this account to control anonymous access. Anonymous access is considered a local logon.

- **Basic**   Basic (Clear-Text) authentication requires the user to submit a valid Windows username and password. The username and password are sent across the network as unencrypted clear text, though, so this is not a preferred security method. Basic authentication is often used because it is supported by all browsers and operating systems.

- **Digest**   HTTP Digest authentication is an Internet standard that allows authentication of clients to occur using a series of encrypted challenges and responses over HTTP. It is intended primarily as a means of allowing users to log on when they must connect through an HTTP proxy server. Unlike with Integrated Windows authentication (discussed next), users configured to use Digest authentication must always supply a username and password to log on to a site.

- **Integrated Windows** Integrated Windows authentication (known as Windows NT Challenge/Response in previous versions of Windows) also requires the user's computer to provide a valid Windows username and password. However, the user's credentials are never sent across the network. If you are running a mixed-mode Windows 2000 network, this method uses the NTLM authentication protocol used by Windows NT 4.0. If your network is running in native mode, this method uses Kerberos V5.

IP and Domain Name Restrictions

You can also restrict access to sites according to a client's IP address or domain name. There are actually two methods for doing this. The first is to open up a site to general traffic but deny access to specified IP addresses or domain names. The second method is to close a site to general traffic but to allow access by specified individuals or groups.

Whichever method you employ, you'll set it up by switching to the Directory Security tab of a site's Properties dialog box and clicking the Edit button in the IP Address And Domain Name Restrictions section. Figure 9-8 shows the IP Address And Domain Name Restrictions dialog box that opens.

First, specify whether all computers are to be granted or denied access by default. Once this is done, use the Add button to add individual or group restrictions in one of three ways:

- Specify a single computer by IP address.
- Specify a group of computers using a network ID and subnet mask.
- Enter a domain name, which could indicate a single computer or an entire domain.

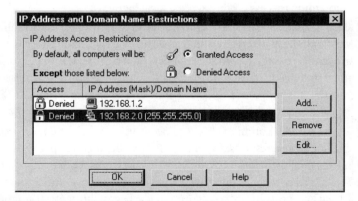

FIGURE 9.8 Restricting access to a site according to IP address or domain name

Access Permissions

Yet another method of controlling access to a site is by assigning permissions governing what users can do with particular parts of the site. As you saw in the previous sections "Web Home Directory" and "FTP Home Directory," when we talked about managing Web and FTP sites, there are a number of different permissions you can assign to a directory (check that section for descriptions). What's really interesting is that you can assign these types of permissions on just about any object you find in the hierarchy of folders under a Web site in ISM, including virtual directories and the like. This means that you can assign parts of your site one set of permissions and parts of your site other sets of permissions. By default, the parts of your site lower in the hierarchy will inherit permissions assigned in higher parts of the hierarchy. For example, if you create a virtual directory in a site, the virtual directory will inherit the permissions assigned to the site as its default permissions. You can, of course, change these. Permissions assigned to a specific object always override any inherited permissions that may be in place.

Exam Tip

As mentioned previously, permissions are almost always handled in the real world using NTFS permissions. NTFS permissions provide much better access control than using the access permissions built into IIS. You should know this information for the exam, but understand that even Microsoft no longer recommends the practice of relying on IIS permissions.

SSL

The Secure Sockets Layer (SSL) protocol lets you configure sites to encrypt data that is transferred between the sites and clients. SSL is used on many Internet sites to provide secure transactions. To use SSL on a site, you must first obtain a server certificate that authenticates the identity of the server and contains the public keys used to encrypt data. You can configure a Windows 2000 server to issue certificates using the Windows 2000 Certificate Services, or you can obtain certificates from a third-party vendor such as VeriSign.

Travel Assistance

You can learn more about Microsoft's implementation of SSL from the Windows Web Services section of Microsoft's TechNet at http://www.microsoft.com/technet/treeview/default.asp?url=/TechNet/prodtechnol/iis/maintain/featusability/c06iis.asp.

Troubleshooting Internet Information Services

The most common type of IIS problem you will run into is when users can simply not connect to a site. Of course, there may be many reasons for this. You will also run into the occasional other problem, as well. Table 9-2 presents some of the common problems and possible solutions.

TABLE 9.2   Problems Encountered with IIS

Problem	Possible Cause	Solution
A single user cannot connect to a site.	Networking problem	See the troubleshooting section in Chapter 3 for recommendations on troubleshooting networking problems.
	Using alternate port number	If an alternate port number is being used, make sure users are pointing their browsers to it correctly. Also make sure the correct port number is being used.
	Name resolution problem	If basic networking is intact and IIS is running, make sure client is resolving names properly. See Chapters 5 and 6 for more on this.
Multiple users cannot connect to a site.	Networking problem	It is possible for a networking problem to affect multiple users. See Chapter 3.
	IIS service stopped	Check the IIS server to see whether the service is started. If it is not started and should be, check the System log in Event Viewer for possible errors. If the service is started, try restarting it to reset the services.
	Name resolution problem	If basic networking is intact and IIS is running, make sure clients are resolving names properly. See Chapters 5 and 6 for more on this.
Clients can connect to a site but cannot access content.	Authentication problem	Make sure the authentication and encryption set for the site match the types the client supports and is configured to use.
	Anonymous access problem	Make sure anonymous access is allowed if you want it to be. Also, make sure the anonymous user account exists (on the IIS server or in the Active Directory) and is properly configured.

TABLE 9.2	Problems Encountered with IIS *(continued)*	
Problem	**Possible Cause**	**Solution**
	Web permissions problem	Check the Web sharing permissions on any Web folders to make sure they enable the appropriate client access (such as permissions to read and execute.
	Local permissions problem	Make sure NTFS permissions are configured properly on Web folders.
	Content is not present	Make sure the home directory for the site exists and is correctly identified. Also make sure virtual directories are correctly configured.
	SSL problem	If SSL is being used, make sure the server is properly configured. Also, make sure clients are accessing secured portions of the site using the URL format https instead of http and that the proper port number is being used in the URL.

CHECKPOINT

✔ **Objective 9.01: Configure and Troubleshoot Internet Information Services**
This objective looked at Internet Information Services (IIS), a component of Windows 2000 that provides a world-class Web, FTP, and SMTP service. You learned how to install IIS and how to create and manage Web and FTP sites. You also learned the security measures available for controlling access to a site and how to troubleshoot basic user connection problems.

REVIEW QUESTIONS

1. Your intranet site has grown to the point where numerous users need to publish information to the site. You would like them to be able to publish information directly without it having to go through an administrator and without the users having access to the IIS server or

the home directory. Which of the following methods would make things easier for your users?

A. Create a new virtual server for each user where they can publish information.

B. Create one or more virtual directories where users can store information.

C. Install IIS on each user's computer and then redirect certain URLs to the new servers.

D. Configure an FTP site for users to send in information to be published.

2. You are planning to create a Web server that will also handle some Internet e-mail services. Which of the following protocols is used to transport e-mail messages?

A. HTTP

B. NNTP

C. FTP

D. SMTP

3. You have set up a Web server, created a virtual directory, and established permissions for Web folders. However, when users begin trying to publish their own documents using Microsoft FrontPage, many report incompatibility problems. Which of the following might be the cause?

A. You must assign a special FrontPage (FP) permission to the virtual directory in ISM so that FrontPage users can connect.

B. You must enable the Allow FrontPage Clients to Connect option on the Web Site tab of the site's Properties dialog box.

C. You must make sure that FrontPage server extensions are installed on the IIS server.

D. You must make sure that the Execute permission is enabled on the virtual directory in ISM.

4. One of your users reports that he cannot connect to the company Web site using his browser. You try to access the site using the browser on your computer and the site won't load for you either. You check and find that the IIS service is running. What should be your next step?

A. Restart the IIS service.

B. Reboot the computer.

    C. Make sure that authentication is correctly configured.

    D. Make sure NTFS permissions are correctly configured.

5. You have created a new Web site on a Windows 2000 server that is to be used only by the executives in your company, on whatever computer they happen to be using. They will not need to access the company site from outside the company network. You want to ensure that all other users cannot access the site. What is the best way to do this?

    A. Use an alternate port number for the site and configure only the executives' Web browsers to use this number.

    B. Deny all users access to this site and then grant access only to the IP addresses of the computers the executives will use.

    C. Configure the Web site to use SSL.

    D. Configure the Web site to use Integrated Windows authentication and assign access permissions only to the executives' user accounts.

6. Which of the following types of authentication methods require users to have a valid Windows 2000 user account?

    A. Anonymous

    B. Basic

    C. Digest

    D. Integrated Windows

7. Which of the following protocols defines how messages are transmitted over the Web and how Web browsers should respond to those messages?

    A. FTP

    B. HTTP

    C. NNTP

    D. SMTP

8. You have configured your Web site with only the Read permission enabled. You have configured a virtual directory inside that Web site with only the Write permission enabled. What are the effective permissions on the virtual directory?

    A. Read

    B. Write

    C. Read and Write

    D. This directory will be inaccessible because read permission must be enabled on virtual directories.

9. You have just created a new Web site using the default values. Which of the following permissions are enabled for the site?

   A. Read

   B. Write

   C. Script Source Access

   D. Directory Browsing

10. You have just created a new Web site using the default values. Which of the following authentication methods are enabled for the site?

    A. Anonymous

    B. Basic

    C. Digest

    D. Integrated Windows

REVIEW ANSWERS

1. **B** Creating virtual directories would be the best of the options offered. Users could put information directly into the virtual directories, where it would be immediately available on the site. This would prevent users from needing access to the IIS server. Note that a much better solution would be using NTFS permissions instead of relying on IIS permissions at all.

2. **D** Simple Mail Transfer Protocol (SMTP) is used to send e-mail between computers on a network. A is wrong because HTTP is used to transfer information between a Web server and client. B is wrong because NNTP is used for hosting electronic discussion groups. C is wrong because FTP is used for transferring files between a client and a server.

3. **C** The only thing that needs to be done in order for FrontPage users to connect and publish pages is for the FrontPage Server extensions to be installed. FrontPage extensions are installed automatically on the default site when installing IIS. You can install them on additional sites. A and B are wrong because these options do not exist. D is wrong because execute permissions are not needed for running FrontPage.

4. **A** Restarting the IIS server provides a way to reset the services without rebooting the computer. To be kind to your users, you might want to pause the services first to allow any users that are connected to disconnect before restarting the server.

5. **D** Integrated Windows authentication requires that a user provide a valid Windows username and password to access the site. A is wrong

because using an alternate port number would not really prevent anyone from accessing the site that really wanted to. B is wrong because this would not allow executives to access the site from any computer they logged onto, but only from certain computers. C is wrong because SSL would encrypt data passed between the site and clients but would not control access to the site.

6. **C D**   Both Digest and Integrated Windows authentication require a valid Windows 2000 account. A is wrong, because although an anonymous user account is required, the users do not require an account. B is wrong because Basic authentication requires a username and password, but not a Windows 2000 account.

7. **B**   HTTP is used to transfer information between a Web server and client. A is wrong because HTML is the format used to build Web pages. C is wrong because NNTP is used for hosting electronic discussion groups. D is wrong because SMTP is used to send e-mail between computers on a network.

8. **B**   The permissions on the virtual directory override the permissions on the Web site, so the effective permissions are only Write. A is wrong because the Web site permissions do not override the virtual directory permissions. C is wrong because the permissions are not combined. D is wrong because you do not have to have the read permission on a virtual directory.

9. **A**   When creating a new Web site using the default settings, only the Read, Log Visits, and Index This Resource permissions are enabled.

10. **A D**   When you create a new Web site using the default settings, both the Anonymous and Integrated Windows authentication methods are enabled.

Configuring, Managing, Securing, and Troubleshooting Active Directory Organizational Units and Group Policy

Managing Active
Directory Objects

	NEWBIE	SOME EXPERIENCE	EXPERT
ETA	6 hours	3 hours	2 hours

Active Directory is one of the most significant changes offered by Windows 2000. This chapter starts with an overview of Active Directory. It then examines the management of users and groups, including creating user and group accounts, changing account settings, and controlling access using groups. Finally, it covers ways to delegate authority within Active Directory to other administrators, both using the Delegation of Authority wizard and through manual configuration.

Create, Manage, and Troubleshoot User and Group Objects in Active Directory

Objective 10.01

U ser accounts provide a way to validate the users that log on to a network, control what resources those users can access, and provide all kinds of information about the users. *Groups* are used to efficiently organize collections of users that share common needs. On a Windows 2000 network, user and group accounts are stored in a database named Active Directory. Understanding how Active Directory works is essential to understanding how to manage the resources it contains. This section begins with an overview of Active Directory that discusses the various structures used to provide directory services to a Windows 2000 domain. Following this overview, we'll talk about how to configure users and groups.

Active Directory Overview

A directory is really just an easy way to look things up. There are directories everywhere, ranging from the phone book sitting on your desk to the kind of directories used on your computer to organize files. Like these, the Active Directory is a collection of information—in this case, a collection of information about the resources available on a Windows 2000 network.

Resources are stored in the Active Directory as objects. There are several different classes of objects, including computers, users, servers, and printers. The object class defines a consistent set of attributes available for configuring an object of its class. For example, a user class defines the user object as a collection of attributes—name, password, phone number, group membership, and so on. The classes and the attributes that they define are collectively referred to as the *Active Directory Schema*—in database terms, a schema is the structure of the tables and fields and how they are related to one another.

Objects are stored in the Active Directory in a hierarchical structure of containers and subcontainers, making the objects easier to find, access, and manage—much like organizing files in a set of Windows folders. You can tailor a directory structure to meet the needs of your organization and scale that structure to easily accommodate a network of any size.

What makes Active Directory so powerful, and so scalable, is that it separates the logical structure of the Windows 2000 domain hierarchy, which is made up of domains, trees, forests, and organizational units, from the physical structure of the network itself. The logical structure of Active Directory does not take into account the physical location or network connectivity in the domain and, thus, does not depend on the size or complexity of your physical network. In this chapter, we are going to discuss the logical structure of Active Directory. We'll get into the physical side in Chapter 12.

Domains

A Windows 2000 *domain* is a group of computers that share a common security and user database and are the primary defining element on a Windows 2000 network. A domain must have at least one domain controller running some edition of Windows 2000 server. Within the boundaries of a domain, all domain controllers hold a replica of the Active Directory database, and information in the database can be updated on any of them.

Using domains allows administrators to divide the network into security boundaries. In addition, administrators from different domains can establish their own security models; security from one domain can then be isolated so that other domains' security models are not affected.

Domains use a naming structure that most network administrators are already familiar with: the same Domain Name System (DNS) used on the Internet (and covered in detail in Chapter 6). The domain, when created, is given a name that follows the DNS structure. For example, a server named Server1 in a domain named headrest.com would have the fully qualified domain name (FQDN) server1.headrest.com.

Travel Advisory

Active Directory supports two domain modes: native and mixed. Native domains are those that contain only Windows 2000 domain controllers and boast the full functionality of Windows 2000's domain features. Mixed-mode domains can contain both Windows 2000 and Windows NT domain controllers and have a subset of the functionality found in native mode domains. Throughout this chapter, particularly in the discussion of group objects, we will point out where the two modes are different.

Trees

Multiple domains are organized into a hierarchical structure called a *tree*. The first domain you create in a tree is called the root domain. The next domain that you add becomes a child domain of that root. This expandability of Windows 2000 domains makes it possible to have many domains in a tree. Figure 10-1 shows an example of a tree. Headrest.com was the first domain created in Active Directory in this example and is therefore the root domain. All domains in a tree share a common schema and a contiguous namespace. In the example, all of the domains in the tree under the headrest.com root domain share the namespace headrest.com.

Domains establish trust relationships with one another that allow objects in a trusted domain to access resources in a trusting domain. Windows 2000 and Active Directory support transitive, two-way trusts between domains. When a child domain is created, a trust relationship is automatically configured between that child domain and the parent domain. This trust is two-way, meaning that resource access requests can flow from either domain to the other. The

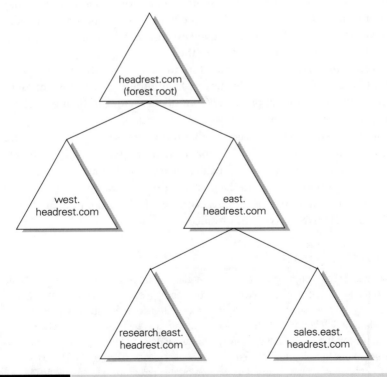

FIGURE 10.1 An Active Directory Tree with several domains

trust is also transitive, meaning that domain controllers in a trusted domain pass along authentication requests to domain controllers in trusting domains.

Forests

A *forest* is a group of one or more domain trees that do not form a contiguous namespace but may share a common schema and global catalog. There is always at least one forest on the network, and it is created when the first Active Directory–enabled computer (domain controller) on a network is installed. This first domain in a forest, called the *forest root domain,* is special because it holds the schema and controls domain naming for the entire forest. It cannot be removed from the forest without removing the entire forest itself. Also, no other domain can ever be created above the forest root domain in the forest domain hierarchy.

Figure 10-2 shows an example of a forest with two trees. Each tree in the forest has its own namespace. In the figure, attech.com is a second tree in the headrest.com forest and has two domains that share its namespace: sales.attech.com and research.attech.com.

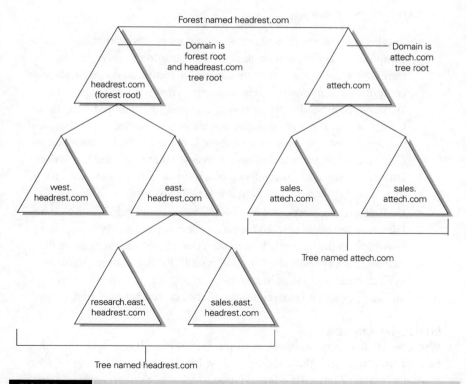

FIGURE 10.2   An Active Directory forest

A forest is the outermost boundary of Active Directory; the directory cannot be larger than the forest. You can create multiple forests and then create trust relationships between specific domains in those forests; this would let you grant access to resources and accounts that are outside of a particular forest.

Exam Tip

The exam assumes that you know and understand all of these concepts: domains, trees, forests, and schema. The exam uses these terms even in questions that don't have directly to do with AD, so take your time to ensure you understand the logical structure of AD.

User Accounts

User accounts provide users with the ability to log on to the domain or a local computer and access resources. They hold information about users and dictate certain options the user is given when logged on. Windows 2000 provides two main types of user accounts:

- **Local user accounts** Local user accounts are created within a particular computer's security database and govern access to resources on that computer. Local user accounts are intended to control access on stand-alone computers or computers in a workgroup. When you initially install a Windows 2000 Server, local accounts are used and managed using the Computer Management console, under the node named Local Users and Groups. When you promote a server to become a domain controller, the Computer Management tool denies access to that node, and the Active Directory Users and Computers tool is used instead (as user accounts on domain controllers are stored in the Active Directory).

- **Domain user accounts** Domain user accounts are created within Active Directory and allow users to log on to a domain and access resources anywhere on the network. You create a domain user account using the Active Directory Users and Computers tool. User accounts are replicated to all domain controllers in a domain, so any domain controller can authenticate a user once replication of the account has occurred.

Built-in Users

Windows 2000 automatically creates a number of default user accounts called *built-in* user accounts. Both locally and within a domain there are two key accounts created: Administrator and Guest.

The Administrator account is the most powerful user account, as it is automatically made a member of the Administrators group (discussed a bit later in the chapter). This allows the ultimate level of control over an individual computer and grants all user rights to a user. The domain-level Administrators account has ultimate control over the entire domain; it belongs to the Domain Administrators group and the Enterprise Administrators group by default. The Administrators account cannot be deleted, but you can (and for security purposes, should) rename the account. You should also ensure that this account does not have a blank password, nor should you distribute the password to others.

The Guest account is the other basic built-in user account and is used to provide a single set of permissions to any users who must log on to the network occasionally, but who do not have regular user accounts. The Guest account is given this ability by being included automatically in the local Guest group (discussed later in the Groups section). The Guest account is disabled by default and is really meant to be used only on low-security networks. You cannot delete the Guest account, but you can disable and/or rename it.

Travel Advisory

Two other user accounts, IUSR_*computername* (IUSR stands for Internet User) and IWAM_*computername* (IWAM stands for Internet Web Application Manager), are also created when Internet Information Services is installed on a domain controller. IUSER_*computername* is used to provide access to IIS services (such as for browsing Web sites). IWAM_*computername* provides anonymous access to IIS out-of-process applications.

Creating Users

Creating a user account is easy. In Active Directory Users and Computers, select the container (or OU, which is discussed later in the chapter) into which you want the account to go or simply choose the built-in Users container. Select Action | New | User or right-click the Users container to access the same command. A wizard walks you through the creation of the account, including creating a name and a password, and configuring some password options. Items you will need to configure when creating a new user are described in Table 10-1.

TABLE 10.1	Items You Can Configure During User Account Creation

Option	Description
First Name, Initial, Last Name	These fields simply represent the parts of the user's full name.
Full Name	When you create a domain account, Windows 2000 builds this name for you from the user's First Name, Initials, and Last Name. You can change it if necessary.
User Logon Name	This is the logon name used when logging on from Windows 2000 systems. The drop-down list presents a list of User Principle Name (UPN) suffixes that can be appended to the name. This list is created on the basis of available domains the user account could be stored in. The default selection is based on the domain in which you are creating the account. However, you can use any domain in which you have permissions to create domain user accounts.
User Logon Name (pre–Windows 2000)	This is the logon name used when logging on to Windows NT or Windows 9x systems. Typically, you should specify the same name as used for Windows 2000 logins.
Password (and confirm password)	Enter a password to be used for the user account.
User Must Change Password at Next Logon	Forces users to change their passwords the first time they log on. You can also enable this setting later via the user account's Properties dialog box to force users to change their passwords the next time they log on.
User Cannot Change Password	Prevents users from changing the password, which is good for temporary workers.
Password Never Expires	Overrides the password expiration policy that may be set for the system or domain.
Account is Disabled	Prevents the account from being used to log on. This is useful for template accounts that you copy to create multiple users with the same settings and for temporarily suspending the logon rights of a user.

Managing Users

To manage the account further, right-click the account and use the shortcut menu that appears. This shortcut menu provides a number of commands:

- **Reset Password** This allows you to change a password if a user forgets it, which happens more often than you'd think.

- **Unlock User Accounts** You can set a user account to become locked if someone makes too many unsuccessful attempts to log on with it (this is covered in Chapter 11). If an account becomes locked, use this option to restore it.

- **Delete** You can delete an account, but doing so is not usually the best option. Instead, when a user no longer needs an account (such as when the user leaves the company), it is better to simply disable the account. If the person comes back, you can reenable the account. If a new person takes over the position, you can rename the account. This saves the hassle of reconfiguring the account with all of the options and permissions it may have held. Be particularly careful when deleting a user account that may have been used to encrypt files, as a designated recovery agent must then be used to access those files (see Chapter 8 for more on this).

- **Rename** This is a good option for users that are turning their jobs over to someone else and for name changes.

- **Copy** This function is quite useful when you create an account to use as a template for your organization. Once you create an account and configure it with all the common configurations that users require, you can copy the account, rename the copy, and then have to configure only the unique settings required for the new account.

- **Disable/Enable** As mentioned earlier, there are times when you may want to disable an account rather than delete it. A disabled account retains all of its settings but is unusable until reenabled.

- **Properties** This command opens a Properties dialog for the account that lets you configure all available attributes for an account.

Exam Tip

Spend some time exploring all the options you can configure for a user account using the Properties dialog box, particularly the Account tab for Domain users and the General tab for local users. These tabs let you modify much of the information you configured while creating the user, and they hold some additional options, such as configuring allowable logon hours. While there are no questions that ask this information directly (i.e., where would you configure a person's phone number), many questions rely on your knowing this information.

Organizing Users with Organizational Units

Objects within a domain are often organized into *organizational units (OUs)*. Organizing objects in this manner is done both to make resources easier to find in Active Directory and to delegate administrative control of those resources. Using OUs, you can achieve the following:

- Organize objects by type, location, or other criteria.
- Delegate administrative control to objects placed inside the OU. As you'll learn in the later section "Manage Object and Container Permissions," you control administrative access to Active Directory objects by assigning permissions. Grouping objects allows you to assign permissions more easily.
- Group resources according to the group and security policies that you need to apply to them. OUs represent the smallest scope to which you can apply group policy settings in Active Directory. Group Policy is covered in Chapter 11.
- Make it easier to assign permissions to resources by assigning permissions to the OU and then placing the resources inside.

When Active Directory is installed, the setup process creates a default structure with six containers and one OU, all of which you can see by opening the Active Directory Users and Computers tool. Table 10-2 lists these default containers and OU.

Planning an OU structure for your organization is the hard part. You must consider permissions, delegation of administrative authority, and assignment of policy. Actually creating an OU is simple but requires that you be a member of the Domain Admins group (for domains) or the Enterprise Admins group (for forests). In Active Directory Users and Computers, just right-click the node or container in which you want to create the OU and select New | Organizational Unit. The OU is created, much as a folder is created in Windows Explorer, and all you have to do is name it by clicking the default name and typing.

Creating User Profiles

A *user profile* is a set of folders that contain data about a user's desktop environment, Start Menu items, application settings, and personal files. User profiles allow multiple users to work on the same computer, yet maintain their own

TABLE 10.2	Default Containers and OUs in Active Directory

Default Container/OU	Description
Builtin	This container holds the default built-in local security groups for the domain controller.
Computers	This container holds computer accounts created when computers running Windows 2000 join the domain.
Domain Controllers	This OU holds computer accounts for domain controllers in the domain. These accounts are also found in the Computers container.
ForiegnSecurityPrincipals	This container holds security identifiers (SIDs) of trusted domains external to the domain.
Users	This container holds user and group accounts created in the domain.
LostAndFound	This container holds objects that have been orphaned. See Chapter 12 for more on this container.
System	This container holds built-in system settings, such as DNS SRV record objects and IPSec objects.

customizations. On computers running Windows 2000, a user profile is created automatically the first time that a new user logs on to a computer. User profiles can also be stored on a server, so that profile settings are accessible on any attached computer a person logs on to. As an administrator, you can create profiles that have the appropriate default configurations for users and even make those profiles mandatory.

There are three types of user profiles:

- **Local user profile**   Created by Windows 2000 when a user first logs on to a computer. The local user profile is stored on the hard drive of the local computer in the \Documents and Settings folder. Changes that a user makes to a local profile are available only on the local computer.

- **Roaming user profile**   A copy of a local user profile that is stored on a server on the network. When a user logs on, the roaming profile is copied to the \Documents and Settings folder of the local computer and is used just like a local profile. The first time a user logs on to a computer, the entire profile must be copied. Following that, only changes to the profile are copied to the local computer. When a user logs off, changes made to the local copy of the roaming profile are copied back to the network server. You can create a roaming profile for a user by opening that user's Properties dialog in Active Directory Users and Computers, switching to the Profile tab, and entering the UNC path for the location the roaming profile should be stored.

- **Mandatory profile** A read-only roaming profile that a user may not permanently modify. You can use mandatory profiles to enforce settings for a user. While logged on, users can make changes to settings (desktop, applications, and so on), but these changes are not copied back to the network version of the roaming profile. Thus, users receive the same settings every time they log on. To create a mandatory profile, you simply rename the ntuser.dat file (which stores the current user's profile in the Registry) in the folder containing the roaming profile to ntuser.man. The real benefit to this type of profile is that you can create a single profile for multiple users, and no single user can alter settings that affect everyone else. While mandatory profiles could be used in a limited way to lock down the abilities a user has, group policies (covered in Chapter 11) are better suited to this purpose.

Home Directories

It is much easier to back up one server than to back up hundreds workstations. Home folders let you provide centralized storage to users so that their documents are not saved on their own computers. Centralized storage makes backups easier to configure and also provides continued access to data should a user's computer fail or should the user need to access data from a different computer.

Creating a home folder for a user is simply a matter of going to the Profile tab of a user's Properties dialog in Active Directory Users and Computers and entering a path for the folder you want to use. You can either enter a local path on the server or specify a drive letter to connect to a UNC path. The UNC path follows the convention:

*server_name**folder_name**user_logon_name*

In place of the actual user's logon name, you can also use the variable %username%, which automatically names each user's home folder with the user's logon name.

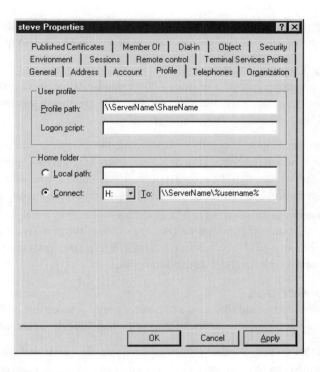

Travel Advisory

Although home folders are still available for Windows 2000 and you should know about them for the exam, Microsoft actually recommends that you have users within a domain store their data in their My Documents folders. Then, you should establish a Group Policy setting that redirects the My Documents folder on users' computers so that it works like a shortcut to a shared network location. Group Policy is discussed in Chapter 11.

Group Objects

Groups simplify the assignment of permissions by organizing users. It is much easier, for example, to assign permissions to one group and then to include users in that group than it is to assign and manage permissions for many users individually. Changing a particular permission for all of those users becomes a single step when those users are members of a group.

As with user accounts, there are both local and domain-level groups. Local groups are stored in a local computer's security database and are intended to control resource access on that computer. Domain groups are stored in Active

Directory and let you gather users and control resource access in a domain and on domain controllers. This chapter focuses primarily on domain groups.

Group Types

When you create a group in Windows 2000, you must specify two things: the type of group you want to create and the scope the group will assume.

Windows 2000 includes two group *types*:

- **Security groups** Security groups are used to group domain users into a single administrative unit or as a placeholder for rights and permissions. Security groups can be assigned permissions and also used as e-mail distribution lists. Windows 2000 itself uses only security groups.

- **Distribution groups** These are used for nonsecurity purposes by applications other than Windows 2000. One of the primary uses is within an e-mail server as an e-mail distribution list. You cannot assign permissions to a distribution group.

Group Scopes

Group *scopes* determine where on a network a group is accessible and what objects can be placed into the group. Windows 2000 includes three group scopes:

- **Global groups** Global groups are used to gather users that have similar permissions requirements. Global groups can contain user and computer accounts in both mixed and native domains. In native domains, global groups can also contain other global groups from the local domain (the domain in which the group is created). Global groups can be assigned permissions or added to local groups in any domain.

- **Domain local groups** Domain local groups exist on domain controllers and are used to control access to resources located on domain controllers in the local domain (for member servers and workstations, you will use local groups on those systems, instead). Domain local groups can contain users and global groups from any domain in a forest in both mixed and native domains. In native domains, they can also contain other domain local groups and universal groups.

- **Universal groups** Universal groups are available only in native mode domains. They exist outside the boundaries of any particular domain and are managed by Global Catalog servers (discussed in Chapter 12). Universal groups are used to assign permissions to related resources in multiple domains. Universal groups can contain users, global groups, and other universal groups from any domain in a forest. You can grant permissions for a universal group to any resource in any domain.

Table 10-3 summarizes the items that groups of different scopes can contain in mixed and native mode domains.

Travel Assistance
Since distribution groups are not used for permissions, they are not subject to the same restrictions in mixed-mode domains that security groups are.

How to Use Groups

So, now that you know the group types and group scopes, how does all this fit together? Here are some recommended guidelines for using groups:

- First, try not to ever assign permissions to user accounts. Assigning permissions to groups provides a much more flexible and easy-to-manage permissions structure. This is possible with a carefully designed group structure.

- Create domain local groups that represent the domain controller resources you want to control access to and how those resources will be used. For example, you might create a domain local group called Color

TABLE 10.3	Rules for Group Scope Membership	
Scope	**Items Group Can Contain in Native Mode**	**Items Group Can Contain in Mixed Mode**
Global (G)	User accounts and global groups from the local domain	Users from the same domain
Domain Local (DL)	User accounts, universal groups, and global groups from any domain. Domain local groups from the same domain	Users and global groups from any domain
Universal (U)	User accounts, universal groups, and global groups from any domain	You cannot create universal groups in mixed mode.

Printers High Priority for a printer installed on a domain controller. Assign the appropriate permissions on the resource to the group. If resources are on a member server or workstation, you will use local groups instead of domain local groups.

- Create global groups that help organize users. For example, you might create a group named Executives. Place the appropriate users (or other groups) inside the group.
- Place global groups inside domain local groups. For example, putting the global group Executives inside the domain local group Color Printers High Priority would give members permission to use the color printers and (as the name suggests) give them a higher priority than other users.

Of course, no one can force you to follow these recommendations, but it is in your best interests in the real world and you'll be expected to understand these practices on the exam.

Exam Tip

You can remember Microsoft's guidelines for using groups with one simple acronym: AGLP. (A)ccounts go into (G)lobal groups, which go into (L)ocal groups, which are assigned (P)ermissions. Just keep in mind that on domain controllers, the (L)ocal group is a domain local group; on member servers and workstations, the (L)ocal group is simply a local group.

Exam Tip

Draw out the domains and the groups on the exam to help ensure that you choose the correct solution to a question. Remember what can and cannot be done in native and mixed modes. Know your group types and scope types. Finally, remember the best practices (not enforced rules) for permission placement and groups.

Creating Groups

To create a new domain group, you will use Active Directory Users and Computers (use Computer Management for local groups). Find the OU in which you want to create the group (or just choose the Users container) and select Action | New | Group. This opens the dialog box shown next. Enter a group name and optionally a different group name used for pre–Windows 2000 servers). Select a group scope and a group type, and click OK to create the group.

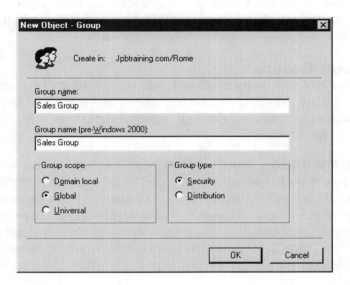

Managing Groups

When a group is created, it has no members and is not a member of any other groups. Configuring this is up to you and is performed (along with other management functions) using the group's Properties dialog box, which contains the following tabs:

- **General**   This tab lets you configure the pre–Windows 2000 name of the group, the description of the group that appears in the AD Users and Computers window, and an e-mail address for using the group as a distribution list. The General tab also shows the type and scope for the group, though you cannot change these after the group's creation.
- **Members**   This tab lists the members of the group. To add a new member, click Add and select a user or group from the dialog box that opens. Select any member and click Delete to remove that member from the group. You can also add user accounts or other group accounts to the membership by using the Member Of tab on their Properties dialog boxes.
- **Member Of**   This tab lists the groups that this group is a member of. Use the Add and Remove buttons to control membership.

- **Managed By** This tab lists the manager of the group. The manager shows the person responsible for managing the membership of the group. By default, no manager is listed. Making someone a group's manager provides a way to delegate control of the group's management to someone else—a department head, for example.

Default Groups

Windows 2000 includes many default groups that contain predetermined sets of user rights, permissions, and group memberships. These default groups are broken down into four categories: built-in global, built-in local, built-in domain local, and special identity.

Built-in Global Groups *Built-in global* groups (referred to in most MS documentation as predefined groups) are found in the Users built-in container within AD Users and Computers. You can control who has access to what by adding these built-in global groups to domain local groups or local groups. The difference between the built-in domain groups and these built-in global groups is that these groups have a global rather than a domain scope. By default, predefined groups do not have any rights or permissions. These groups are listed in Table 10-4.

Built-in Local Groups *Built-in local* groups are created on stand-alone and member servers, and on computers running Windows 2000 Professional. If you are following the recommended group practices, you will not add users to any of these groups (since users are added only to global groups). Built-in local groups include the following:

- **Administrators** The king of all local groups, allowing members to perform all administrative tasks. The local Administrator account is automatically made a member of this group, as are the Domain Admins and Enterprise Admins global groups discussed in the previous section.
- **Backup Operators** Allows members of this group to back up and restore data on the local system.
- **Power Users** Can create and modify local user accounts on the computer, share resources, and install drivers for legacy software. This group exists only on Windows 2000 Professional workstations and on member servers, but not domain controllers.
- **Users** Allowed to perform the most common of tasks like running applications and accessing resources. They cannot share out folders or

TABLE 10.4	Built-In Global Groups		

Predefined Group	Description	Default Members of This Group	Members of These Groups by Default
Cert Publishers	Short for Certification Publishers, this group is populated by programs and services that issue security certificates.	None	None
Domain Admins	Designated administrators for the domain.	Administrator account for domain	All local and domain local Administrators groups in the domain
Domain Computers	When you add a computer to the domain, the account is added to the Domain Computers group.	All computers joined to the domain	None
Domain Controllers	When a server becomes a domain controller, the account is added to this group.	All domain controllers in the domain	None
Domain Guests	Used for managing guest access to resources in a domain.	Guest accounts on computers in domain	Local Guests groups on computers in domain
Domain Users	By default, when you add a user to the domain, the account is added to the Domain Users group.	All domain users	Local Users groups on computers in domain
Enterprise Admins	Designated administrators of the enterprise (the AD forest).	Domain Administrator account in root domain	All local and domain local Administrators groups in the domain
Group Policy Creator Owners	Used to create and manage group policy for the domain.	Administrator account for domain	None
Schema Admins	Designated administrators of the AD schema.	Administrator account for forest root domain	None

printers, or create local printers. All authenticated users are made members of this group, by default.

- **Guests**   Allow for temporary or single access for persons through the Guest account. The Guest account is made a member of this group, by default.
- **Replicator**   Supports the directory replication service.

Built-in Domain Local Groups   *Built-in domain local* groups (sometimes just called built-in groups in Microsoft documentation) include domain local variations on all of the groups listed in the previous section on built-in local groups, with the exception of the Power Users group. These groups are used to control access on domain controllers and are found in the Built-in container in the Active Directory Users and Computers tool. In addition to the built-in local groups listed in the preceding section, built-in domain local groups include the following:

- **Server Operators**   Members of this group have administrative rights on domain controllers in the local domain.
- **Account Operators**   Members can create, manage, and delete user accounts and groups, although not the Administrators account, the Domain or Local Administrative groups, the Account Operators, Print Operators, or Backup Operators groups.
- **Print Operators**   Members can create, manage, delete, and share printers.

Special Identity Groups   *Special identity* groups exist on all computers running Windows 2000. These groups do not have memberships that you can modify, but rather the membership depends on the actions you perform. Unlike with other groups, you can't add users to or remove users from special identity groups. Instead, special identity groups represent different users at different times. In fact, you can't even see the special identity groups when you're administering groups. The only time you'll ever see them is when you assign permissions to resources. Special identity groups include the following:

- **Anonymous Logon**   Those that are logged on anonymously, as in IIS Web- or FTP-connected users.
- **Authenticated Users**   All users that have been given access to the system through authentication means. When assigning permissions, you can use the Authenticated User group in place of the Everyone group to prevent anonymous access to resources.
- **Creator Owner**   Refers to the user who created or took ownership of the resource to which you're assigning permissions.
- **Dialup**   Includes anyone who's currently connected to the network through a dial-up connection.

- **Everyone** Includes all users who access the system. Be careful about assigning resources to Everyone, because you could accidentally allow unauthenticated users to access the system. One way of reducing this problem is to disable the Guest account. Remember that the Guest is a part of Everyone; and in some cases, Windows 2000 represents anonymous users as a guest.

- **Interactive** Anyone logged on to the computer locally.

- **Network** Basically the opposite of the Interactive group, this group includes any users who are accessing a computer from another computer. Remember that just because users are on the network, they aren't necessarily members of the Network group. The Network group is specific to each computer. Therefore, a user isn't a member of a computer's Network group unless the user is currently accessing resources on that machine.

 **Objective 10.02** # Manage Object and Container Permissions

Just as you can place permissions on network resources to determine who has access to those resources, you can place permissions on Active Directory objects to determine who can access and manage those objects. You apply permissions on Active Directory objects (for example, an OU) for the purpose of delegating administrative authority.

The five standard permissions that can be applied to an object described in the following list:

- **Full Control** Allows the user to view objects and attributes, the owner of an object, and the AD permissions, as well as to change any of those settings. In addition, a user with Full Control can literally change permissions on the object and take ownership of an object.

- **Write** Allows the user to view objects and attributes, the owner of an object, and the AD permissions. Also allows the user to change any of those settings.

- **Read** Allows the user to view objects and attributes, the owner of an object, and the AD permissions.

- **Create All Child Objects**   Allows the user to create additional child objects to an OU.
- **Delete All Child Objects**   Allows the user to delete existing objects from an OU.

All objects within the AD have an owner. The owner of an object can change permissions on the object and how those permissions are handed out. Logically, the initial owner of any object is the one who created it. So, if a user creates an OU named Legal, that user's account is registered as the owner. Any user that is granted the Full Control permission has the ability to take over the ownership of an object and thus become the object's new owner.

Assigning Permissions to Objects

You can set permissions on objects in two ways. The first is manually, by directly adding users and configuring their corresponding permissions. This method is most often used to assign permissions on a container or OU, as the permissions will be inherited by the objects inside. To do this, open the Properties dialog box for the object, switch to the Security tab, and modify the permissions the same way you would for a file or folder in Windows Explorer.

The second way to set permissions (other than by inheritance) is by using the Delegation of Control wizard. This wizard offers an easy way to assign sets of permissions to administrators on organizational units. Once set on the OU, permissions flow down to the objects inside (more about this in the next section). The following steps describe the use of the Delegation of Control wizard:

1. In Active Directory Users and Computers, find the organizational unit for which you want to delegate control.

2. Select Action | Delegate Control or right-click the object and select Delegate Control.

3. Click Next to skip the opening page of the wizard.

4. On the Users and Groups page, you are prompted to select a user, several users, a group, or several groups (the choice depends on your needs). Click Add, and select some users or groups. Then click Next.

5. The Tasks To Delegate screen (shown in Figure 10-3) presents your options for delegation. Select what you need and then click Next.

6. Review your selections and then select Finish.

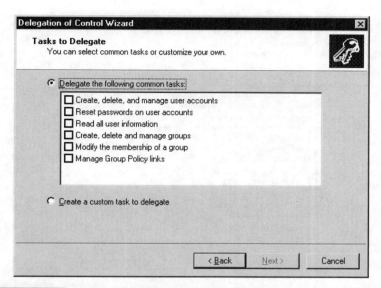

FIGURE 10.3 Delegating administration of an OU

Exam Tip

There are specific questions related to the type of task you need to choose for users to perform certain functions. The options here are relatively self-explanatory, but you need to memorize them so that a false option doesn't trick you.

The basic task options (selected in step 5 in the preceding procedure) allow for common tasks you may need to assign. However, there are times when you may need a more granular level of delegation. You can achieve this from within the wizard. On step 5 of the procedure just described, you would choose the option Create A Customized Task To Delegate. This option presents you an additional wizard page (shown next) that provides two options. The first specifies that permissions be set on the current folder, everything in it, and new objects created in the folder. The second option lets you specify the exact objects in the folder to choose from.

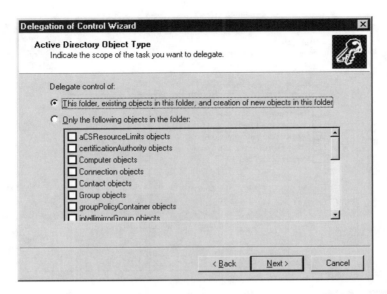

Another extra wizard page (shown next) presents you with a number of de-tailed permissions you can assign. Notice the three options of permission detail: General, Property-Specific, and Creation/Deletion Of Specific Child Objects. Each of these options toggles the display of additional permissions in the window.

Permissions Inheritance

Inheritance of permissions is automatic for child objects within parent containers. Put simply, if a parent OU has permissions assigned to it, the child objects beneath automatically inherit those permissions. The benefit of inheritance is that permissions need to be applied only at high-level containers, and they flow down throughout child containers already in existence. This makes the administrative task of delegating authority much easier

---

Exam Tip

Remember how these permissions flow from above for the exam and keep in mind that you have the ability to change this.

There are times when allowing permissions inheritance does not make sense for child objects. On the Security tab of the Properties dialog for an object (shown in Figure 10-4), you can choose whether permissions from parent containers

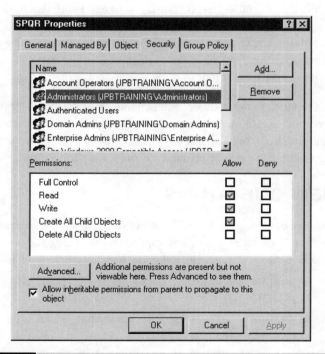

FIGURE 10.4 The OU's permissions are being inherited from the parent OU.

should affect an object. When this box is selected, permissions are inherited. Remove the check in this box to remove the permission inheritance.

When you remove the check in the box, a separate dialog box appears that offers you three choices:

- **Copy** Retain permissions that were already inherited, but do not inherit future permissions from the parent container.
- **Remove** Remove already inherited permissions and do not inherit future permissions from the parent container.
- **Cancel** Cancel the inheritance removal and return to the Security tab.

CHECKPOINT

✔**Objective 10.01: Create, Manage, and Troubleshoot User and Group Objects in Active Directory**   This objective provided an overview of Active Directory vocabulary and concepts. Next, we covered different user account issues, including creating, deleting, renaming, disabling, enabling, resetting passwords for, and copying accounts. Finally, we discussed the use of groups and covered the two types and three scopes of groups and how they work in both native and mixed modes.

✔**Objective 10.02: Manage Object and Container Permissions**   This objective covered the use of permissions on Active Directory objects to delegate administrative control. This can be done manually or using the Delegation of Control wizard. We also covered the inheritance of permissions.

REVIEW QUESTIONS

1. You are designing an Active Directory structure and need to configure two domains with separate namespaces: bigshoes.org and smallsocks.org. How would you need to configure the domains?

    A. As separate trees

    B. As separate forests

    C. As domains in the same tree that use separate schemas

    D. As domains in the same forest that use separate schemas

2. Joe is leaving the company. He vows never to return. He does this every other week. What should you do with Joe's account?

   A. Disable the account.

   B. Delete the account.

   C. Copy the account and give his replacement the new one and then delete the old one.

   D. Rename the account and change the password.

3. You are working in a mixed-mode domain and would like to create a Universal group. However, when you go to create one, the option to create a universal security group is unavailable. The option to create a universal distribution group, on the other hand, is available. What is the likely problem?

   A. This is the default behavior for universal groups. There is no such thing as a universal security group.

   B. The use of universal security groups is disabled by default. You must enable it using Active Directory Users and Computers as a member of the Enterprise Admins group.

   C. Universal security groups are not available in mixed mode.

   D. You are not a member of the Domain admins group.

4. You are the administrator of a domain tree with five domains, all of which are in native mode. Each domain has one or more users who run the help desk for your organization. Each domain has a global group named Help Desk that contains the user accounts of the help desk users from the local domain. There is an OU named Sales in the root domain. You want all help desk personnel to be able to reset passwords for user accounts in the Sales OU. What type of group will you need to use to group together the users from different domains?

   A. Global

   B. Local

   C. Domain Local

   D. Universal

5. You are the administrator of a Windows 2000 network. You create global groups and domain local groups for the Sales and Research departments. The domain local group named Sales has Change permission for a folder named Brochures. The Sales global group is a member of the Sales domain local group. The domain local group named Research has Read permissions on the Brochures folder.

A user named Joe is a member of the Sales department and is transferred to the Research department. Joe now needs only Read access to the Brochures folder but is still able to change items inside. What are two possible causes of this problem?

A. Joe's user account has explicit permissions on the Brochures folder.

B. Joe's user account belongs to another group that gives him permissions on the Brochures folder.

C. The Brochures folder is not published in Active Directory.

D. The Sales domain local group is not a member of the Sales global group.

6. You have a Windows 2000 domain in mixed mode and you would like to create a group for an e-mail group list. Which of the following types and scopes could you choose?

A. Distribution group

B. Security group

C. Domain Local

D. Global group

E. Universal group

7. You are setting up a group structure for a mixed-mode domain. Which of the following are you not allowed to do? (Choose all that apply.)

A. Put users into Domain Local

B. Put Global groups into Universal

C. Put Global groups into Domain Local

D. Put Global groups into Global groups

8. You are setting up your Active Directory structure so that your junior administrators can handle much of the routine administrative work. Which of the following has the primary function of easing the process of delegating authority?

A. Domains

B. Forests

C. Global Catalog Servers

D. OUs

9. You are setting up delegation of administrative control in Active Directory. Which of the following tools would you use to view Active Directory permission settings on objects?

   A. Active Directory Users and Computers

   B. Computer Management

   C. Active Directory Sites and Services

   D. Windows Explorer

10. You are trying to view an object's permission settings by going into its Properties dialog box in Active Directory Users and Computers. You cannot see the Security tab. What is the solution to this problem?

    A. You need to install the Windows 2000 Resource Kit.

    B. You need to log in using an account that has the right to change permissions.

    C. You need to turn on Advanced Features in Active Directory Users and Computers.

    D. You are need to log on locally to a domain controller.

REVIEW ANSWERS

1. **B**   In Windows 2000, a forest has two or more trees that do not share a common domain namespace. They do, however, share the same Active Directory database, configuration, schema, and Global Catalog.

2. **A**   Because this is a common occurrence, you can disable the account until Joe comes back. If he never does come back, then you can delete the account or rename it for his replacement.

3. **C**   Universal groups are not possible in mixed mode. The reason it is grayed out is because you are in mixed mode, so you need to convert it to native.

4. **D**   Universal groups allow users and groups from different domains to be grouped together. Universal groups are allowed only in native mode.

5. **A** **B**   The most likely cause of the problem is that Joe was added to the Research global group but not removed from the Sales global group (answer B). The least restrictive combination of permissions apply (refer to Chapter 8), so he has Change permissions. It is also possible that Joe's user account has been given specific permissions on the folder.

6. **A** **C** **D** **E**   For e-mail distribution, it is best to use the distribution group type and, regardless of the mode, all three group scopes will be available for you.

7. **B** **D**   Using mixed mode means you cannot use Universal groups at all and you cannot put Global groups into each other. Answer A is incorrect because this is a possible solution in both mixed and native modes. Answer C is also incorrect because in both mixed and native modes, you can place Global groups into Domain Local groups.

8. **D**   Assigning control at the OU level is the best way to administer control over objects within Active Directory, although it is possible to assign permissions directly to objects, such as a user or a printer.

9. **A**   Active Directory Users and Computers lets you create OUs, delegate control over those OUs, and view that delegation of control.

10. **C**   By default, you cannot see the Security tab for objects. It's turned on using View | Advanced Features in Active Directory Users and Computers. Answer D is incorrect because the scenario doesn't mention who you are logged on as, so it would be unwise to automatically conclude in this case that you have the wrong permissions.

Using Group Policies

CHAPTER 11

ETA

	NEWBIE	SOME EXPERIENCE	EXPERT
	5 hours	3 hours	2 hours

279

In the preceding chapter, you learned what Active Directory is and how users and groups are configured and organized. This chapter introduces group policies, which you can use to manage Windows settings for users, deploy and update applications, and apply security settings throughout an organization.

Group Policy Overview

Before moving into planning and creating group policies, it is essential that you understand what group policies are and what they are used for. *Group policies are user and computer configuration settings that you can link to computers, sites, domains, and organizational units (OUs) in Active Directory. A collection of group policy settings is called a *Group Policy Object (GPO).*

Any computer running Windows 2000 (whether it is part of Active Directory or not) contains one local GPO with policies applied to that computer. If the computer is a part of Active Directory, then any number of additional nonlocal GPOs may also apply to that computer.

As an example, assume that a user named Jenny has just logged on to a computer named Lab1, which is running Windows 2000 Professional and is part of Active Directory. The local GPO on the Lab1 computer contains a collection of policies. Another GPO has been configured in Active Directory that applies to a group of computers, of which Lab1 is a member. Yet another GPO has been linked to an OU that Jenny's user account is a member of. When Jenny logs on to the computer, the settings in all three of these GPOs are combined and applied.

We'll get to how those GPOs are combined a bit later. First, let's take a look at the tool used to configure group policy and the kinds of settings you can apply.

Using the Group Policy Snap-In

Group policy is managed using a Microsoft Management Console snap-in named Group Policy, shown in Figure 11-1. This snap-in works both as a stand-alone snap-in (meaning that you can open a console window and access the snap-in) and as an extension snap-in (meaning that you can access it via an object in another type of console).

The Group Policy snap-in used when managing local GPOs (those stored on local computers running Windows 2000) and when managing GPOs in the Active Directory is the same. However, the procedures for accessing the snap-in depend on the GPO you want to view.

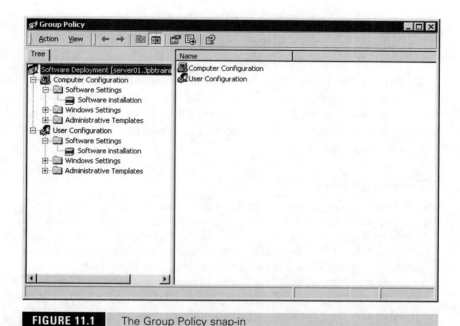

FIGURE 11.1   The Group Policy snap-in

You can open a local GPO for the computer at which you are sitting or for another computer on the network using roughly the same procedure:

1. Click Start | Run.

2. In the Run dialog box, type **mmc** and press ENTER. This starts a Microsoft Management Console.

3. Click Console | Add/Remove Snap-In to open the Add/Remove Snap-In dialog box.

4. On the General tab of the Add/Remove Snap-In dialog box, click Add. This opens the Add Standalone Snap-In dialog box.

5. Select the Group Policy entry and click Add.

6. The local computer is automatically selected. Click Finish to open the Group Policy snap-in with the local computer as the focus, and start editing.

7. To view the local GPO for a remote computer, click Browse instead of clicking Finish in the previous step. This opens the Browse For A Group Policy Object dialog box.

8. Switch to the Computers tab. Choose whether to open the GPO for This Computer (which does the same thing as clicking Finish in step 7) or Another Computer (which requires that you supply the name of the remote computer). Click OK to close the Browse For A Group Policy Object dialog box.

Travel Advisory

For the most part, you will not bother with setting local group policy, since it is more effective and efficient to set policies within the Active Directory. You can use the other tabs of the Browse For A Group Policy dialog box (Domains/OUs, Sites, and All) to open or create GPOs that are part of Active Directory. However, to keep things straight, it is better to do this using the Active Directory Users and Groups tool or the Active Directory Sites and Services tool. In this chapter, we'll be covering the creation and management of group policy within Active Directory.

Group Policy Settings

As you can see from the example in Figure 11-1, there are two basic types of group policy settings:

- **Computer configuration settings** Used to set group policies that apply to specific computers, regardless of who logs on to them.
- **User configuration settings** Used to set group policies that apply to specific users, regardless of which computer they log on to.

No matter which type of setting you are configuring (computer or user), there are three categories of settings available: Software, Windows, and Administrative Templates.

Travel Advisory

Computer configurations are saved in the Registry in the HKEY_Local_Machine subtree. User configurations are saved in HKEY_CURRENT_USER.

Software Settings

By default, the Software Settings node contains only one item: Software Installation. This item has configuration settings that help you specify how applications are installed and updated throughout an organization. You'll learn more about this in the section "Deploy Software by Using Group Policy," later in the chapter.

Windows Settings

Windows settings let you change a number of configurations related to the Windows environment. These settings include the following:

- **Scripts**   When setting up a computer configuration, you can identify scripts that should run at startup or shutdown of a computer. When setting up a user configuration, you can identify scripts that run when the user logs on or off. Scripts can be written in any ActiveX scripting language, including VBScript, Jscript, Perl, MD-DOS batch files, and others.

- **Security settings**   There are a host of security settings for both computer and user configurations. These are covered in the section "Implement and Manage Security Policies by Using Group Policy," later in the chapter.

- **Internet Explorer Maintenance**   This setting is available only for users. It lets you manage and customize Internet Explorer on client computers.

- **Remote Installation Services**   This setting is also available only for user configurations. It controls the behavior of remote operating system installations.

- **Folder Redirection**   Also available only for user configurations, this setting lets you redirect Windows 2000 special folders (such as My Documents, the Start menu, and Application Data) from their default location in a user's profile to an alternative network location. This lets you centrally manage folders for users.

Administrative Templates

The Administrative Templates node (available for computer and user configurations) contains all Registry-based group policy settings. Table 11-1 lists the Administrative Templates settings available for both user and computer configurations.

TABLE 11.1		Administrative Template Settings	

Node	Computer Configuration	User Configuration	Description
Control Panel		✓	Determines the Control Panel tools available to a user
Desktop		✓	Controls the appearance of a user's desktop
Network	✓	✓	Controls settings for Offline Files and Network and Dial-Up Connections
Printers	✓		Controls printer settings
Start Menu & Taskbar		✓	Controls configuration settings for a user's Start menu and taskbar
System	✓	✓	Controls logon/logoff (for users), startup/shutdown (for computers), and group policies themselves
Windows Components	✓	✓	Controls built-in components of Windows, such as Windows Explorer, Internet Explorer, and Windows Installer

Exam Tip

While you need to understand the types of settings you can make, you are not responsible for knowing the individual settings for the exam. After all, there are over 450 settings for Administrative Templates alone. Spend some time exploring and making sure you understand what's available.

How Multiple GPOs Are Combined

Since GPOs can come from different sources to apply to a single user or computer, there must be a way of determining how those GPOs are combined. GPOs are processed in the following order on a computer running Windows 2000.

1. **Local GPO** First, the local GPO on the computer is processed and all settings specified in that GPO are applied.

2. **Site GPOs**   Next, any GPOs that have been linked with the site in which the computer resides are processed. Settings made at this level override any conflicting settings made at the preceding level. For example, if the local GPO specifies that a computer does not have access to a printer and a site GPO specifies that the computer does have access, the site GPO "wins." If multiple GPOs are linked to the site, the order of processing is determined by the administrator (you'll see how later).

3. **Domain GPOs**   Next, GPOs linked to the domain in which the computer resides are processed and any settings are applied. Settings made at the domain level override conflicting settings applied at the local or site level. Again, the administrator will specify the order if multiple GPOs are linked to the domain.

4. **OU GPOs**   Finally, GPOs linked to any OUs that contain the user or computer object are processed (see Chapter 10 for more on OUs). Settings made at the OU level override conflicting settings applied at the domain, local, or site level. It is possible for a single object to be in multiple OUs. In this case, GPOs linked to the highest level OU in the Active Directory hierarchy are processed first, followed by the next highest level OU, and so on. If multiple GPOs are linked to a single OU, the administrator gets to specify the order in which they are processed.

Exam Tip

An easy way to remember the order in which GPOs are processed is that first the local GPO is processed, and then Active Directory GPOs are processed. Active Directory GPOs are processed starting with the farthest structure from the user (the site), then the next closer structure to the user (the domain), and—finally—the closest structure (the OU).

Exam Tip

Since it is possible to link any number of GPOs to a single OU, using multiple policies per OU and using many levels of OUs can get confusing quickly. For this reason, Microsoft recommends that you not use more than three levels of nested OUs.

Group Policy Inheritance

Within the Active Directory hierarchy, group policy flows down from parent to child containers in a process called *inheritance*. For example, assume that you link a GPO to an OU named Research and that the Research OU contains a child OU named Engineers. By default, the Engineers OU inherits settings specified in the GPO linked to the Research OU.

Continuing that example, if you were to link another GPO to the Engineers OU, settings in that GPO would override settings inherited from the Research GPO. Make sense so far? It gets better.

Within a GPO, you can specify that a particular setting is enabled, disabled, or not configured (you'll see how later). Settings that are not configured for the parent container are not inherited at all by the child container. Settings that are enabled or disabled are inherited as such.

If GPOs are configured for both a parent and a child, settings in the GPOs are combined if the settings are compatible. For example, a setting on the parent OU that calls for a certain desktop wallpaper and a setting on the child OU that calls for a certain background window color would both be used. When settings are incompatible, the default configuration is for settings linked to the child container to override settings linked to the parent container. For example, if a GPO linked to the parent container specified that one wallpaper be used and a GPO linked to the child container specified another wallpaper, the GPO linked to the child would "win."

Of course, inheritance as just described is only the default mechanism. As you'll see in the upcoming sections on creating and managing GPOs, you can specify a number of exceptions that modify the way inheritance works.

Exam Tip

Know the proper order of group policy inheritance in the way policies are applied to a system. Keep in mind that policies cannot directly be linked to users or groups or to built-in containers (such as the Users or Computers container) in Active Directory. Policies can be linked only to a site, domain, or OU.

How Group Policy Is Applied

Obviously, processing GPOs when a user logs on is a pretty complicated endeavor. After all, a large number of GPOs may be linked (either directly or through inheritance) to the computer that a user is logging on to and to the user account being logged on with. The following steps describe how group policy is applied when a computer that is part of Active Directory starts and a user logs on.

1. During startup, the computer obtains an ordered list of GPOs. This is based on whether the computer is a member of Active Directory or not. If not, only the local GPO is processed. If the computer is a member of Active Directory, the list of GPOs to process is based on the AD structure and inheritance, as you have learned in the preceding sections.

2. If the GPOs linked to the computer have not changed since the last time the computer started, no processing is done. If the GPOs have changes, they are all processed again.

3. The computer applies any Computer Configuration settings. This occurs in the familiar order: local, site, domain, OU.

4. Startup scripts specified by any GPOs now run. Each script must complete or time out before the next script begins.

5. The logon screen is displayed to the user. The user presses CTRL-ALT-DEL and enters credentials to log on to the network.

6. Once the user is authenticated, the computer loads the user profile (which is governed by GPOs in effect).

7. The computer receives an ordered list of GPOs that are linked to the user. Again, if no GPOs have changed since the last time the user logged on, no processing is done. If the GPOs have changed, they are all processed again.

8. The computer applies any User Configuration settings in this order: local, site, domain, and then OU.

9. The computer runs any logon scripts associated with GPOs and then the desktop appears.

Creating and Managing a Group Policy Object

A GPO is broken down into two distinct parts stored in different locations: the Group Policy Container (GPC) and the Group Policy Template (GPT).

- **Group Policy Container (GPC)**   The GPC is stored in Active Directory and is displayed as a container in Active Directory Users and Computers (you must choose View | Advanced Features to see it).

The GPC keeps track of various policy attributes and extensions, including the location of the GPT. Each GPC is given a globally unique identifier (GUID), which is a long number identifying the GPC uniquely within Active Directory.

- **Group Policy Template (GPT)** The GPT is contained in the SYSVOL folder, which is a special folder in the system root on all domain controllers. This folder replicates to every DC in the domain. The GPT folders contain the actual settings specified in a GPO.

Creating a GPO

Policies are created and stored and then linked with the appropriate structure in Active Directory. Because the Group Policy snap-in works as both a stand-alone and extension snap-in, there are a two ways to go about creating a GPO. First, you could open an MMC console, load the Group Policy snap-in, create a group policy, and then go into Active Directory Users and Computers or Active Directory Sites and Services to link the GPO to a container. However, since you will almost always create a GPO to be used with a particular container, it is much easier to create and link the GPO as a single step from within one of the two Active Directory tools. This is the method we'll discuss here.

You'll use Active Directory Users and Computers to create and link GPOs with a domain or OU. To do this, you must be a member of the Domain Admins group or have been given specific permission to modify the GPO.

You'll use Active Directory Sites and Services to create and link GPOs with a site. To do this, you must be a member of the Enterprise Admins group.

Whichever tool you are using, the process for creating and linking a GPO is almost the same. Just right-click the site, domain, or OU for which you are creating a GPO and choose Properties from the shortcut menu. Switch the Group Policy tab, shown in Figure 11-2.

Use the following basic controls on the Group Policy tab to work with GPOs.

- **New** Click New to create a GPO directly in the list and give the new GPO a name.
- **Add** By default, GPOs you create are linked only to the container whose Properties dialog box is open. If you right-clicked an OU, the new GPO is linked to that OU. Click Add to link to other sites, domains, or OUs.
- **Edit** Click Edit to open the Group Policy snap-in (refer to Figure 11-1), which lets you modify the settings for the GPO. A new, unedited GPO will have no effect, since all the settings in the GPO default to a not-configured state.

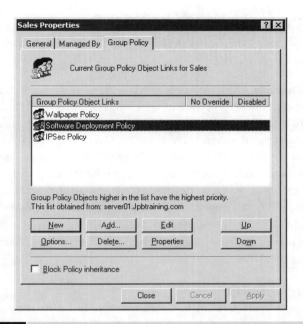

| **FIGURE 11.2** | Creating a GPO |

The other options on the Group Policy tab are discussed in the next few sections.

Controlling Order of GPO Application

When multiple GPOs are applied to a container (site, domain, or OU), those policies are processed from bottom to top. The lowest GPO on the list is processed first. The next higher GPO is then processed, and settings override those that conflict with the lower-level GPO. You can rearrange the order in which GPOs are evaluated using the Up and Down buttons.

Blocking Inheritance

The Block Inheritance option on the Group Policy tab prevents the current container from inheriting GPO settings from any parent containers (sites, domains, or OUs). This creates a powerful exception to the inheritance rule and should be used only in rare circumstances. Note that if a parent container has the No Override option set, the child container cannot block inheritance from this parent. The No Override option is discussed in the next section.

Setting Group Policy Options

Clicking Options on the Group Policy tab brings up a simple dialog box with two options:

- **No Override** This option prevents settings made in GPOs linked to child containers from overriding settings made by GPOs linked to the current container. This essentially forces child containers to inherit settings from the parent. Using the No Override option overrides the use of the Block Inheritance option on a child container. As with other options that create exceptions to policy inheritance, you should limit the use of the No Override settings to rare situations where, for example, you may need to enforce policy for an entire domain.
- **Disabled** This option provides a means of disabling a GPO (and thus preventing its settings from being applied) without having to delete the GPO.

Deleting a GPO

Clicking Delete opens a dialog box with two options for deleting a GPO. The first option is to simply remove the link to the GPO from the current container. This option leaves the GPO intact but removes it from the list of GPOs that are processed for the container. The second option is to remove the link and delete the GPO itself.

Travel Advisory

Policies under NT 4 were called System Policies and they performed a process called "tattooing" of the Registry. Policy changes affect a system's Registry, and under NT 4, the Registry was permanently altered unless you manually fixed the edits or you created another policy to revert back. Group policies under Windows 2000 do not tattoo the Registry but overlay it, which means the system will revert to its normal functions if a policy is deleted.

Disabling Unused Policy Settings

Select any GPO and click Properties on the Group Policy tab to open a Properties dialog for that GPO. The General tab of the GPO presents information about the GPO (such as the dates it was created and modified) and presents options for disabling unused computer and user configuration settings in the

GPO. Most policies that you create will use only a fraction of the available settings. Since all settings in all policies must be processed, requiring a computer to process unconfigured settings requires unnecessary system resources. By disabling the unused settings, you can ease the load on client computers having to process the policy.

Finding Links to a GPO

The Links tab of the Properties dialog box for a GPO lets you list all of the containers (sites, domains, and OUs) to which the GPO is linked. Because generating this information can take some time, the list on this tab is left unpopulated until you select the domain and click Find Now.

Delegating Control of a GPO

The Security tab of a GPO's Properties dialog box lets you assign administrative permissions to the GPO. By default, the following permissions are assigned to any new GPO:

- **Authenticated Users group**   This group is given the Read and Apply Group Policy permissions, enabling authenticated users in a domain to process group policy.
- **Creator Owner**   This user is given a number of special permissions in addition to those assigned to the Authenticated Users group. Click the Advanced button to list them.
- **Domain Administrators group, Enterprise Administrators group, and SYSTEM account**   The Domain Administrators and Enterprise Administrators groups are given the Read, Write, Create All Child Objects, and Delete All Child Objects permissions so that members may create and manage GPOs. The SYSTEM account is also given these permissions so that the computer has the ability to permit these actions.

Filtering GPOs with Permissions

One potential problem with group policy can arise when you want to apply a policy to, for example, an OU that has 100 users and 15 groups and you don't want to have the policy applied to all of those objects. For example, assume you have a policy that governs dial-in access. Ten people need access. The rest do not. Do you have to move them out of the OU to remove the policy from applying to them? No. Fortunately, the designers of Active Directory thought of this.

To prevent a policy from applying to either a user or a group, you can change permission settings for those users. Two permissions are needed for a policy to apply: the Read permission on the policy (because, logically, if you cannot read a policy, then you cannot apply it) and the Apply Group Policy permission (which kind of speaks for itself). The way to prevent a user or group from having a policy applied is to change permissions so that you deny the ability to read or apply the policy in question.

To filter accessibility to a GPO, assign permissions using the following procedure:

1. On the Group Policy tab for the container, select the GPO you want to manage and click Edit. This opens the Group Policy snap-in.

2. Right-click the root node in the snap-in window (it will bear the name of the GPO) and click Properties.

3. Use the Security tab of the Properties dialog box to assign the appropriate permissions to user or group accounts. Accounts that are granted the Read and Apply Group Policy permissions will have the GPO applied to them. Accounts that are denied these permissions will not have the GPO applied to them. Accounts where these permissions are not specified may or may not have the GPO applied, depending on other group memberships.

Refreshing Group Policy

Policy changes are recorded immediately, but these changes are not automatically passed on to the users or computers. The following is a list of the times when policies are updated:

- When a computer starts
- When a user logs on
- When an administrator forces an update through the use of the Secedit command (covered later in the section "Using the Secedit Tool")
- When an application requests a policy refresh
- When a policy interval has been reached

Policy intervals define how often policies are refreshed. The default intervals are 5 minutes for domain controllers and 90 minutes for all other computers running Windows 2000. You can change the group policy settings that affect the users and computers by going through User or Computer configuration and choosing Administrative Templates – System – Group Policy and changing the Group Policy Refresh Interval.

Objective 11.01 Deploy Software by Using Group Policy

With Windows 2000 Active Directory, you can deploy software to your clients using group policies. This requires that the client computers be running Windows 2000 and that they be members of Active Directory. You can specify which users or computers will get the software, you can specify upgrades when necessary, and you can even remove the software. Two components work together to provide this function:

- **Windows Installer Service**   This is a Windows 2000 service that uses Windows 2000 packages (described next) as instruction sets to deploy and update software.

- **Windows Installer Packages**   These are self-executing script files that contain all the instructions necessary for the Windows Installer Service to carry out installation, updating, or repair of software. Windows Installer Package files have the file extension .msi.

Once the Windows Installer Service installs an application, it tracks the state of the application. It can be used to reinstall an application, to repair missing or corrupted files, and to remove the application when it is no longer needed.

Travel Advisory

For information about using Windows Installer and about creating packages, visit the Windows 2000 site at http://www.microsoft.com /windows2000 and search using the phrase "Windows Installer."

Windows 2000 provides two ways to deploy software: *publishing* and *assigning*. When an application is assigned to a user, a shortcut becomes available to the user and appears on the user's Start menu or desktop. This appearance is called *advertising* the application to the user. When the user starts the shortcut (or opens a file associated with the program), the installation routine is started. When an application is assigned to a computer, the application is installed the first time the computer starts up following the assignment.

When you publish an application, you make it available for users to install when they want to. Applications can be published only to users; you cannot publish an application to a computer. The application becomes available in the Add/Remove Programs Control Panel tool and will also be installed on demand if a user opens a file associated with the program.

Exam Tip

Assigned applications are *resilient.* If a user uninstalls the application, the application is published or assigned to them again when the computer processes group policy. If program files become deleted or corrupted, Windows Installer repairs the application. Published applications are not resilient by default but can be made so. The procedure is discussed a bit later.

Deploying Applications

As with other group policies, you must create or select a GPO to configure for application deployment. After opening the GPO in the Group Policy snap-in, find the Software Settings node under either Computer Configuration or User Configuration (depending on whether you want to deploy to a computer or user). Refer back to Figure 11-1 for a refresher. Under the Software Settings node, right-click Software Installation and choose New | Package from the shortcut menu. This opens a short wizard that steps you through the process. The first step of the wizard is to select an .msi file to use for the deployment. Remember, you should check out Microsoft's Windows 2000 site for information on creating these.

The second (and final) step of the wizard is to select whether you want to publish, assign, or deploy with advanced options. If you select the advanced option for assigning or publishing an application, the Properties dialog box for the new software installation opens immediately for configuration. If you select one of the basic options (publish or assign), the software installation is created immediately and stored in the Software Installations folder. You can open the same Properties dialog for it at any time following the installation from that folder. The options in this dialog box are discussed in the next section.

Setting Properties for a Specific Software Installation

A number of tabs appear in the Properties dialog box for a specific software installation that let you configure how an application is deployed. These tabs include the following:

- **General** This tab shows basic information about the software installation, such as the name of the product and information about the application being deployed.

- **Deployment** This tab, shown next, lets you change the type of deployment (published or assigned). You can disable on-demand installation (installing the application when a user opens an associated file), flag the application to be uninstalled when the user or computer falls out of the scope of the GPO (say, when a user object is moved to another domain), and specify that a program not be displayed in the Add/Remove Programs tool. You can also specify the level of influence a user has when the program is being installed. The Basic option limits the user to default configuration settings; the Maximum option lets the user configure anything that would be configurable during a regular installation of the application.

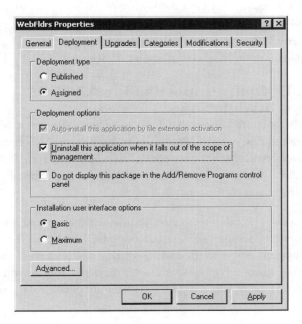

- **Upgrades**   This tab lets you specify that the software installation is an upgrade to one or more existing packages. Click Add to specify the GPO containing a package that this package will be an upgrade for. Use the Required Upgrade For Existing Packages option to make the software installation package you are working on a mandatory upgrade; in this case, the update is applied as soon as a user opens the application. If the upgrade is not mandatory, the user can elect whether to install it or not. Requiring updates applies only to user configurations; since computer configurations are assigned and not published, updates are always applied when the computer starts. The bottom of this dialog lists other software installation packages that are designated as upgrades to the package on which you are currently working.

- **Categories**   This tab lets you sort applications according to categories you set up by modifying the default properties for new software installation packages (discussed in the following section). Applications are grouped by category in a user's Add/Remove Software tool. For example, you might make the categories Graphics Tools, Database Tools, and Office Tools.

- **Modifications**   This tab lets you specify additional .msi packages that work as custom sets of instructions to modify how an application is installed. Again, check out the Windows 2000 Web site to learn more about creating .msi files.

- **Security**   This tab specifies the users and groups that have permission to manage the software installation package.

Setting Default Properties for All New Software Installations

You can also configure settings that apply to all new software installations. To apply default settings, open the Properties dialog box for the Software Installation item directly under the Software Settings node in the Group Policy snap-in (this is the container in which you create individual software installations). The following tabs let you configure default options:

- **General**   This tab, shown next, shows the default package location where new packages are stored. It also specifies how the default deployment type is selected when creating new packages (assign, publish, advanced options, or display the dialog box for you to choose). Finally, you can specify the amount of control the user has and whether applications are uninstalled when they fall out of the scope of a GPO. These options are identical to those discussed in the preceding section on configuring individual packages; these options are just the defaults applied to new packages.

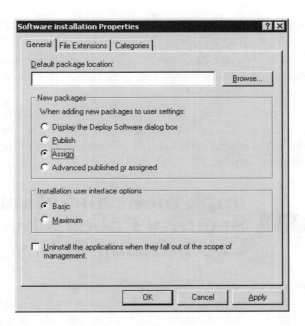

Travel Advisory

Make sure you put in a network share with a proper Universal Naming Convention (UNC) path for the package (i.e., *servername**sharename*) rather than a local drive, because the user's system will see the local drive path and will actually look for that path locally rather than going out to the server with the .msi package.

- **File Extensions**   This tab is used to associate file extensions with the package so that when a user opens a file of that type, the installation of the package is invoked on demand.
- **Categories**   This tab lets you configure the categories used on the Categories tab of individual software packages' Properties dialog boxes. Categories are discussed in the preceding section.

Removing Applications

Removing a package from a given GPO is simple. Just right-click the package and select All Tasks | Remove from the shortcut menu. When you do this, you are given two options:

- *Immediately Uninstall Software from Users and Computers*   This option does just what it says. It removes the software installation package (preventing new installations from occurring) and then uninstalls the application identified in the package from all users or computers for which it has been installed.

- *Allow Users to Continue to Use the Software but Prevent New Installations*   This option removes the software package (preventing new installations) but leaves the application untouched on the computers where it has already been installed.

Implement and Manage Security Policies by Using Group Policy

Just as you can create GPOs that control configuration settings and deploy software, you can create GPOs that prevent users from modifying a computer's configuration or from accessing network resources that they should not. GPOs configured for security are called *security policies* and follow the same rules as other types of policies. They can be configured locally on individual Windows 2000 computers or configured within Active Directory for sites, domains, and OUs.

Exam Tip

Just like other group policies, security policies are applied in the following order: local, site, domain, and then OU. After the local settings, policies are applied starting with the furthest structure from the user and working closer.

To modify a local security policy, you would use the Local Security Policy tool found in the Administrative Tools folder on a Windows 2000 computer. However, Microsoft suggests that you not use local security policies for the same reason that they suggest you not use other types of local policy: having lots of local policies is tough to administer. Instead, it is much more effective to create group security policies on Active Directory containers.

Travel Advisory

Before you can modify the local security policy on a Windows 2000 Professional computer, you must add the Local Security Policy snap-in to an MMC console. The preconfigured console is included only on Windows 2000 servers.

Security Policies are configured like any other group policy—using the Group Policy snap-in. Particularly, security policies are configured using either the Computer Configuration/Windows Settings/Security Settings node or the User Configuration/Windows Settings/Security Settings node, depending on whether you are configuring a policy for computers or users.

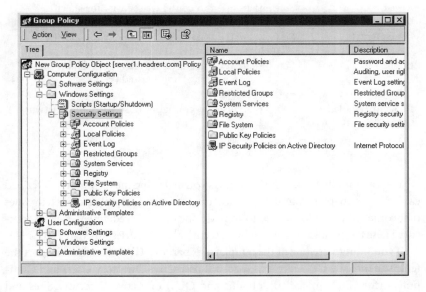

If you are configuring a user configuration, there is only one setting available to you, and that is used to configure public key policies. Since public key policies are outside the scope of this exam, we're going to focus on the settings you can make for computer configurations. The categories of computer configuration settings that you can set for a GPO are listed in Table 11-2. These categories correspond to the nodes under the Computer Configuration/Windows Settings/Security Settings node in the GPO snap-in.

TABLE 11.2	Categories of Security Policy Settings

Category	Description
Account Policies	Settings in this category are used to configure password policies and other account policies such as locking a user out after repeated unsuccessful attempts to log on.
Local Policies	These settings are used to configure auditing, user rights and permissions, and other local security options (both locally and through GPO).
Event Log	Settings are used to configure Event Viewer log settings, such as log size and access.
Restricted Groups	Settings are used to configure membership for some security groups, including Administrators, Power Users, Server Operators, Domain Admins, and so on.
System Services	Settings are used to configure security and startup settings for such services as file and print access, and Internet.
Registry	Settings are used to configure security for specific Registry keys.
File System	Settings are used to configure security for specific file paths.
Public Key Policies	Settings are used to configure encrypted data recovery agents (see Chapter 8) and trusted certificate authorities.
IP Security Policies on Active Directory	Settings are used to configure IP security for a network.

You can modify these security settings yourself using the techniques described earlier in the chapter. Alternatively, you can use one of several security templates that come with Windows 2000 to provide one of four predefined levels of security. These templates and the four basic security levels are described in Table 11-3.

If you want to use one of the templates as part of a GPO, you must import the template into the GPO. For this, you will use Active Directory Users and Computers (for GPOs linked to domains and OUs) or Active Directory Sites and Services (for GPOs linked to sites). Open the Group Policy snap-in for the appropriate GPO by selecting the GPO and clicking Edit on the Group Policy tab of the container's Properties dialog box (see Figure 11-2 for a refresher). Right-click the Security Settings node under Computer Configurations/Windows Settings and select Import Policy from the shortcut menu that appears. Select a template from the list and click Open to apply the template to the GPO. The next time the computer starts or the GPO is refreshed, the settings are applied.

TABLE 11.3	Default Security Templates in Windows 2000		
Security Level	**Level Description**	**Template**	**Template Description**
Basic	Default level of security applied to all new installations of Windows 2000 on an NTFS partition (see Chapter 8 for more on NTFS). These templates are also intended for resetting security levels back to their defaults.	basicwk.inf	The default basic workstation template.
		basicsv.inf	The default basic server template.
		basicdc.inf	The default basic domain controller template.
Compatible	Provides a higher level of security than Basic but still ensures that standard applications will run successfully.	compatws.inf	Can be applied to workstations or servers. By default, this template allows all users to run Windows 2000–certified applications but allows only power users to run noncertified applications.
Secure	Adds an additional layer of security to the Compatible level and may restrict some applications from functioning properly.	securews.inf	The Secure workstation and server template.
		securedc.inf	The Secure domain controller template.
Highly Secure	Provides a maximum level of security for network traffic and communication protocols without regard for application compatibility.	hisecws.inf	Highly Secure template for workstations and servers.
		hisecdc.inf	Highly Secure template for domain controllers.

Travel Advisory

If the default security templates do not meet your needs, you can import, modify, and then export a template to create your own. You can also use the Security Templates snap-in to create your own from scratch. For more on this, see Microsoft's Windows 2000 site at http://www.microsoft.com/Windows2000.

Using the Security Configuration and Analysis Tool

Before implementing any GPO, you must test it to make sure it performs as you expect. This is particularly true of security policies. Fortunately, Windows 2000 provides a special snap-in named Security Configuration and Analysis to help you do just that. This tool uses security templates to analyze, configure, and secure the computer, and then generates a text file report and graphically displays consistencies and inconsistencies.

After you add the Security Configuration and Analysis snap-in, you create a new database with a security template. The database is used to analyze the security settings on the computer, and the security template compares its security information with the computer's security information. Consistencies and inconsistencies between the security template and the computer system can be analyzed. The following methods are used to create a new database and install a security template, to analyze a computer, and to configure a computer.

To create a new database with the Security Configuration and Analysis tool, follow these steps:

1. Open an MMC console and add the Security Configuration and Analysis snap-in.
2. Right-click the Security Configuration and Analysis snap-in.
3. Select Open Database.
4. In the Open Database dialog box, type the name of the new database and click Open.
5. Select the basicsv.inf security template and click Open. The following section discusses how to configure your own security template.

> **Travel Advisory**
>
> basicsv.inf is a preconfigured security template that defines a set of default security settings for a Windows 2000 Server. There are 13 templates to choose from initially. You can edit these or create your own.

To analyze the computer's current security settings to the security template, follow these steps:

1. Right-click the Security Configuration and Analysis snap-in.

2. Select Analyze Computer Now.

3. Click OK to save the error log at the designated path.

4. To check the log file, right-click the Security Configuration and Analysis snap-in and select View Log File.

5. To view analyzed information, browse through the Security Configuration and Analysis snap-in. Figure 11-3 displays the different responses to the original configuration using the basicsv.inf file.

To understand the analysis, use the following:

- A red X signifies that there is a difference between the current configuration and the security template.

- A green check signifies that the current configuration meets or exceeds the setting in the security template.

- If an icon does not appear, this fact indicates that the configuration option was not included in the security template.

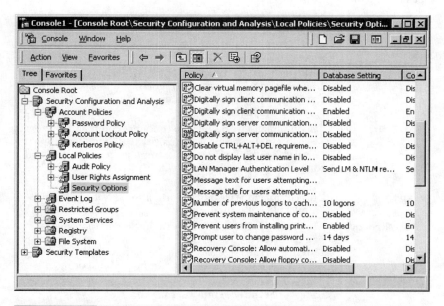

| **FIGURE 11.3** | The analysis of your server through the Security Configuration and Analysis tool |

To configure a computer with the new database and security template information, follow these steps:

1. Right-click the Security Configuration and Analysis snap-in.
2. Select Configure Computer Now.
3. Click OK to save the error log at the designated path.

Using the Secedit Tool

Secedit.exe is a command-line tool that provides many of the same functions as the Security Configuration and Analysis tool and boasts a few extra functions, as well. The six main command options that can be used with Secedit are described in Table 11-4.

TABLE 11.4	Command Options Used with Secedit

Command Option	Description
/Areas	Identifies specific areas of security settings to configure on a computer or to export. Available areas include security policy, group_mgmt, user_rights, regkeys, filestore, and services.
/Analyze	Performs the same functions as the Analyze Computer Now command in the Security Configuration and Analysis tool. It is used with /db to specify a database and with /cfg to specify a template to import.
/Configure	This command works like the configure command in the Security Configuration and Analysis tool. It lets you apply a template's settings to the local computer. It is also used with /db to specify a database and with /cfg to specify a template to import.
/Export	This command is used to export template settings to a new template file. It is used with /db to specify a database.
/Refreshpolicy	This command, available only in the Secedit tool, allows you to force GPOs associated with a computer to be refreshed. When it is used with the /enforce option, GPOs are refreshed whether they have been modified or not.
/Validate	This command verifies the syntax of a template created using the Security Templates snap-in.

Travel Assistance

You can examine the syntax for using the Secedit command and all available options in the Windows help files on any Windows 2000 server.

Objective 11.03

Monitor and Manage Network Security

Security on a Windows 2000 network can take many forms, including the physical security of servers and clients, protection from outside access, user education, and more. The focus of this section is on using a Windows 2000 feature called *auditing* to monitor security. Auditing a computer provides one of the best ways to monitor the effectiveness of your security implementation and helps you improve the security practices. Auditing lets you track the activities of users and operating systems on a computer.

In Windows 2000, auditing is enabled using a policy, whether that be a local policy for auditing resources on a particular computer or a group policy for setting up auditing on a group of computers. In the same way that you create security policies and other types of GPOs, you can create GPOs that specify resources to be audited. GPOs configured for auditing are called *audit policies* and follow the same rules as other types of policies. They can be configured locally on individual Windows 2000 computers or configured within Active Directory for sites, domains, and OUs.

Exam Tip

Just like other group policies, audit policies are applied in the following order: local, site, domain, and then OU. After the local settings, policies are applied starting with the furthest structure from the user and working closer.

To modify a local audit policy, you would use the Local Security Policy tool found in the Administrative Tools folder on a Windows 2000 computer. Group audit policies are configured like any other group policy—using the Group Policy snap-in. Audit policies are applied only to computer configurations (not to user configurations) and are found in the Computer Configuration/Windows Settings/Security Settings/Local Policies/Audit Policies node, as shown here:

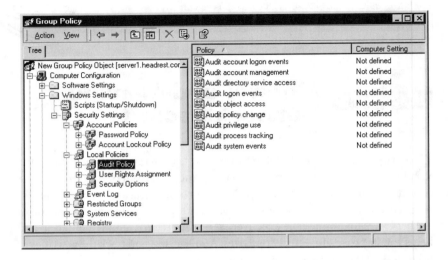

Table 11-5 details the events that you can audit. When you turn on auditing for an event, you can elect to audit for success, failure, or both. What you audit depends on your needs, but keep in mind that auditing events you don't need to audit will just fill up your audit logs (using up system resources and creating more log entries you have to sort through). For example, you may want to audit unsuccessful logon attempts because an unsuccessful attempt is more likely than a successful attempt to be a security problem. Auditing only failed attempts would prevent your logs from being filled with all the successful logon attempts. To turn on auditing, just double-click an event to open its dialog box and select the kinds of attempts you want to audit (success, failure, or both).

Travel Advisory

Auditing can really tie up your system resources. Requiring the logging of every successful and unsuccessful access of every file and object (or process) can keep your computer busy and quickly fill up an audit log. Don't audit more than you have to.

The type of policy you use to configure auditing depends on what you are attempting to audit and where you are looking for a problem. For example, if you

TABLE 11.5	Available Auditing Policies	
Audit Policy	**Logs an Event When**	**When Policy Becomes Active**
Account logon events	A domain controller receives a request to validate a user account.	Immediately for all events.
Account management	An administrator creates, changes, or deletes a user account or group. Also when an administrator renames, disables, enables, or changes the password for an account.	Immediately for all events.
Directory service access	A user accesses an Active Directory object.	You must configure objects in Active Directory for audit logging after setting up the policy. Only those objects are logged.
Logon events	A user logs on or off, or makes or cancels a connection to another computer.	Immediately for all logon attempts.
Object access	A user attempts access to a file, folder, or printer.	You must configure objects that you want logged after setting up the policy. Only configured objects are logged.
Policy change	A change is made to the user security options, user rights, or audit policies.	Immediately for all events.
Privilege use	A user exercises a right, such as shutting down a system.	Immediately for all events.
Process tracking	A program performs an action. (This auditing feature is really used only in development.)	Immediately for all events.
System	A user restarts or shuts down a computer, or an event occurs that affects Windows 2000 security or the security log.	Immediately for all events.

are worried that an unauthorized user is attempting to log on to the domain, you should audit account logon events on domain controllers (you can use the Default Domain Security policy for this).

Auditing Files, Folders, and Printers

Some types of auditing, such as directory service access and object access, require that you first set an audit policy and then activate auditing on the specific objects you want to track (because you wouldn't want to track access to all objects on a computer). For example, if you wanted to audit access to an object like a file, folder, or printer, you would have to configure auditing in two steps. First you would have to enable Audit Object Access using a policy, and then you would have to configure auditing for the object itself.

Files, folders, and printers that are on an NT File System (NTFS)–formatted volume can be audited. Auditing files and folders enables you to monitor successful and failed attempts to access the resources. To enable local auditing for an object, follow these steps:

1. Right-click any NTFS file, folder, or printer and choose Properties from the shortcut menu.

2. On the object's Properties dialog box, click the Security tab.

3. Click Advanced to open the Access Control Settings dialog box for the object.

4. Click the Auditing tab.

5. Click Add and choose a group or user you want to audit in association with the object. Access by those groups and users will be audited.

6. Choosing a user or group opens an Auditing Entry dialog box that lists many different types of access audits you can enable. Check the boxes for auditing successful or failed events and click OK when you are done.

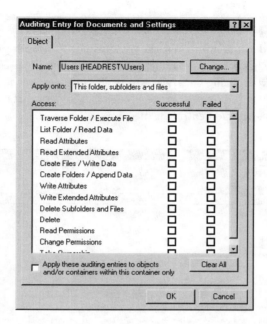

7. Click Add to add other users or groups or click OK to return to the object's Properties dialog.

8. Click OK to return to Windows.

The audit event list is known as the System Access Control List (SACL) and represents the security descriptor for auditing information for the object. The SACL identifies the following items:

- The group or user accounts to audit when the object is accessed
- The access events to be audited for each group or user
- A success or failure attribute for each access event

Travel Advisory

If you are not using an NTFS volume, no Security tab is available in an object's Properties dialog, even if you've turned auditing on.

Auditing Active Directory Objects

As with file, folder, and printer objects, you can audit Active Directory objects to determine who has performed certain activities on them. Right-click the object, open its Properties dialog box, switch to the Security tab, click Advanced, and then switch to the Auditing tab in the advanced dialog box that opens. This tab, shown next, lists the audit entries in effect for the object.

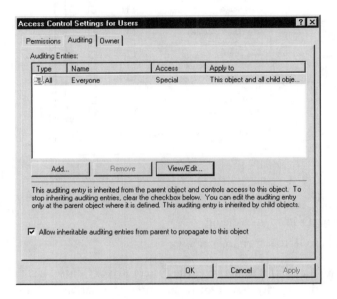

Audit settings (much like GPOs) are inherited by child objects in Active Directory from their parent objects. The list on the Auditing tab shows entries inherited from any parent objects. You cannot modify entries that are inherited from parent objects unless you first disable the Allow Inheritable Auditing Entries From Parent To Propagate To This Object option. If you disable this option, you are given the choice of retaining or discarding the current inherited audit entries; either way, the object will no longer inherit new entries.

You can add new entries for an object that will work in combination with inherited entries. Audit settings from various entries are combined to determine what will be audited for a particular object. Click Add to add a new entry; click View/Edit to modify an existing entry. Both of these commands open the same dialog box (shown next), which lists the particular types of access you can audit. Use the Apply These Auditing Entries To Objects And/Or Containers Within This Container Only option to specify whether child objects of this object should inherit audit settings.

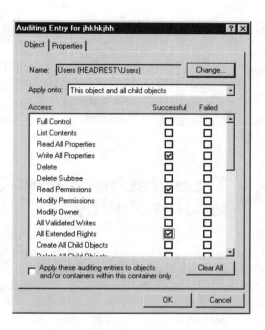

Reviewing Audited Events with the System Security Log File

Event Viewer displays audited events once auditing has been configured. You can access Event Viewer by selecting Start | Programs | Administrative Tools | Event Viewer. You can learn more about the standard use of Event Viewer in Chapter 2. Notice from the image that follows that the Security Log makes it very easy for you to track both successes (indicated by a key icon) and failures (indicated by a lock icon) for an audited event.

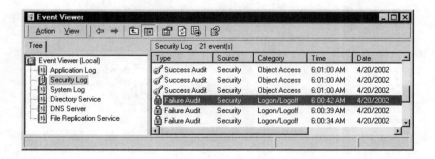

Exam Tip

Turn on auditing on your computer and spend some time looking through the audit logs. Understanding the various types of entries of the Security log and the information available will help you on the exam and will prepare you for setting up a good audit plan in the future.

 **Objective 11.04** # Troubleshoot End-User Group Policy

Troubleshooting end-user group policy is largely a matter of understanding how different policies are applied and how different levels of policy affect one another. You must take into consideration how multiple GPOs that affect the same computer or user are resolved and how GPO inheritance works. Table 11-6 presents some of the more common problems you might run into with group policies.

TABLE 11.6   Troubleshooting Group Policy

Problem	Possible Cause	Solution
You cannot open a GPO in the Group Policy snap-in.	Permissions are not assigned correctly.	Administrators must have both Read and Write permissions for the GPO in order to manage the GPO.
A Failed To Open The Group Policy Object message appears when you try to edit a GPO.	Networking problem, usually with Domain Name System (DNS) configuration.	Make sure the DNS server is working and that your computer is resolving DNS names. See Chapter 6 for more on this.
Group policies are not being applied to users and computers in a security group, even though a GPO is linked to that group.	No problem.	This is commonly mistaken for a problem with group policy, but it is by design. GPOs can be linked only to sites, domains, and OUs.
Group policy is not affecting users or computers in a site, domain, or OU.	GPO not linked.	First, make sure that the GPO is actually linked to the appropriate container.

TABLE 11.6	Troubleshooting Group Policy *(continued)*	
Problem	**Possible Cause**	**Solution**
	Inheritance problems.	Make sure no policy set at a higher level has been configured with the No Override option. Also make sure that the Block Policy Inheritance option is not turned on for the container.
	Permissions problems.	Make sure that the users or computers are not members of a group for which the Apply Group Policy permission is denied. Make sure they are members of at least one group where the Apply Group Policy permission is granted and one group where the Read permission is granted.

Travel Assistance

Obviously, no one chapter can make you an expert in group policy deployment. Check out *Windows 2000 Group Policy, Profiles, and IntelliMirror* by Jeremy Moskowitz (Alameda, CA: Sybex, 2001), which includes information on ADM Templates, NT 4 System Policies, and just about every thing else you could want to know about using group policies to administer your organization and deploy software.

CHECKPOINT

✔**Objective 11.01: Deploy Software by Using Group Policy**   This objective looked at how applications can be deployed, updated, repaired, and removed using group policy. It also examined the different deployment methods, including publishing and assigning applications.

✔**Objective 11.02: Implement and Manage Security Policies by Using Group Policy**   This objective looked at the use of the security policies, which are essentially GPOs used to provide security. It covered the use of security templates, the Security Configuration and Analysis tool, and Secedit.

✔**Objective 11.03: Monitor and Manage Network Security** This objective covered how to configure auditing in Windows 2000 using group or local policy. Auditing is used to log the successes and failures of users and computers when accessing system resources, logging on the network, and many other actions.

✔**Objective 11.04: Troubleshoot End-User Group Policy** This objective looked at a number of issues that might arise when deploying group policy and basic methods for resolving those issues.

REVIEW QUESTIONS

1. You create a group policy that should change the desktop settings for a computer. You're sitting at the computer waiting for the policy to refresh so that you can test it. What can you do to force the policy to refresh?

   A. Run secedit /refreshpolicy MACHINE_POLICY.

   B. Run secedit /refreshpolicy USER_POLICY.

   C. Run ntdsutil /refreshpolicy USER_POLICY.

   D. Log out and log back in.

2. You need to deploy an application using a group policy object. Which of the following file types contain the instruction sets used to control deployment?

   A. .msi

   B. .msp

   C. .mst

   D. .zap

3. You've been using the security templates provided with Windows 2000 on your domain. You have a complete Windows 2000 domain in native mode using the High Security template policy settings on your domain controllers. Your domain is using trust relationships with an NT domain. Users configured in the NT domain complain that they cannot access your Windows 2000 domain. What do you need to do?

   A. Use a lower-level security template on all domain controllers in the Windows 2000 domain that the NT domain accesses.

   B. Use a higher-level security template on the NT server domain.

   C. Change the NT domain to native mode.

   D. This is not a possible situation.

4. Your company is constantly moving people from one OU to another. Each OU has its own set of software policies assigned so that users get the software they need. You want to ensure that if a user is moved from one OU to another, software that is not part of the user's new policy is removed. How would you do this?

A. Create a logon script that checks for applications that the user shouldn't have and then deletes them.

B. Configure the Group Policy setting to uninstall the application if it falls out of the scope of management.

C. Manually check each user's machine to ensure software compliance.

D. This is not possible within Windows 2000; you will need to purchase third-party software to accomplish this task.

5. You need to install an update patch for Windows 2000 on all your systems in your organization. The patch is an .msi file. Your organization consists of a single domain with 250 workstations. How would you go about installing the update in the best possible way?

A. Create a group policy for the Computers container in Active Directory Users and Computers.

B. Create a group policy at the domain level that will specify software settings for Computer Configuration.

C. Just let the software update automatically because of Windows Installer.

D. You need to manually apply updates to the operating system. Only applications can be updated through group policy.

6. Bob is a network administrator who wants to install Microsoft Word on all the computers of all the users in the Document Processing department. Most of the computers are contained in an OU named Document Processing. Which of the following methods of deployment would be the best approach for group policy deployment of this software?

A. Configure the policy to publish the software under the Computer Configuration options for the document-processing OU.

B. Configure the policy to assign the software under the Computer Configuration options for the document-processing OU.

C. Configure the policy to publish the software under the User Configuration options for the document-processing OU.

D. Configure the policy to assign the software under the User Configuration options for the document-processing OU.

7. You are the administrator for an organization. You are setting a group policy to specify that all users in one OU must not have access to the Run option from the Start menu. You want to be certain that administrators lower down in the hierarchy cannot negate this policy. Choose the best action from the following:

   A. Configure a GPO filter to stop all groups but Enterprise Administrators from overriding the policy.

   B. Use the Block Inheritance option.

   C. Right-click the policy and choose No Override.

   D. Choose Disable Inheritance Blocking.

8. How do the predefined IPSec policies Server (Require Security) and Server (Request Security) differ? (Choose all correct answers.)

   A. Server (Request Security) will first attempt to implement secure communications but will use unsecured communications if it cannot negotiate security settings.

   B. Server (Request Security) will request the security settings of a client computer if the client computer is configured improperly, and then the server will time out.

   C. Server (Require Security) will allow unsecured communications, but only if the client computer is on the same subnet.

   D. Server (Require Security) will not allow unsecured communications, even if a peer is not IPSec enabled.

9. You have recently installed and configured several network printers. Auditing has been enabled for the printers, to track their usage and potential security hacks. You find that someone has been modifying permissions on your network printers. When looking through the Event Viewer Security log, which icon would you look for to indicate Successful access to the printer's permissions?

   A. An open lock

   B. A key

   C. A stop sign

   D. A green light

10. Joe is the network administrator in a company called RollingTech. He is concerned that users are accessing files on a Windows 2000 Member Server. Which of the following choices should Joe perform to audit the server?

A. Go to the Local Policy of the Member Server and select Audit Object Access.

B. Go to the Domain Policy of the Member Server and select Audit Object Access.

C. Go to the Domain Controller Policy of the Member Server and select Audit Object Access.

D. Go to the Local Policy of the Member Server and select Audit File and Folder Access.

REVIEW ANSWERS

1. **B** You can use the Secedit.exe command to force a policy. You can force either the computer or user policy, depending on what you need. To refresh policies under the Computer Configuration node, type **secedit /refreshpolicy MACHINE_POLICY** and then click OK. You would type **secedit /refreshpolicy USER_POLICY** to refresh policies under the Computer Configuration node.

2. **A** Package files (or .msi files) contain the instructions used by Windows Installer to control the deployment of an application.

3. **A** Keep in mind that if you are using a High Security policy template, then down-level clients will have difficulty communicating and this may lead to problems. This is especially a problem for situations when you have trust relationship with a Windows 2000 domain and an NT 4 domain and your Windows 2000 DCs have the Highly Secure template applied. The NT Servers will not be able to access the Windows 2000 DCs. The best solution is to choose a lower-level security policy to apply. Answer B is incorrect because you cannot use these security templates with NT. Answer C is also not accurate because you cannot make an NT domain native mode. Answer D is incorrect because the problem is fixable by making some slight changes on the systems that require those changes.

4. **B** By enabling the setting Uninstall This Application When It Falls Out Of The Scope Of Management, you force the software to remove itself when a user is moved from one OU to another that doesn't allow for the same software applications. Answer A is incorrect because it's not a practical solution for your needs. Answer C is incorrect because it would take way too long and is unnecessary. Answer D is incorrect because you don't need to purchase anything extra.

5. **B** Considering the fact that the update should affect all computers in the domain, you want to establish the policy at the domain level. Keep in mind that you cannot establish a policy on containers that are not OUs, like the Users container or the Computers container.

6. **D** In this scenario, because you want to ensure that users get the software, rather than computers, you want to make sure you assign it to the OU and establish the settings of the policy under the User Configuration. Answer A is incorrect because you cannot publish to computers. Answer B might appear to work, but you cannot assume that all the computers used for document processing are in the OU for it, especially given the scenario. Answer C is incorrect because it publishes the software, which doesn't conform to the scenario.

7. **C** To make a GPO apply to all child objects, go to the Group Policy tab in the properties of the object to which you are linking the policy. Right-click the policy and choose No Override. Answer A is incorrect because it makes the scenario too complicated and doesn't work in the end. Answer B is incorrect because it blocks, rather than forces, the application. Answer D is incorrect because there is no such thing as Disable Inheritance Blocking as a option.

8. **A D** A computer that is configured with Server (Request Security) tries to negotiate secure communications with a client computer but uses unsecured communications if security settings cannot be negotiated successfully. A computer that is configured with Server (Require Security) does not allow unsecured communications, even if a peer is not IPSec enabled. Answers B and C are incorrect because Server (Request Security) will use unsecured communications if necessary to establish the connection between a client and itself. A time-out is not the result of negotiation conflicts and Server (Require Security) does not allow unsecured communications.

9. **B**   A key indicates a successful attempt in auditing terms. Answer A is incorrect because an open lock indicates a failed attempt. Answer C is incorrect because this indicates system errors in other logs but has no place in auditing. Answer D is incorrect because this is not a correct symbol for Event Viewer.

10. **A**   Being that you are auditing a specific system, you want to establish auditing on the Local Security Policy of the Member Server and then audit files you want with Audit Object Access. Answer B is incorrect because the Domain Policy should be used primarily for account access control and isn't required on this scenario. Answer C is incorrect because the Domain Controller Policy will not affect the Member Server anyway. Answer D is incorrect because it chooses a fictitious policy setting.

Managing Active Directory Replication

CHAPTER 12

	NEWBIE	SOME EXPERIENCE	EXPERT
ETA	6 hours	4 hours	2 hours

Active Directory uses multiple domain controllers for fault tolerance and load balancing. It is essential, therefore, that every domain controller hold a complete copy of the Active Directory database. Whenever changes are made to the database on one domain controller, those changes must be replicated to all other domain controllers. Replication occurs automatically among all domain controllers in a domain. However, you can group domain controllers into sites and subnets to help control the flow of replication on large networks.

This chapter introduces the creation of sites and subnets to control replication in a domain. It also discusses some of the specialized roles that can be assumed by domain controllers and covers backing up and restoring Active Directory.

Diagnose Active Directory Replication Problems

T he Active Directory replication process is fascinating. Consider all the various objects that make up Active Directory (users, computers, printers, and so on) and all the attributes that go with those objects (such as a user's name, address, and so on). All of these objects and attributes need to be replicated to all the domain controllers in a domain. That is a tremendous amount of data moving around, and with it comes the huge task of keeping track of the data.

Windows 2000 uses a replication model called *multimaster replication,* in which all replicas of the Active Directory database are considered equal masters. You can make changes to the database on any domain controller, and the changes are replicated to other domain controllers in the domain.

Travel Advisory

In Windows NT 4.0, a single domain controller (the Primary Domain Controller) contained the only write-enabled copy of the domain accounts database. This meant that all changes had to be processed by a single server, a fact that proved to be a limitation on the size of any single NT 4.0 domain.

Overview of Replication

In Active Directory, a site is a set of domain controllers (DCs) that are well connected, which essentially means that all the DCs are connected by a local area network (LAN). Domain controllers on the same site replicate on the basis of notification. When changes are made on a DC, that DC notifies its replication partners; the partners then request the changes and replication occurs. Because of the high-speed connections assumed within a site, replication occurs as needed rather than according to a schedule.

Unless you configure your own sites in Active Directory, all domain controllers are automatically made a part of a single site—a default site created when you create the first domain named Default-First-Site-Name.

You should create additional sites when you need to control how replication traffic occurs over slower WAN links. For example, suppose you have a number of DCs on your main LAN and a few DCs on a LAN at a branch location. Those two LANs are connected to one another with a slow (say, 256K) WAN link. You want replication traffic to occur as needed between the DCs on each LAN, but you do not want it to occur as needed over the WAN link. To address this situation, you set up two sites—one site that contains all the DCs on the main LAN and one site that contains all the DCs on the remote LAN.

To clarify this, let's look first at replication within a single site (called intrasite replication) and then compare that with replication between sites (intersite replication).

Intrasite Replication

Intrasite replication sends replication traffic in an uncompressed format. This is because of the assumption that all DCs within the site are connected by high-bandwidth links. Not only is the traffic uncompressed, but replication occurs according to a change notification mechanism. This basically means that if changes are made in the domain, those changes are quickly replicated to the other domain controllers. Now, as we will see shortly, this isn't completely devastating to your network bandwidth, because Microsoft has really tried to tone down the amount of traffic generated by replication.

Exam Tip

For the exam, remember that Microsoft considers any connection less than T1 to be a slow connection link that hence requires separate sites. Any networks connected by T1 and above Microsoft will normally consider as a single site.

Intersite Replication

Intersite replication sends all data compressed. This shows an appreciation for the fact that the traffic will probably be going across slower WAN links (as opposed to the LAN connectivity intrasite replication assumes), but it increases the load on the server side because compression/decompression is added to the processing requirements. In addition to the compression, the replication can be scheduled for times that are more appropriate to your organization. For example, you may decide to allow replication only during slower times of the day. Of course, this delay in replication (based upon the schedule) can cause latency between servers in different sites.

Replication Protocols

All communication within a network requires some protocol to carry the information. The same is true of AD replication traffic. The two protocols that are used to replicate data are RPC and SMTP.

Internet Protocol traffic uses Remote Procedure Calls (RPCs) for sending replication messages within a site and between sites. RPC is the default protocol for all AD replication because it is an industry standard and is compatible with most network types.

Simple Mail Transfer Protocol (SMTP) can be used for replication between sites that are not connected with permanent connections (which are required for RPCs). One caveat to SMTP is that it doesn't replicate domain partition information to DCs in the domain. Because SMTP is used only for replication between sites, this is not a problem for replication of domain partition information within the domain (because this will automatically use RPC); however, it shows that SMTP is useful only for replication of the Schema and the Global Catalog.

Configuring Sites, Subnets, and Site Links

Unlike most Active Directory objects—sites, subnets, and associated objects are not displayed in Active Directory Users and Computers (the tool used for other AD object creation and management). Instead, you will use a tool named Active Directory Sites and Services to create and manage sites and to configure replication.

Creating a Site Object

When you install Active Directory service on the first domain controller on a network, Windows 2000 creates a site object named Default-First-Site-Name in the Sites container of the Active Directory Sites and Services tool, shown in the following illustration. The first domain controller (which is created by installing Active Directory for the first time) is placed into this default site. You can rename the site by right-clicking it and choosing Rename.

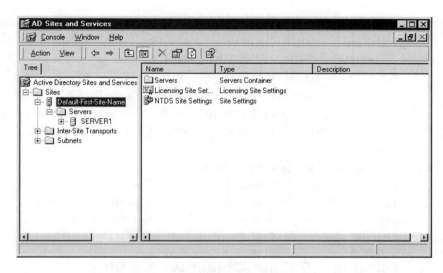

You can create a new site using the following procedure:

1. Click Start | Programs | Administrative Tools | Active Directory Sites and Services.

2. Right-click the Sites folder and select New Site from the shortcut menu. This opens the New Object – Site dialog box, shown here:

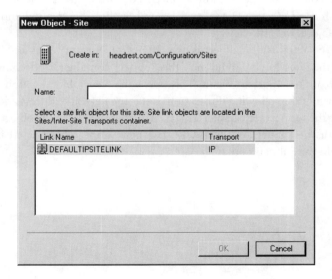

3. Type a name for the new site. Names must be under 63 characters and cannot contain spaces or periods or be all numbers. In addition, names must conform to DNS naming standards if the network is to interoperate with networks using non-Microsoft DNS servers.

4. From the Link Name list, select a site link object. A site link object is used to configure a link between sites. Site links are covered in more detail in the section "Creating and Configuring Site Links" later in the chapter.

5. A dialog opens letting you know that the site has been created and pointing you toward other tasks you may need to perform, such as linking the site to other sites, adding subnets to the site, and placing domain controllers in the site. These tasks are discussed in upcoming sections. Click OK to return to Active Directory Sites and Services.

Associating a Subnet Object with a Site

Computers on Active Directory networks based on TCP/IP are assigned to sites according to their local IP subnet (or subnets). You can learn more about subnets in Chapter 3, but basically they provide ways to segment a network into more manageable pieces reflecting the physical proximity of computers. For example, all the computers on one floor (or in one building, or whatever) might be part of one subnet.

A site consists of one or more subnets. You specify the subnets associated with each site in Active Directory Sites and Services by creating and linking subnet objects with site objects.

Creating a new subnet object is easy. In Active Directory Sites and Services, expand the sites folder, right-click the Subnets container, and choose New Subnet from the shortcut menu. This opens the New Object – Subnet dialog box shown in the following illustration. Enter the network address and subnet mask for the subnet (see Chapter 3 for help on these). Select a site object to associate with the subnet and click OK. The new subnet object is created and appears in the Subnets container.

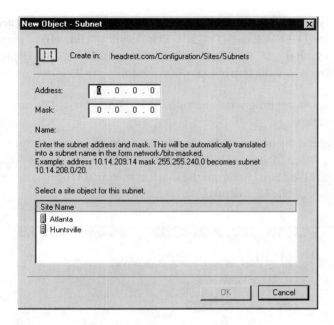

You can also associate an existing subnet object with a site (or change the association) by right-clicking the subnet object in the Subnets container and selecting Properties. On the General tab of the subnet object's Properties dialog box, use the Site drop-down menu to change the site association.

Creating and Configuring Site Links

Within a site, replication happens automatically. For replication to occur between sites, you must establish a link between the sites. There are two components to this link: the actual physical connection between the sites (usually a WAN link) and a site link object. The *site link* object determines the protocol used for transferring replication traffic (IP or SMTP) and governs when replication is scheduled to occur. It is possible to use a single site link object to control more than a single pair of sites. For example, if your network consists of four sites that all use the same protocol, are connected with the same type and speed WAN link, and should follow the same schedule, you could configure a single site link object to connect all the sites.

When you install Active Directory, a default site link object is created for IP and is named DEFAULTIPSITELINK. This default site link object is associated with the default site. No default site link object is created for the SMTP protocol.

To create a new site link object, use the following procedure:

1. Click Start | Programs | Administrative Tools | Active Directory Sites and Services.

2. Expand the Inter-Site Transports container, right-click the protocol container (IP or SMTP) for the type of site link you want to create, and select New Site Link from the shortcut menu. This opens the New Object – Site Link dialog box.

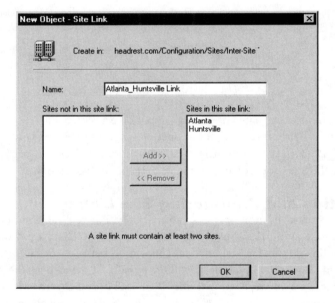

3. Type a name for the new site link object. This name should describe the use of the object. For example, you could name it after the two sites being connected or for the replication schedule you will configure.

4. Use the Add and Remove buttons to choose which sites are associated with the site link object (on the right) and which sites are not (on the left). Note that a site link object must be associated with at least two sites.

5. Click OK to create the new site link object. The object appears inside the container for the protocol (IP or SMTP) of which the link is a type.

You can also associate a site with an existing site link object. Just right-click the site link object and choose Properties. On the General tab of the site link object's Properties dialog box (shown in the following illustration), you'll find the same kind of interface for choosing sites to associate with the site link object.

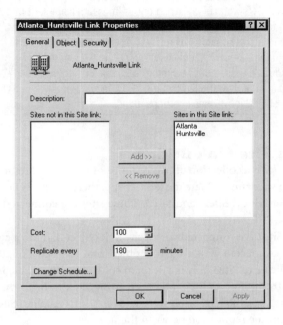

The General tab of a site link object's Properties dialog box also contains other parameters you can configure:

- **Cost**   Used to assign the cost of using the site link relative to other site links. If you have multiple site links that connect the same sites (for redundancy and load balancing), you can specify that one site link be used in favor of another by assigning it a lower cost. Lower-cost site links are always tried before higher-cost site links.

- **Replicate Every**   Used to specify the interval, in minutes, between replications over the site link. Valid entries are between 15 and 10,080 minutes (one week). For example, if the interval is set to 60 minutes, replication occurs every hour. The default value is 180 minutes.

- **Change Schedule**   Used to specify periods during a week that replication is allowed. This button opens a calendar control that lets you select the specific hours during each day of a week that replication can and cannot happen. During the periods that replication is allowed, it occurs according to the interval specified in the Replicate Every setting.

Travel Advisory

Because the SMTP protocol is asynchronous (messages are sent through e-mail), SMTP is set to ignore schedules by default. You can change this setting by opening the Properties dialog box for the SMTP protocol container and changing the Ignore Schedules setting on the General tab. You can also set IP-based links to ignore schedules using the Properties dialog box for the IP container. For the most part, though, you should leave these settings alone.

Creating Site Link Bridges

A site link *bridge* is a collection of two or more site links used to build transitive links between sites and evaluate the least-cost path. As an example, suppose you have three sites: Site1, Site2, and Site3. These sites are connected as shown in Figure 12-1.

Site1 and Site2 are connected with a site link object that has a cost of 5. Site2 and Site3 are connected with a site link object that has a cost of 10. By default, Site1 can replicate to Site3 only if a domain controller is available in Site2. Data is replicated from Site1 to Site2 and then from Site2 to Site3. Assuming that every domain controller in Site2 were suddenly unavailable, Site1 and Site3 could not continue replication between them.

You could solve this problem in one of two ways. Obviously, you could just go ahead and create a site link object between Site1 and Site2, so that replication could occur directly. The other solution is to create a site link bridge. The bridge would imply a transitive link between Site1 and Site2 with a cost of 15. The cost is a combination of the costs of the individual site links; this combination is

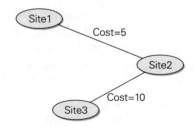

FIGURE 12.1   Using site link bridges

used to ensure that the bridge cost is always higher than the individual site link cost. Also, once site links are bridged, all site links for a specific protocol implicitly belong to the bridge.

In a simple example like this one, it would be just as easy to configure an additional site link as it would be to configure a site link bridge. On more complex networks, however, the site link bridge is easier to administer because you don't need to create and configure site links between all sites (configuring site links between just five sites would require eight site links).

By default, all sites in Active Directory are considered part of one large bridge. If you want to create your own bridges (for example, to create a kind of disjointed network on which you could control replication traffic even further), you need to disable this default behavior and then create your site link bridges. To disable the default behavior, open the Properties dialog box for a particular transport protocol (IP or SMTP) and disable the Bridge All Links option on the General tab.

Once you have disabled the Bridge All Links option, you can configure a site link bridge using the following procedure:

1. Click Start | Programs | Administrative Tools | Active Directory Sites and Services.

2. Expand the Inter-Site Transports container.

3. Right-click the IP or SMTP container and select New Site Link Bridge. This opens the New Object – Site Link Bridge dialog box.

4. Type a name for the site link bridge.

5. Use the Add and Remove buttons to configure which sites belong to the bridge. You must have at least two sites in a bridge.

6. Click OK to create the site link bridge object.

The new site link bridge object appears in the container for the transport protocol you selected. You can open the object's Properties dialog box to change the sites that belong to the bridge.

Designating a Preferred Bridgehead Server

By default, Active Directory lets all domain controllers in a site exchange information directly with domain controllers in other sites with which a site link is configured. However, you can control this flow of replication traffic between sites to occur only using select domain controllers. For example, assume you have five controllers in one site and five controllers in another, as shown in Figure 12-2.

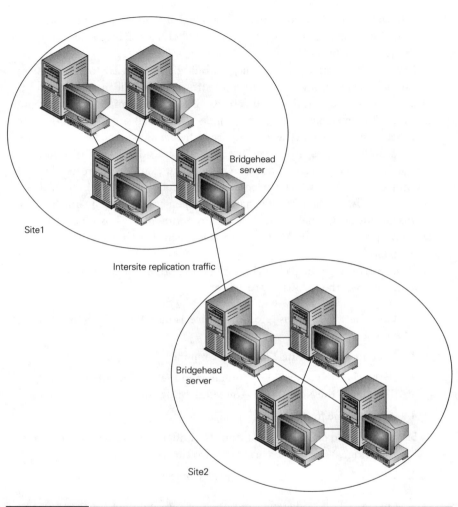

FIGURE 12.2 Using bridgehead servers to control replication traffic between sites

You could configure one controller in each site to pass replication traffic to the other site. Servers configured in this way are called *bridgehead servers.*

When bridgehead servers are configured, all domain controllers in a site pass replication traffic to their site's bridgehead server, which then passes it on to a bridgehead server in a remote site. You can configure multiple servers in a site to work as bridgehead servers, but only one is active at a given time. If the active bridgehead server is unavailable, an alternate bridgehead server is used. If no designated bridgehead servers are available, a nondesignated domain controller in the site is picked to act as a bridgehead server.

Use the following procedure to set up a designated bridgehead server:

1. Click Start | Programs | Administrative Tools | Active Directory Sites and Services.

2. Expand the Sites container, the container for the site containing the server you want to make a bridgehead server and then the Servers container for that site.

3. Right-click the domain controller you want to make a bridgehead server and select Properties from the shortcut menu.

4. On the Server tab of the Properties dialog box that opens, select a transport protocol (IP or SMTP) and click Add to make the server a bridgehead server for that protocol.

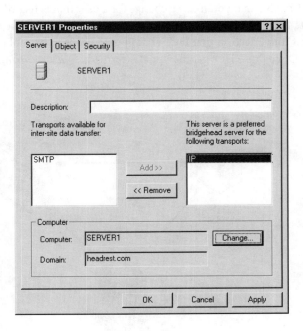

5. Click OK.

Exam Tip

If you have a firewall set up between sites, you must configure bridgehead servers. It is recommended that you configure your firewall proxy server as the preferred bridgehead server.

Replication Convergence and Latency

Microsoft never promises total convergence (the state where all domain controllers are 100 percent up to date). Instead, Windows 2000 offers what's known as *loose convergence*, which basically means Windows does its best to keep domain controllers fully replicated and up to date. The delay time between updates is known as *latency*.

Consider the diagram shown in Figure 12-3. To start with, what is an update? An update can be the addition of a new object (as when a new user is added to AD), the deletion of a user, the modification of a user (let's say a person's phone number is changed), or just about any other change you can make in the Active Directory. Imagine that you make a change for a user that is recorded on DC1. This update is considered an originating update for DC1 because the change was first put into effect on that DC. That update needs to be replicated to the other DCs. Once those DCs get the update (termed *replicated updates* on those

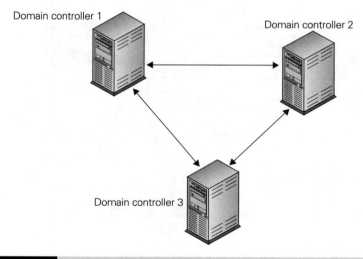

Domain controller 1

Domain controller 2

Domain controller 3

FIGURE 12.3 Servers that replicate data

controllers because the update occurs but does not originate at the DC), they make the change. The benefit here is that the DCs who receive the replicated updates will make the change until all DCs are updated.

You'll notice in Figure 12-3 that two-way arrows connect the DCs. This simply indicates that replication traffic between DCs can flow both ways. Thanks to a service named the Knowledge Consistency Checker (KCC), which automatically creates these two-way connections, multimaster replication can occur without a lot of administrative overhead.

Within a site, the connections allow all DCs to be connected in a circle. The KCC creates this circle so that there is never more than a three-server hop for an update to reach all servers. Up to seven DCs can be connected in a circular connection ring because of the three-hop rule, but once the eighth DC is added to the mix, the KCC creates a shortcut connection within the ring, as shown in Figure 12-4.

Every five minutes (by default), the DCs notify their closest neighbors on the circle of any changes that have occurred since the last update. The DCs use the "tell a friend" method so that the change propagates through the topology with one DC notifying another, which then notifies another, and so on. In a matter of about 15 minutes, all the DCs within a site should be up to date with the new information.

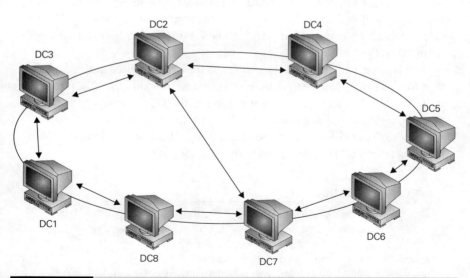

FIGURE 12.4   The KCC topology

Travel Advisory

You can force the replication to occur without waiting for the five-minute cycle by going into the AD Sites and Services tool. Expand the site, find the server and the NTDS Settings, and then choose the connection link you wish to replicate. Right-click the connection and choose Replicate Now.

All the objects in AD, and all of their attributes, are given special numbers called Update Sequence Numbers within the domain controllers so that the DCs can keep track of the changes they have received for a particular object. This prevents the circle of servers from continuing with the update past the point at which all controllers are updated. In Figure 12-4, if DC1 gets an update and the update replicates around to DC8, DC8 sees that the originating update came from DC1. If DC6 checked with DC7 and the update had already reached DC7, the two systems would be able to establish that by checking the Update Sequence Number.

When you make a change to an object's properties, the property change includes the identity of the originating server. Remember that a change to a directory occurs first on the originating server, as opposed to the replication update that occurs on the replicated DCs. When a DC hears of a new change to the directory, it takes note of both the GUID of the originating server and the USN of the property. By utilizing these pieces of information, an Up-to-Date Vector (UTD) table is created that indicates the highest originating update from a domain controller.

At this point, you are familiar with the way the USNs are used during replication to make sure that the updates are performed only on target DCs that require the change. The UTD Vector combines the USN knowledge with the GUID knowledge and determines whether an update request is just propagating back to the originator. If that is true, the loop is broken and the update isn't sent. Therefore, UTD vectors prevent update loops of the same change.

Travel Assistance

There is a good deal of information written about AD replication, USNs, UTDs, Watermark Vectors and such. If you need to learn more about these topics, we recommend researching them through Microsoft's Knowledge Base at http://support.microsoft.com/. Another great resource for replication is *Windows 2000 Active Directory Design and Deployment* by Gary Olsen (Indianapolis: New Riders, 2000).

Replication Conflicts

Thanks to good engineering, replication conflicts are not too common, but they can happen when the same attributes are updated on more than one DC simultaneously. After all, what are the chances of two administrators make a change on the same attribute of the same object within just a couple of minutes of one another? Not too high, but high enough that a good conflict resolution mechanism needs to be in place. The conflicts can, and do, happen though, and Microsoft has provided methods to handle them.

The way AD replication determines the winner of a conflict starts off simply. If two different domain controllers have different values for the exact same object attribute, then eventually replication will bring those changes to a confrontation. The DC that receives the conflicting changes has to compare the two, make a decision, and replicate that decision off to the other DCs. The initial resolution attempt is by timestamp: whichever change was made last wins. Each update gets a stamp that includes the version number, the timestamp, and the Server GUID (which is the ID of the server where the change originated). If the timestamps on both are exactly the same, right down to the second (a virtual impossibility), the change with the highest globally unique identifier (GUID) is accepted.

The LostandFound Container

Sometimes a conflict occurs when you delete a container object that has child objects inside that are not considered part of the deletion. These child objects become orphaned objects and go into a special container named LostandFound. This happens rarely, but it can happen. As an example, suppose you delete or move an OU named Paris. All inner OUs are deleted or moved with it. However, before that change can be replicated to all the DCs, another admin goes in and adds an OU to the Paris OU called Sales. When the replication catches up to that DC, there will be a conflict. To resolve it, the Sales OU goes into the LostandFound container.

By default, you cannot see the LostandFound container. To make it visible, you need to go into AD Users and Computers and select View | Advanced Features.

> **Exam Tip**
>
> You do not need to know the detailed mechanics of conflict resolution. You should know that conflicts occur at the attribute level, that the first attempt to resolve conflicts is by time, and that orphaned objects go to the LostandFound container.

Sibling Rivalry

Yet another interesting replication problem can occur when two objects with the same name try to go into the same container. For example, suppose you have a user object named Kevin in the Sales OU and a user object named Kevin in the Marketing OU. You decide to combine these two OUs into a new OU named Combo and move the users into the Combo OU. There will be a conflict.

The resolution is interesting. The servers check the objects' timestamps, and the object with the latest timestamp wins and gets to stay; the object that loses gets a square box (along with a CNF entry and a the GUID of the object) included in the name to give the object a unique name. This makes the object immediately stand out as different. As an administrator, you must determine if this is an object you want to keep, in which case you manually change the name, or if not, delete.

Operations Master Roles

Running contrary to the model that multimaster replication provides, there are times when you can perform a task only on a particular domain controller. These domain controllers fill what are known as Operation Master (or Flexible Single Master Operations, FSMO) roles. Operation Masters are domain controllers that are assigned to complete certain tasks for a domain or forest; an Operation Master's duties are always specific to the domain or forest, and no other computer is allowed to complete these tasks. The tasks are separated into manageable areas, and because one server is responsible for one task, no other computer can take on that role.

Forest-Wide Operation Master

There are two forest-wide Operation Master roles:

- **Schema Master** The first domain controller in the forest holds the role of the Schema Master and is responsible for maintaining and distributing the Schema to the rest of the forest. It maintains a list of all the possible classes of attributes that define the objects found in AD. If the Schema needs to be updated or changed, as in the case of installing an application that must make modifications to the classes or attributes within the Schema, it must be updated on the Schema Master (that is, the DC serving as the Schema Master must be available), and the update must be performed by a member of the Schema Admins group. If the DC serving as the Schema Master is unavailable and you must make the changes to the Schema, then you can move this role to another available DC.

Travel Advisory

One caveat to updating the Schema is that it causes an immediate replication of the entire Schema to all the DCs in the entire forest. Therefore, it is recommended that any time you must make changes to the Schema (or in the case of installing an application that modifies the Schema significantly), these changes be performed at a time when the replication will not hinder your production.

- **Domain Naming Master**   The domain controller for the forest that records the additions and deletions of domains to the forest, this Operation Master is important in maintaining the integrity of the domain. The Domain Naming Master is queried when new domains are added to the forest. Keep in mind that if the Domain Naming Master is not available, then new domains cannot be added; however, this role can be moved to another system if necessary. Another important point to remember about the Domain Naming Master (in a multiple domain environment) is that it must also be a Global Catalog (GC) server. This is because it queries the GC to verify that the creation of any additions to the forest is unique.

Domain-Wide Operation Masters

The three domain-wide Operation Master roles control activity inside a domain. Tasks range in scope from keeping track of domain controllers in a domain to assisting non–Windows 2000 users. There are three domain-wide Operation Master roles:

- **Relative Identifier (RID) Master**   Responsible for assigning blocks of RIDs to all domain controllers in a domain. A Security Identifier (SID) is a unique identifier for each object in a domain. SIDs in Windows 2000 are made up of two parts. The first part is common to all objects in the domain; a unique identifier (the RID) is then suffixed to create the unique SID for each object in a domain. They uniquely identify the object and specify where it was created.

- **Primary Domain Controller (PDC) Emulator**   Responsible for emulating an NT 4.0 PDC for clients that have not migrated to Windows 2000. One of the PDC emulator's primary responsibilities is to log on non–Windows 2000 clients. The PDC emulator will also be consulted if a client fails to log on. This gives the PDC emulator a chance to check for any last-minute password changes for non–Windows 2000 clients in the domain before it rejects the logon request. The point is that the PDC emulator will always receive priority password replication. In addition, the PDC emulator is the system on which GPT changes (discussed in Chapter 11) are made.

- **Infrastructure Master**   Records changes made concerning objects in a domain. All changes are reported to the Infrastructure Master first, and then they are replicated out to the other domain controllers. The Infrastructure Master deals with groups and group memberships for all domain objects. It is also an Infrastructure Master's role to update other domains with changes that have been made to objects. An important point is that the Infrastructure Master and the Global Catalog should not be on the same DC. This is because the Infrastructure Master will not work properly if it contains any references to objects that are not part of the domain. If the Infrastructure Master is on the same system as the GC, then the GC will have objects that the Infrastructure Master doesn't hold and it will interfere with the job of the Infrastructure Master.

Moving and Seizing FSMO Roles

Once a domain controller is configured to fill an Operations Master role, you can change that role. There are three primary reasons why you might need to change the FSMO role of a system:

- Because you know that the system is going to be down for a brief or extended period of time and you want that role available on another server
- Because you are following the rules of FSMO placement to move the Infrastructure Master off a GC or to ensure that the Domain Naming Master is on the same server as the GC
- Because you want to balance the roles across various systems or because you want to ensure that if a system went down, all roles wouldn't be lost

Transferring a role is easy if you know where to look. To find and change the location of a FSMO role, you use different tools for different roles. To find and move the RID master, PDC emulator, and Infrastructure Master roles, you must use AD Users and Computers. To find and move the Domain Naming Master, you must use AD Domains and Trusts. To find and move the Schema Master, you must use the AD Schema snap-in tool.

If, for some reason, you cannot transfer a role (such as when a server is down and critical network services are lost), you can seize a role. To *seize* a role, you should first disconnect the server that is down. Then, on the server that will assume the role, use the ntdsutil command. There is a potential for data loss, so perform this action only if necessary. The following steps are used to seize a role:

1. Open a command prompt, type **ntdsutil**, and press ENTER.

2. Type **roles** and press ENTER.

3. The FSMO Maintenance prompt appears. Type **connections** and press ENTER.

4. Type **connect to server** followed by the FQDN of the server that is going to hold the new role and press ENTER.

5. Type **quit** and press ENTER to return to the FSMO Maintenance prompt.

6. Type **seize FSMO_role_name** and press ENTER. Role names include RID master, PDC, Infrastructure Master, Domain Naming Master, and Schema Master.

7. Type **quit** until you are completely out of the command prompt.

Exam Tip

Understand the benefits of multimaster replication, along with the caveats that come with it in replication. Also, familiarize yourself with the single master operation roles.

Global Catalog Server

Another server function that can be assigned to a domain controller is the Global Catalog server. The Global Catalog server maintains a subset of Active Directory object attributes that are most commonly searched for by users or client computers, such as a user's logon name. Global Catalog servers provide two important functions. They allow users to log on to the network and they allow users to locate AD objects anywhere in a forest.

The Active Directory is composed of three partitions:

- **Schema Partition**   This partition stores the definitions of all objects that can be created in a forest along with their attributes. There is only one schema partition for a forest. A copy is replicated to all domain controllers in the forest.

- **Configuration Partition**   This partition defines the Active Directory domain, site, and server object structure. There is only one configuration partition for a forest. A copy is replicated to all domain controllers in the forest.

- **Domain Partition**   This partition identifies and defines objects specific to a domain. Each domain has its own domain partition and a copy of it is replicated to all domain controllers in a domain.

The Global Catalog contains a subset of information in the domain partition and is replicated amongst domain controllers in the domain. When a user attempts to log on or to access a network resource from anywhere in the forest, the Global Catalog is consulted for the resolution to the request. Without the Global Catalog, that request for access would have to be fielded by each domain controller in the forest until a resolution could be found. If your network uses a single domain, this function of the Global Catalog isn't really necessary because all domain controllers in the domain would have information on all users and objects on the network. With multiple domains, however, this function of the Global Catalog is essential.

The other function that the Global Catalog provides, which is useful whether you have one or many domains, is to assist in the authentication process when a user logs on to the network. When a user logs on using a User Principal Name (such as user@domain.com), that name is checked against the Global Catalog before the user is resolved. This provides the ability for users to log on from computers in domains other than where their user accounts are located.

The first domain controller installed in a forest becomes the Global Catalog server by default. Unlike Operations Master roles, however, you can assign multiple domain controllers to serve as Global Catalog servers.

You can make any domain controller a Global Catalog server using the Active Directory Sites and Services tool. Expand the container for the domain controller and locate a folder named NTDS inside. Right-click the NTDS folder and choose Properties from the shortcut menu. On the General tab of the NTDS Settings Properties dialog box that opens, select the Global Catalog option.

Exam Tip

You can create as many Global Catalog servers as you want to achieve load balancing and redundancy of services. Microsoft recommends placing at least one Global Catalog server in each site.

While you can make any domain controller a Global Catalog server, you should be careful when deciding which servers should fill the role. To start with, you cannot make the same domain controller an Infrastructure Master and a Global Catalog server. See the previous section, "Domain-Wide Operation Masters," for an explanation. Also, you should note that being a Global Catalog server uses a significant amount of resources on the domain controller. For this reason, you would probably not want to make a Global Catalog server out of a domain controller that was fulfilling other demanding roles.

Backup and Recovery of Active Directory

The Windows 2000 Backup program protects against data loss due to user error, disk failure, viruses, power failure, and natural disasters. There should be onsite backups for quick restoration of data and offsite backups for recovery from disaster. To ensure that you can recover your data to the best of your ability, backups should be scheduled on a regular basis (daily if possible). Another important method to ensure recovery is to have a documented plan of restoration in the event that one is needed and then to test that plan and verify that your plan works and the backups are successful. This may involve a bit of work, and some hardware to test the recovery on, but it will benefit you in the long run. Backup also includes features for handling the backup and restoration of Active Directory information on domain controllers.

Travel Assistance

This chapter cannot go into all the details of using Windows Backup. For more details, check out *Mike Meyers' MCSE Windows® 2000 Server Certification Passport (Exam 70-215)* by Dan Newland and Rob Scrimger (Berkeley: Osborne/McGraw-Hill, 2001).

By default, only two local groups have rights to restore information from a backup:

- **Administrators**   Who logically have the ability to handle all procedures, including backup/recovery
- **Backup Operators**   Who can back up and restore files and folders, even if they cannot access those files because of permissions.

Exam Tip

You can also create a local group and assign it specific user rights to perform backup/recovery procedures, although this is not a requirement. It's important in the Microsoft exams to know the default methods and default user rights for certain situations. Try not to think beyond the question. Just because you have the ability to perform a workaround doesn't mean it's in the scenario. If asked who can handle backup/recovery procedures, by default the answer is Administrators and Backup Operators.

System State Data

System State refers to data that is a combination of important Windows 2000 Server system information. The System State data should be backed up regularly because it contains vital components for recovery. The following system components combine to make up System State data:

- **Windows Registry**   The hierarchical database that is made up of hives, keys, subkeys, and values. It contains the computer's configuration for hardware, software, user information, and installed application information.

- **System Startup files**   Includes the system and boot files to start the server.

- **Component Services Class Registration database**   Component Object Model (COM) is a binary standard for writing component software in a distributed systems environment. There are two Component Services elements on each system: the component binaries, including DLLs and executable files (EXEs), and the Component Services database. The components are backed up as a part of normal file enumeration. The Component Services database, however, is backed up and restored as a part of the System State data.

- **Certificate Services database**   Contains X.509 certificates issued to the domain controller.

- **Active Directory database**   This is included on domain controllers only. The file on domain controllers containing the database is the ntds.dit file.

- **SYSVOL directory**   The Windows 2000 System Volume, or SYSVOL, is built during the creation of a domain controller by Dcpromo.exe. It is a tree of folders containing files that need to be available and synchronized between domain controllers in a domain or forest. This directory includes the NETLOGON share, Windows 95/98/NT system policies, Windows 2000 group policies, and user logon/logoff scripts.

Travel Advisory

One point we'd like to make here is that there is a System State on all Windows 2000 systems, Professional, Server (Stand-Alone, Member, and DC). The distinction with DCs is that the System State includes the AD and the SYSVOL folder.

When backing up a Windows 2000 Server, the Backup program gives you the option to back up the System State data, as shown in Figure 12-5. The example in the figure is from a domain controller and includes Active Directory and the SYSVOL directory.

The System State can be backed up only on the local computer. It cannot be backed up from a remote computer. The System State is backed up and restored as a package; you cannot back up or restore single parts of the System State data.

Restoring System State Data on a Domain Controller

When you back up the System State data for a domain controller, the restore process becomes slightly more complicated. There are two approaches to the restore process, depending on your circumstances: authoritative or non-authoritative restores.

Each domain controller has a replica of all the objects in a domain. This might lead you to believe that each DC is exactly the same, which is not entirely correct. Each domain controller keeps track of the objects using its own unique

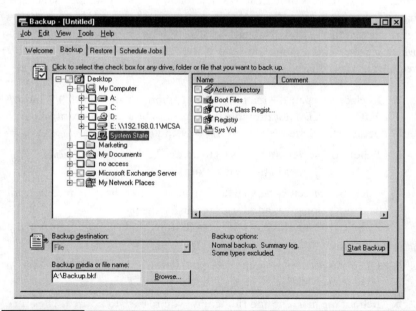

FIGURE 12.5   Backing up the System State data on a domain controller

numbering system. When an object is changed (for example, if a person moves and you have to change the address on the user's object in AD), the domain controller that records the change notifies the other DCs using Update Sequence Numbers (USN). These numbers are associated with the objects.

Performing a Nonauthoritative Restore of Active Directory   If a DC crashes and you have to restore it from a backup, there is a period of time that the domain is still functioning and updates are still occurring. In other words, if you don't bring back a single DC, the entire domain will not crash; however, that DC probably served a valuable purpose and so you want it up and running. When you recover the server and restore the System State (including the AD) nonauthoritatively, the server checks in with the other DCs to see where the USNs are. The other DCs then update the server that has been out of the loop.

A *nonauthoritative* restore restores the System State data to the USN from when the objects were created, but the restored information is not replicated throughout the domain, because the USN is outdated according to the other servers, who are aware of the deletion of that object. Nonauthoritative restores are perfect for situations in which a server crashes and you want it back up and running. The procedure is simple enough. The following steps assume that the server has had a hardware malfunction of some sort, although you could restore the System State for other reasons. Nonauthoritative restores are perfect for situations in which a server crashes and you want it back up and running, and you don't require any objects to be retained that may have changed within the domain.

1. Replace or repair the malfunctioned equipment and reinstall Windows 2000 Server. Do not promote the system to be a domain controller, because the System State restore will handle this.

2. Reboot the server, and press F8 to access the Advanced Options (discussed further in the next section).

3. Select the Directory Service Restore mode. After the system restarts in safe mode, log on as administrator, using the password you initially supplied for the Directory Services Restore Mode password during the promotion to AD.

4. Open the Backup program, select the Restore tab, and click the System State data check box.

5. Reboot the machine and (hopefully) you're back to normal. The other DCs will bring the restored one up to date.

Travel Advisory

If the failed system was just a domain controller and served no other role, all you really have to do is reinstall Windows 2000 and promote the system to be a domain controller. The new domain controller will receive a replicated copy of the Active Directory database and resume its role as a domain controller.

Performing an Authoritative Restore of Active Directory Imagine the following situation. You get an e-mail asking you to delete the Sales OU, which is located inside the Paris OU (which incidentally holds 4,000 objects all totaled). Due to some distraction, you accidentally delete the entire Paris OU instead.

You come back later and realize your error, but the update is already replicating throughout the domain. You try to perform a nonauthoritative restore, but every time you reboot the system and it has the Paris OU, the other DCs happily inform your server that the Paris OU needs to be deleted because the restored DC is considered out of date. What do you do? This is where the authoritative restore comes into play.

An *authoritative* restore assigns new USNs to the restored System State data so that the old USNs are not used. If the old USNs were used, the rest of Active Directory would know not to replicate the changes because of the outdated sequence number. An authoritative restore assigns the new USN so that the rest of the domain controllers know that the restored replicated information is valid and should be replicated throughout the domain.

If OUs or other objects are accidentally deleted from Active Directory, an authoritative restore must be performed to force the restore of that object back on the domain controller. To perform an authoritative restore, follow these steps:

1. Reboot the server and press F8 to access the Advanced Options.

2. Select the Directory Service Restore mode. After the system restarts in safe mode, log on as administrator using the password you initially supplied for the Directory Services Restore Mode password during the promotion to AD.

3. Open the Backup program, select the Restore tab, and click the System State data check box.

4. After the data is restored, *do not reboot*. Rather, type **ntdsutil.exe** at a command prompt and press ENTER.

5. At the prompt, type **authoritative restore** and press ENTER.

6. At the Authoritative Restore prompt, type **restore** followed the name of the object to restore and press ENTER. An example is "restore subtree OU=Paris,DC=Server1,DC=coriolis, DC=com".

7. Exit ntdsutil and reboot. The authoritative restore ensures that the OU=Paris is restored to its original backed up condition and is replicated throughout Active Directory. Thus it looks new to the other DCs, although it is really not.

Travel Assistance

You should know how to use ntdsutil to restore Active Directory OUs and objects. The ntdsutil command is used for authoritative restores, for AD defragmentation, and for moving the AD database. It is a very powerful tool that you will do well to understand when managing AD domains. You can learn more about using ntdsutil by going to http://www.microsoft.com/technet and searching using the term "ntdsutil."

CHECKPOINT

✔ **Objective 12.01: Diagnose Active Directory Replication Problems** This objective looked at the difference between intrasite and intersite replication and the benefits of each. It then covered Active Directory replication—what it is and the various types of conflicts that can arise during replication. It also covered the method AD uses to resolve these conflicts—timestamps, name extensions, and the LostandFound container. Finally, it looked at how to use the Windows 2000 backup with AD and the difference between nonauthoritative and authoritative restores.

REVIEW QUESTIONS

1. You have three branch offices connected with permanent T1 connections. You also have a remote location with 56K dialup connectivity. Which of the following solutions would provide the best replication results?

   A. Place the three branch offices with strong connectivity within a single site and create another site for the remote location with dialup. Use RPC replication for all connectivity.

   B. Place all four offices within their own sites and use SMTP connectivity between the offices.

   C. Place the three branch offices with strong connectivity within a single site and create another site for the remote location with dialup. Use the default RPC connectivity for the first site and use SMTP replication for the site that uses dialup.

   D. Place the three branch offices with strong connectivity within a single site and create another site for the remote location with dialup. Use the default SMTP connectivity for the first site and use RPC replication for the site that uses dialup.

2. Your domain is growing, and you are adding new DCs to handle the large number of user authentication requests coming from the increase. You've just added your eighth DC. What must you do to ensure a well-balanced replication topology?

   A. Force the KCC to create a shortcut connection object between the third DC of your bidirectional ring and your new DC.

   B. Create a connection object manually between any two DCs within the bidirectional ring that the KCC has automatically created.

   C. On the new server, under the NTDS Settings within AD Sites and Servers, select the check box to allow this server to become a Global Catalog server.

   D. Nothing. The KCC will automatically create a shortcut connection object within the automatically generated bidirectional ring.

3. A change is made on a user object—the address of the person is changed. Right afterward, another administrator changes the user's phone number on a different server. When the two replications meet, which update will be retained by the DCs?

   A. Only the address change will be retained because the address was made first, giving it the priority setting.

   B. The phone number will be retained because the phone number is considered, by default, a highly important property for contact use.

   C. Both will be retained because the change was made on different properties of an object and these will not cause a replication conflict.

   D. Neither will be retained, because the changes cancel each other out.

4. You have two DCs within your company, DC1 and DC2. They are connected by a high-speed T3 link and are in the same site. DC1 and DC2 are at a state of convergence at 7 P.M., when the connection between the two servers goes down. Three hours later, the connection is restored. How much of the directory will need to be replicated to bring these two DCs back to a state of convergence with each other?

A. The entire directory will need to replicate between them because the lost connection forces a directory split that removes all preceding replicas between these two servers.

B. None of it. The domain controllers will not allow any changes to be made to the directory when a replication partner is not accessible.

C. Only those changes that have occurred since the last replication before the connection was lost.

D. Directory replication transcends the physical boundaries of a network and can replicate, even when the physical side is down, so all will be fine.

5. You work for a company called SiteConnect that handles consulting services. You've been called in to assist in a company's new establishment of AD replication. The company has three offices: one in San Francisco, one in Los Angeles, and one in Dallas. Subnets have not been fully decided upon, and making this decision is part of your services. San Francisco and Los Angeles are connected by a T1 connection. Dallas is connected with a 56K connection. What type of solution would you recommend under these circumstances for the best replication possibilities?

A. Establish two sites, one for Los Angeles and San Francisco and one for Dallas.

B. Create three sites, one for each location.

C. Create a single site that encompasses all three locations.

D. Establish two sites, one for Los Angeles and Dallas and one for San Francisco.

6. You have a schedule for maintenance for one of your DCs to update the hardware on this system, and the server will be offline for about four hours. The DC happens to be the Schema Master. Currently, there are no planned modifications to the Schema. Which of the following should you do?

    A. Move the role of the Schema Master to another system prior to the shutdown of the DC.

    B. Move the role of the Schema Master to another system after the shutdown of the DC.

    C. Seize the role of the Schema Master from another system using the ntdsutil.exe command.

    D. Do nothing, considering the fact that the server will be offline for only four hours.

7. An OU named Marketing has been deleted from DC1 for the Corp domain. Just prior to deletion, all user accounts were moved out of the OU and into the Users container. On DC2, prior to replication of the OU's deletion, an administrator creates a user named Kenny in the Marketing OU. After the replication is complete, the OU is gone and the users are moved to the Users container. Where is the user object named Kenny?

    A. In the User's container

    B. In the LostandFound container

    C. In the Deleted OU's container

    D. Gone forever

8. Which of the following tools allows you to perform an authoritative restore of your Active Directory System State?

    A. Secedit

    B. Regedit

    C. Cipher

    D. Ntdsutil

9. Your company has three locations (England, Ireland, and Scotland) connected by 56K connections. You are configured as a single site and have DCs in the Ireland branch office. What can you do to increase logon times for your users at the other two branch offices? (Choose two.)

    A. Configure each location as its own site.

    B. Add more GC servers to the Ireland branch.

    C. Add DCs to each branch office.

    D. Create additional child domains for each location.

10. What are two benefits of intersite replication over slow WAN links?

    A. Compression of all replication

    B. Reduced processing at the bridgehead server

    C. Scheduled replication times

    D. Change Notification ensuring up-to-the-minute convergence

REVIEW ANSWERS

1. **C** Because the connectivity between the three offices is strong, they can remain in their own sites; however, the remote location should be given its own site. In addition, because the connection to the remote site is dialup, it would be better to use SMTP replication for the changes going to this site. Answer A is incorrect because it doesn't use the best replication method for this scenario. Answer B is incorrect because SMTP is not usually necessary unless there is a situation in which intermittent dialup is used for connectivity with a remote site. Answer D is incorrect because it switches the replication protocol. SMTP cannot be used within a site and so is not a possible solution.

2. **D** The KCC handles the automatic generation of the replication topology, including the creation of shortcut connection objects once the number of DCs exceeds seven. This is because the standard number of hops for data between DCs is kept to three and once you have eight DCs, that number is too high, so the KCC automatically generates a shortcut. Answer A is incorrect because you don't have to force the creation. Answer B is incorrect because you don't have to manually create the shortcut, although you can. Answer C is incorrect because, although you can make this DC a Global Catalog server, that will not affect the replication process.

3. **C** Both changes will be retained in this scenario. Remember that replication is not based upon objects themselves, but on the attributes and values within. These settings involve two different types of attributes for the object and do not conflict with each other. The other answers are incorrect because they suggest a conflict at the object level, implying that these changes will cause the DC to choose.

4. **C** When the two DCs are able to communicate with each other again, they will not need to replicate all information, only the updates. Thanks to USNs, the changes that have been made since the last replication will be the only updates needed, and the two DCs will be able to check their UTDs to determine the latest changes. The other answers are incorrect.

5. **A** Sites should be established based upon the physical connectivity and subnets. It is a logical grouping of DCs to ease replication traffic. The best choice here is to allow the two offices with a T1 connection to be in the same site, while keeping Dallas separate. In a real-world scenario, however, you would want to make sure the T1 connection was enough for your needs and that most of the bandwidth was still available to you for replication.

6. **D** Under these circumstances, it is not necessary to move the Schema Master to a different system. The system is not going to be down for any length of time, and this is not an essential system for you to move or seize. Answers A and C are incorrect because you don't have a need to move or seize. Answer B is incorrect because you do not move an operations role after the system is down.

7. **B** When the replication comes through that the OU for Marketing is deleted and the users are moved, the system will place the Kenny object in the LostandFound container. You can decide what to do with the object at that point. Answer A is incorrect because the AD will not know to move it without instructions. Answer C is incorrect because this is fictitious. Answer D is incorrect because Microsoft thought of this and made provision for this type of replication conflict.

8. **D** Without the ntdsutil.exe command, you could not perform an authoritative restore. This tool is invaluable for that reason and many others, including the ability to defragment your AD and move the ntds.dit file. Answer A is incorrect because it is the wrong tool. Answer B is incorrect because it is used to change the Registry. Answer C is incorrect because it is used with EFS for encryption.

9. **A C** In the situation given, you can do two things to enhance the logon process. The first is to create sites for each location, an approach that is better under the low-bandwidth circumstances. The workstations will attempt to log on within their own site, so in addition to splitting the domain into sites, you need to add DCs to each location to enhance the logon process. Adding GCs or breaking the domain into child domains will not assist in this situation, so answers B and D are incorrect.

10. **A C** Intersite replication allows for a scheduling of replication at convenient times and a compression of all updates to preserve bandwidth on the WAN connection. Answer B is incorrect because intersite replication is actually more intensive on the bridgehead, which has to handle the compression/decompression of the updates. Answer D is incorrect because the Change Notification process works only with intrasite replication.

Configuring, Securing, and Troubleshooting Remote Access

Configuring Remote Access

	NEWBIE	SOME EXPERIENCE	EXPERT
ETA	5 hours	3 hours	2 hours

This chapter covers three exam objectives related by their focus on remote access. The largest, by far, is configuring remote access and virtual private network (VPN) connections in Windows 2000. You'll learn how to install and configure the Routing and Remote Access Service and how to configure secure VPN connections. This chapter also covers how to implement and troubleshoot remote access policies, which provide a way of determining who gets to do what with regard to remote access. Finally, this chapter looks at implementing Terminal Services, a feature of Windows 2000 that allows access by terminals to servers that host resources and applications used by the client.

Configure and Troubleshoot Remote Access and Virtual Private Network (VPN) Connections

Objective 13.01

Remote Access in Windows 2000 comes in the form of a service named Routing and Remote Access Service (RRAS). This service runs on a Windows 2000 server and lets other servers or client computers that are not connected via the local network establish temporary connections over phone lines, ISDN lines, Internet connections, or services such as X.25. Once a computer establishes a connection with an RRAS server, that computer can access the resources on the RRAS server and possibly access the other computers on the RRAS server's network, depending on how RRAS has been configured.

As I mentioned in the introduction, RRAS is a pretty bulky topic, especially for a single chapter. This section begins with an overview of remote access that includes an examination of the many features and components that make up RRAS. You will then learn how to install, configure, secure, and manage an RRAS server.

Remote Access Overview

Before you get into the details of installing and configuring a remote access server, it is necessary to understand some of what is going on behind the scenes. Many different protocols are used in remote access, including remote access protocols, networking protocols, and security protocols. This overview provides a look at the features and concepts of remote access.

A Windows 2000 Server running the Routing and Remote Access Service is able to accept connections from users that are physically separated from the main network but still need to connect to the main network to access resources. Once connected, remote access clients use standard tools and applications to access these network resources. For example, once a user is connected to a remote access server, that user can retrieve files with Windows Explorer, connect to a messaging server with a standard e-mail client, and open documents with applications such as Microsoft Word. From the user's perspective, it is just as if he or she were directly connected to the network. In fact, at its heart, RRAS really is just another way to transmit standard networking protocols and commands already in use on the network. Instead of being put onto a network cable by a network interface card, the information is formatted (and possibly secured) by RRAS and transmitted across whatever type of link is configured.

Travel Advisory

The concepts of remote access and remote control are often confused. In *remote access,* a client computer connects to a remote access server using a dial-up or other type of on-demand connection. Once connected to the network, the client can access network resources. All applications still run on the client computer. In *remote control,* a client computer connects to a remote server and actually takes control over that server in a separate window on the client computer. Within this window, it is actually as if the user is sitting at the server computer: all applications are run on the server. RRAS provides remote access and *not* remote control.

Remote Access Connection Methods

Windows 2000 RRAS provides two distinct methods of remote access connections for remote users:

- **Dial-up networking**   With dial-up networking, a client makes a temporary, dial-up connection to a physical port on the RRAS server. This connection uses the services of a public telecommunications provider such as a public-switched telephone network (PSTN), an Integrated Services Digital Network (ISDN), or X.25. A good example of dial-up networking would be if both a client and a server had a standard modem. The client would initiate the dial-up connection using the modem. The connection to the server modem would be made over public phone lines, and the server would authenticate the user and provide the configured access.

- **Virtual private networking**   Virtual private networking provides a way of making a secured, private connection from the client to the server over a public network such as the Internet. Unlike dial-up networking, where a connection is made directly between client and server, a VPN connection is logical and tunneled through another type of connection. Typically, a remote user would connect to an Internet service provider (ISP) using a form of dial-up networking (particularly good for users with high-speed connections). The RRAS server would also be connected to the Internet (probably via a persistent, or permanent, connection) and would be configured to accept VPN connections. Once the client is connected to the Internet, it then establishes a VPN connection over that dial-up connection to the RRAS server.

VPN offers two significant advantages over dial-in access. First, remote users that are not in the same local calling area as the remote access server need not make long-distance calls to connect to the network. Instead, they can make local calls to an ISP. Second, every standard dial-up connection requires that a physical device be present on the RRAS server and devoted to that connection. This places limitations on the number of users that can connect remotely at a single time and also increases the start-up costs and maintenance needed; you must purchase, maintain, and upgrade all the necessary modems and the connection lines they use. Assuming a fairly high-bandwidth Internet connection from the RRAS server to the Internet, more remote users are able to connect at the same time using VPN than dial-up connections.

Protocols Used in RRAS

A *protocol* is simply a defined and often standardized way of communicating between two devices on a network. There are two general types of protocols that you must be familiar with to work with RRAS: remote access (or line) protocols and network transport (or LAN) protocols.

Remote Access Protocols   *Remote access* protocols govern how information is broken up and transmitted over wide area network (WAN) connections, of which a dial-up connection is one type. RRAS supports four remote access protocols:

- **Point-to-Point Protocol (PPP)**   By far the most common remote access protocol in use today. Most dial-in servers, including RRAS, support PPP, and it is generally considered to be the best choice for remote access situations. Windows 2000 RRAS supports PPP for both dial-out and dial-in connections.

- **Serial Line Interface Protocol (SLIP)**   An older protocol developed in UNIX and still in wide use today. Windows 2000 RRAS supports SLIP in dial-out configurations, but you *cannot* use a SLIP client to dial in to an RRAS server.

- **RAS Protocol** Used to support the NetBIOS naming convention and is a proprietary protocol, used only between Microsoft-based networks. It is required to support NetBIOS naming and is installed by default when you install the RRAS server.

- **NetBIOS Gateway** Used to provide compatibility with older versions of RAS server that do not support networking protocols such as TCP/IP and NWLink. The NetBIOS gateway is used to translate data from the NetBEUI protocol to these other protocols.

Network Transport Protocols *Network transport* protocols govern how information is transmitted between devices on a local area network (LAN). You should already be familiar with the major networking protocols available in Windows 2000, but here is a brief description of a few of the protocols you'll need to be familiar with for the exam:

- **TCP/IP (Transmission Control Protocol/Internet Protocol)** An extensive, robust protocol that is ideally suited for connecting different types of computers and operating systems. Thus, it is the standard choice of protocols for networks containing many different types of systems, such as Microsoft systems or those based on UNIX, and it is the standard protocol for the Internet and is also required on Windows 2000 networks.

- **IPX (Internetwork Packet Exchange)** The protocol of choice for networks using versions of Novell's NetWare previous to version 4.11 (newer versions use TCP/IP). If your network is using NetWare and you need your remote clients to be able to access these resources, you must enable IPX.

- **NetBEUI** A simple, efficient protocol that you would primarily use on small networks that consist only of Microsoft clients. Although easy to configure and manage, NetBEUI does not support routing and is therefore not suitable for use on large, varied networks.

Exam Tip

While RRAS supports various LAN protocols, keep in mind that many remote access features (such as VPN and Terminal Services, both discussed later) require the use of TCP/IP.

You must use at least one LAN protocol, but RRAS lets you use all three simultaneously, if necessary. Remember that any remote client dialing in must support one of these protocols. RRAS also supports the Point-to-Point Tunneling Protocol (PPTP), an extension of PPP that you can use to establish a connection such as a virtual private network.

Remote Access Security

Remote access has always been considered one of the weaker points of networking security. While it's always been fairly easy to secure a network from unauthorized physical access, the current popularity of Internet access and remote user access places larger security demands on the modern network. Fortunately, new security technologies and protocols have been developed that ease the problem of remote access security.

Security Through User Authentication   The primary method of securing a remote access connection involves authenticating the user trying to connect. To do this, the user (or the user's client computer) must present some sort of credentials that allow the RRAS server to verify that the user is indeed a valid user. Windows 2000 supports five different user authentication protocols:

- **Password Authentication Protocol (PAP)**   The most basic form of user authentication. A user's name and password are transmitted over the dial-up connection to the RRAS server. This information is transmitted in clear text with no encryption, making it quite vulnerable to snooping. In addition, PAP provides no way for a client and a server to authenticate one another. For the most part, the availability of better authentication protocols is rendering PAP obsolete. In fact, Microsoft recommends that you not use it unless absolutely necessary.

- **Shiva Password Authentication Protocol (SPAP)**   Shiva is a private company (now owned by Intel) that manufactures remote access hardware devices. SPAP is included mainly for compatibility with these devices and really isn't used much on most networks.

- **Challenge Handshake Authentication Protocol (CHAP)**   Considerably more secure that PAP or SPAP. In this form of authentication, the server sends the client a challenge and the client uses its credentials to encrypt the challenge. This encrypted information is then sent across the dial-up connection to the server, which decrypts it and attempts to validate the user. If the outcome matches the challenge, the user is authenticated. Since the challenge and response are encrypted, they are considerably less vulnerable to eavesdroppers. CHAP is also commonly referred to as MD5-CHAP because it uses the RSA MD5 hash algorithm for encryption.

- **Microsoft CHAP (MS-CHAP)**   A modified version of CHAP that allows the use of Windows 2000 authentication information. There are two versions of MS-CHAP. Version 2 is the most secure and is supported only by Windows 2000 (and XP). Version 1 is supported by earlier versions of Windows and other operating systems.

Exam Tip

If you need to know which authentication protocol to use, remember: if all the systems are Windows 2000, use MS-CHAPv2; if some are not Windows 2000 but all are Microsoft, use MS-CHAP; if there are non-Microsoft operating systems, use CHAP.

- **Extensible Authentication Protocol (EAP)**   A general protocol for PPP authentication that supports multiple authentication mechanisms. Instead of selecting a single authentication method for a connection, EAP can negotiate an authentication method at connect time. The computer asking for the authentication method is called the *authenticator* and may require several different pieces of authentication information. This allows the use of almost any authentication method, including secure access tokens or one-time password systems.

Exam Tip

The EAP protocol is required for SmartCard authentication, a feature that many exams (including this one) emphasize.

Security Through Connection Control   In addition to being able to authenticate users in a variety of ways, Windows 2000 RRAS provides a number of methods for securing the actual connection from a client to a server. One such method is the Callback Control Protocol, which allows your RRAS servers to negotiate a callback with the other end. For example, a server may be configured to hang up and call a user back at a specified number whenever that user tries to connect. This provides two advantages. The first is that a successful connection can be made only from a particular number—a good way of ensuring that only authorized users can make the connection. The second advantage is that, for users dialing in from another calling area, the company can foot the bill for the long-distance call.

Another way that you can control connections is by configuring an RRAS server to accept or reject calls on the basis of Caller ID or Automatic Number Identification (ANI) information. For example, a server could be configured to accept calls only from a certain number.

Security Through Access Control   RRAS supports a number of ways to control remote user access to the RRAS server. The primary access control method is enabling or disabling the permission to dial in on individual user accounts. In addition to this basic method, Remote Access Policies (RAPs) enable you to extend control over whether users can dial in or not by setting a number of conditions on the access. You'll learn about RAPs later in the chapter, in the section "Troubleshoot Routing and Remote Access Policy."

Installing Remote Access

Now that you have a basic grasp of the concepts behind the Routing and Remote Access Service, it is time to see how to actually implement and configure it. This is a fairly simple procedure—but unlike other software or Windows components, RRAS is not installed using the Add/Remove Programs component of the Windows Control Panel. Instead, RRAS is automatically installed along with Windows 2000 Server but is left in a disabled state. All you have to do is enable it.

To enable the Routing and Remote Access Service, follow these steps:

1.   Log on as an administrator and click Start | Programs | Administrative Tools | Routing and Remote Access. This utility (shown next) is actually a snap-in for the Microsoft Management Console.

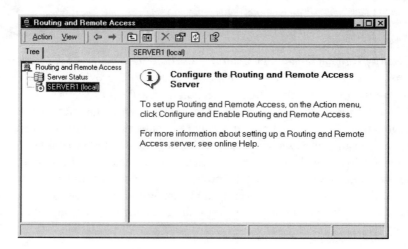

2. Right-click the computer on which you want to enable RRAS and select Configure And Enable Routing And Remote Access from the shortcut menu.

3. Click Next to skip the opening page of the Routing and Remote Access Server Setup wizard that opens.

4. On the Common Configurations page, select the Remote Access Server option and then click Next. Descriptions of the available configurations are shown in Table 13-1, following this procedure.

5. If you are configuring RRAS on a stand-alone server, you will next see a page that asks whether you want to configure RRAS as a basic or advanced server. Choose the advanced server option and click Next. Advanced RRAS servers include all the features of a basic server but also include features like remote access policies.

The rest of this procedure (and chapter) assumes the use of an advanced RRAS server and covers all the options that would be present in a basic server, as well.

TABLE 13.1 Common Configuration Options When Enabling RRAS via the Setup Wizard

RRAS Configuration Option	Description
Internet Connection Server	Allows all of the computers on a network to share the RRAS Server's Internet connection in one of two ways. The first is Internet Connection Sharing (ICS), which prompts you to use the Network and Dial-Up Connections folder to configure and share an Internet connection. The second is Network Address Translator (NAT), which is installed as a routing protocol within RRAS. NAT requires more configuration but also offers more flexibility. ICS and NAT are described in Chapter 14.
Remote Access Server	Used to configure the RRAS server to allow remote clients to dial into the network. This option is the focus of this section.
Virtual Private Networking (VPN)	Used to allow clients to connect to a public network such as the Internet, and then use a tunneling protocol, such as PPTP, to create a secure VPN connection over the first connection. This option is described later in the chapter in the section "Virtual Private Networking."
Network Router	Configures the server to route data to other networks or routers when required. See Chapter 3 for a description of routers.
Manually Configured Server	Lets you manually configure the options you need instead of using the Setup wizard.

6. The next page of the wizard lists the protocols installed on the computer. Make sure that whatever protocols you intend to use are listed. Verify that the Yes, All The Required Protocols Are On This List option is selected and click Next. If you select No, the wizard ends and you must configure the appropriate protocols and restart the wizard.

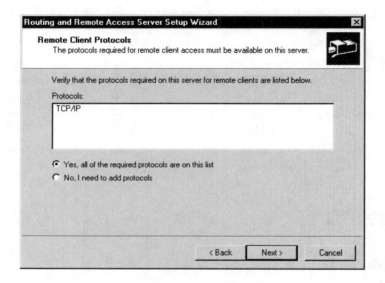

7. Clients that connect to the network must be assigned an IP address if you are allowing TCP/IP-based dial-in clients. RRAS can issue IP addresses itself or make use of a DHCP server on the local subnet. If you choose DHCP, then you will be warned that you should configure the RRAS server with the IP address of a DHCP server. Specify the option you want to use and click Next. If you want RRAS to assign IP addresses, you will be asked (on an extra wizard page) to specify a range of addresses it is allowed to assign. See Chapter 4 for more information on using DHCP.

8. The next wizard page asks whether you want to set your RRAS server up to use Remote Authentication Dial-In User Service (RADIUS), which lets the RRAS server pass authentication requests along to a RADIUS server for validation. A RADIUS server is usually devoted to running a large user account database against which it can identify remote users. RADIUS is an industry-standard protocol that is available on many

different types of operating systems and that can therefore authenticate users against many different types of account databases. Choose your option and click Next. If you choose to use a RADIUS server, you are given the option to configure it on an extra wizard page.

9. Click Finish to exit the wizard and enable RRAS.

Travel Assistance

For an overview of RADIUS and plenty of resources for learning more about its implementation, check out http://www.funk.com/RADIUS.

And that's all there is to it. Once you have enabled RRAS, you can pause or stop the service by right-clicking the server in the Routing and Remote Access snap-in and choosing the appropriate action from the All Tasks submenu on the shortcut menu. In the following section, you will learn to configure connections for the new server.

Configuring Remote Access

Once RRAS is enabled on your server, you will have to configure it to behave the way you want. This configuration is performed in three places:

- **At the server level**   Most of the configuration of inbound connections happens at the server level using the RRAS snap-in that you used to enable the service. In particular, you will use the property pages of the server itself to control whether the server allows connections at all, what protocols it supports and how, security options, and event logging. You will also use RRAS to set up policies and profiles and to monitor the status of a remote access server.

- **At the user level**   A good bit of configuration also happens using the property pages for individual users in the Active Directory Users and Computers snap-in (or the Computer Management snap-in for a stand-alone computer). This is where you'll grant dial-in permissions for individual users, as well as set callback and other dial-in options.

- **At the client**   Once the server and the user accounts are configured for dial-in access, each client also needs to be configured. Fortunately, all versions of Windows and most other operating systems come with some form of dial-in capability built in that is relatively easy to configure.

Travel Assistance

This section focuses on configuring RRAS at the server level and the user level. Configuring clients is very similar between different versions of Windows (and for that matter, on non-Windows clients) and is not featured as part of the exam. The best course of action is to consult the help files for your system.

Configuring Inbound Connections at the Server

Like most objects in Windows 2000, RRAS servers are configured using settings in a Properties dialog box. Open the Properties dialog box for any RRAS server by right-clicking the server in the RRAS snap-in and choosing Properties from the shortcut menu. The next several sections cover the general use of each of the tabs available in the Properties dialog box of an RRAS server.

Setting RRAS General Properties   The first tab you see when you open the properties for an RRAS server is the General tab, shown in Figure 13-1. The most important setting on this tab is the Remote Access Server option, which allows the RRAS service to operate as a remote access server. This means you

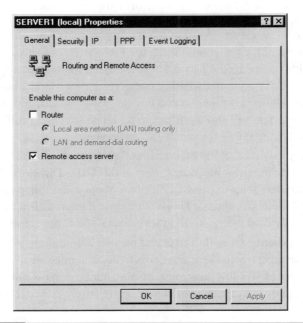

FIGURE 13.1   Setting general properties for an RRAS server

can switch remote access on and off without actually disabling the RRAS service, which cause the service to erase its settings.

The other option on the General tab, Router, lets you choose whether the server is also used as a router. If routing is enabled, you can choose whether to allow routing access only within the confines of the LAN (computers that are directly connected to the computer) or to allow the RRAS server to automatically dial a connection to another network on demand. Demand-dial routing allows the RRAS server to make WAN connections to RRAS servers on other remote networks.

Exam Tip

The General tab of the Properties dialog box for an RRAS server is extremely important, as it plays the deciding role in determining whether remote access is enabled for a server.

Setting RRAS Security Properties   The Security tab, shown in Figure 13-2, is used to specify which authentication and accounting methods are used by RRAS.

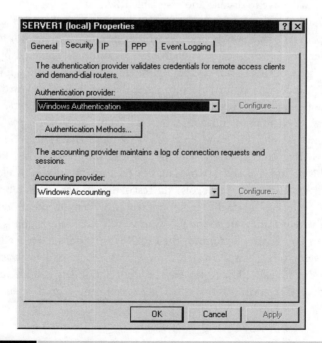

FIGURE 13.2   Setting RRAS security properties

The Authentication Provider menu lets you choose between using Windows Authentication and using RADIUS Authentication. The Accounting Provider drop-down list on the Security page allows you to configure whether connection request events are sent to a log file (the Windows Accounting option) or to a RADIUS server (the RADIUS accounting option).

Exam Tip

If Windows authentication and accounting is used, related events are logged to special log files in the %SystemRoot%\windows32\LogFiles folder on the RRAS server. If RADIUS authentication and accounting is used and the RADIUS server is a Windows 2000 server, events are logged to the same folder on the RADIUS server.

Setting RRAS IP Properties   The IP tab, shown in Figure 13-3, is one of four tabs that control the networking protocols supported by RRAS. The others include IPX, NetBEUI, and AppleTalk. These tabs are shown only if the protocols were installed on the server prior to enabling RRAS. To install protocols after RRAS, you will have to disable and re-enable RRAS.

The Enable IP Routing option controls whether or not RRAS is allowed to route IP packets between networks. For this option to work, the Router option on the General tab must also be enabled. This option is enabled by default, meaning that if the RRAS server is configured to operate as a router, it will route IP packets. Since you can turn on routing for the server itself and turn off routing for the IP and other protocols individually, you can achieve pretty fine control over what clients can and cannot access the network.

The Allow IP-Based Remote Access And Demand-Dial Connections option controls whether TCP/IP-based clients are allowed to connect to the RRAS server at all. If this option is disabled (which may be the case if you want to allow access only for clients using other protocols), the rest of the settings on this tab are moot.

The IP address assignment section controls how remote clients get their IP addresses when connecting to the RRAS server. The default setting is based on the answers you gave while running the RRAS Setup wizard. DHCP allows your RRAS server to refer clients to a DHCP server on your network to be assigned IP addresses dynamically. The Static Address Pool option lets you manually configure a pool of IP addresses that the RRAS server can assign to clients itself.

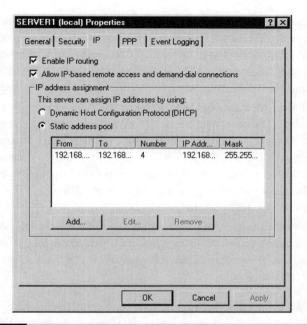

FIGURE 13.3   Setting RRAS IP properties

Travel Assistance

Since TCP/IP is by far the most common protocol used over dial-up connections, it is the only one discussed here. For information on configuring settings on tabs corresponding to other protocols, consult the RRAS help files.

Setting RRAS PPP Properties   The PPP tab is used to control the PPP-layer options available to clients. There are four options on this tab:

- **Multilink Connections**   The PPP Multilink Protocol (MP) is used to combine multiple physical links into a single logical link. For example, two 56KB modem links could be combined into a 128KB link. MP is turned on by default; but if your clients are not using it (or your server does not support multiple physical connections), there is really no reason to leave it turned on.

- **Dynamic Bandwidth Control Using BAP Or BACP** The Bandwidth Allocation Protocol (BAP) and Bandwidth Allocation Control Protocol (BACP) force a client to dynamically add and remove links during a multilink session to adjust for changes in bandwidth needs. This option is available only when the Multilink option is enabled.

- **Link Control Protocol (LCP) Extensions** These extensions include a number of enhancements to the LCP protocol that is used to establish a PPP link and control its settings. One of the primary enhancements included is the ability for the client and server to dynamically agree on protocols used on the connection. This option is turned on by default; and since Windows 9x, NT, and 2000 clients all support the extensions, you will probably want to leave it on.

- **Software Compression** This option controls whether RRAS should allow clients to use the Compression Control Protocol (CCP) to compress PPP traffic. Again, this option is on by default and is usually best left that way.

Setting RRAS Event Logging Properties The Event Logging tab lets you control the level at which events are logged to the Windows Event log. You can have RRAS log only events, log events and warnings, log the maximum amount of information, or log nothing. The more information you log, the more resources must be devoted to logging. For this reason, you should leave the logging set to Log Events Only most of the time and bump the logging to a higher level when you need to troubleshoot some particular problem.

The other option on this tab is to turn on PPP logging. When it is enabled, events in the PPP connection establishment processes are written to a log file named ppp.log, which is found in the %systemroot%\Tracing folder.

Configuring a User for Remote Access

Once you have configured your RRAS server to support remote access, the next step is to configure what users are allowed that access and how. There are three tools you will use for doing this:

- **User accounts** The configuration settings associated with individual user accounts. Each user has exactly one account, which is stored in the Active Directory. These accounts include options such as whether the user can connect remotely, whether callback for the user is enabled, and so on. User accounts are the focus of this section.

- **Remote access policies** Connection rules that apply to groups of users. These are covered in the section "Troubleshoot Routing and Remote Access Policy," later in this chapter.

- **Remote access profiles** These are associated with remote access policies and contain settings that determine what is required during call setup and completion. Remote access profiles are also covered in the later section "Troubleshoot Routing and Remote Access Policy."

If your RRAS server is part of a Windows 2000 domain, user accounts are stored in the Active Directory. In this case, you will use the Active Directory Users and Computers snap-in to manage these accounts. If your RRAS server is not part of a Windows 2000 domain, user accounts are stored on the local computer and are controlled using the Local Users and Groups snap-in. Whichever tool you use, the configuration of the user accounts are the same. Here, we'll assume that you are using the Active Directory Users and Computers snap-in.

While each user account has a host of settings scattered across a number of tabs, the tab we are most concerned with in relation to remote access is the Dial-in tab, shown in Figure 13-4.

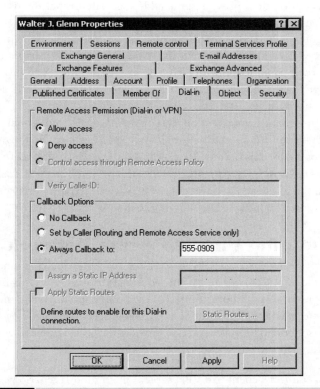

FIGURE 13.4 Setting dial-in properties for a user

The Dial-in tab holds a number of settings that control the user's remote access capability. The Remote Access Permission (Dial-in or VPN) section is used to enable remote access for the user. There are three options. The first two are to explicitly allow or deny access; these options work in conjunction with any policy settings that may apply to the user. The final option is to let a remote access policy control the user's access.

The Verify Caller-ID option lets you enter a phone number that is used to verify the remote caller using the Caller-ID information provided by the phone company. Calls from any other number are automatically rejected. Note that the phone system and modems in use must support the Caller-ID feature.

The Callback Options section provides two ways to use the callback feature of RRAS. The first option is to let the number be set by the caller in the client software. This option does not provide much added security but can be a good way of letting a company be billed for long-distance access instead of the caller. The second callback option sets a specific number that is always called for the user. This option does provide some added security in that the user must be calling from a given number in order to access the network.

The Assign A Static IP Address option is used to provide a user with the same IP address every time the user calls in. While it is generally a better idea to let RRAS work in conjunction with DHCP to assign dynamic IP addresses (this is covered later in the chapter), occasionally a client may need a static IP address for specific applications.

The Apply Static Routes section lets you define a set of routes that are always used to deliver information from the client to specified hosts on the network. If you do not enable this option, the client uses the default gateway that it is assigned by DHCP or is given manually. Once this option is enabled, use the Static Routes button to add and remove routes. This option is typically used for accounts that allow other routers to dial into the RRAS server.

Configuring Virtual Private Networking

Virtual private networking (VPN) offers a way to create a logical connection between two computers over an existing routing infrastructure. This means that two computers that are both connected by a public network like the Internet could create an additional private connection between them that uses TCP/IP or any other supported protocol and also provides authentication and encryption.

VPNs are typically used in one of two contexts:

- **To connect a client to a VPN server**   A common scenario would be a remote user that first connects to the Internet via a local ISP and then establishes an additional, virtual connection over the Internet to a VPN server on the company network.

- **To connect two VPN servers** A common scenario would be a company with two locations (and therefore two LANs) each having Internet access and an RRAS server configured to use with VPN. These servers could be configured to route messages between the two networks over the Internet using VPN.

For both of these contexts, the two main reasons you might want to use VPN instead of traditional dial-up access are security and cost. If you have remote users in separate calling areas from the main network or two networks that are separated by distance, connecting to the Internet locally instead of making long-distance calls means pretty good savings. VPN provides the security necessary to allow a public infrastructure to be used.

VPN Components

Several components make up a complete VPN solution. These include a VPN server, a VPN client, a connection between the two, and the protocols used for that connection.

The VPN Server For the purposes of our discussion, a *VPN server* is a Windows 2000 server running the Routing and Remote Access Service that is configured to support VPN connections. In addition, the server will typically have one connection to the Internet and a separate connection to the local network. When you enable RRAS on a server, VPN ports are automatically created. All you have to do is configure them. You can also specify that a server will become a VPN server during the process of enabling RRAS.

The VPN Client A *VPN client* is any computer that can initiate a VPN connection to a VPN server. This client could be a remote user connecting to a main network or could be a router connecting to another router. Most operating systems have some sort of VPN client available, even if the operating systems themselves do not come with built-in support. Windows 98, Windows 98 SE, Me, NT 4.0, and 2000 all include built-in support for use as a VPN client.

The VPN Connection and Protocols The routing infrastructure for a VPN connection must be a network using a routable protocol, whether this network is the Internet or a private network. This network, often referred to as the *transit internetwork*, serves as the basis for the VPN connection. Once the client and server are both connected to the transit internetwork, the client can use TCP/IP or another networking protocol that it has in common with the server to establish the VPN connection. For example, if the main company network uses IPX as its primary network protocol, the client will likely want to establish a VPN connection using IPX as the transit internetwork.

This capability of VPNs to use one networking protocol on top of another is often referred to as *tunneling*: packets sent across the virtual network are encapsulated for transmission through the actual network. The ability to tunnel is supported through the use of a tunneling protocol, which both sides of the connection use to create, monitor, and maintain the virtual network. Windows 2000 supports two tunneling protocols:

- **Point-to-Point Tunneling Protocol (PPTP)**   PPTP is an extension of the PPP remote access protocol. PPTP uses a TCP connection and allows IP, IPX, or NetBEUI traffic to be encrypted and then encapsulated within an IP header that can be sent across the IP internetwork.

- **Layer 2 Tunneling Protocol (L2TP)**   L2TP is an extension of the PPP protocol that merges the best features of PPTP and another protocol called Layer 2 Forwarding. Although the L2TP specifications support transit internetworks using IP, X.25, Frame Relay, or ATM, Windows 2000 supports L2TP only over IP or ATM. One distinct advantage that L2TP has over PPTP is that L2TP uses IPSec in addition to any higher-level encryption used, while PPTP supports only the higher-level encryption. In addition, L2TP is always used with IPSec, a mode of encryption that is more secure than that used by PPTP, Microsoft Point-to-Point Encryption (MPPE).

Installing and Configuring a VPN Server

If you have installed RRAS on a server, then that server is already configured to use VPN; you may just not know about it. If you have not yet installed RRAS, you can enable it on your server and specify that it be used as a VPN server. Both methods are discussed in this section.

Installing RRAS as a VPN Server   If you do not yet have RRAS enabled on your server, you need to enable it, activate it, and configure it for use with VPN. This is a relatively simple procedure and, for the most part, is the same as the procedure for enabling RRAS as an RRAS server. This procedure was discussed in detail earlier in the chapter, and there's really not much need to go over it again here. The one difference is that when you come to the Common Configurations page of the wizard, you should select the Virtual Private Network (VPN) Server option instead of the RRAS Server option (see Table 13-1 for a refresher on the options). Once you complete the wizard, your new VPN server will be ready to accept connections.

Using VPN on an Existing RRAS Server   If you have already enabled RRAS on your server and you chose something besides the VPN option on the Common Configurations page, you can configure it as a VPN server without having to reinstall the service. All you have to do is open the property pages for the server in the RRAS snap-in and make sure that the Remote Access Server option on the General page is enabled. Once this is done, your server can accept VPN connections.

Configuring VPN Ports   Just like enabling VPN on an RRAS server, configuring VPN is a pretty simple process. If you have enabled VPN on the server using one of the two methods just discussed, then you have a functional VPN server right off the bat. There are a few settings that you can customize, however.

VPN is primarily managed through the Ports container in the RRAS snap-in (it's under the server in the left-hand pane). When this container is selected, as shown in the following illustration, you'll see a number of objects in the right-hand pane named WAN Miniport. Each of these represents a virtual port, which supports either PPTP or L2TP. RRAS is configured by default to accept up to five connections of each type; these default connections are numbered 0–4. Thus, the complete name of a port might be WAN Miniport (L2TP)(VPN3-1).

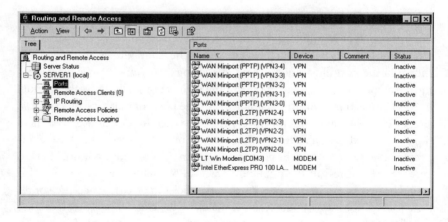

To the right of the device name, columns list the type of port (in this case, VPN) and the status of the port (active or inactive). You can also see a detailed status page for a port by right-clicking the port and choosing Status from the shortcut menu.

To configure settings for the ports on your system, right-click the Ports container itself and choose Properties from the shortcut menu. This opens the Ports Properties dialog box, shown here:

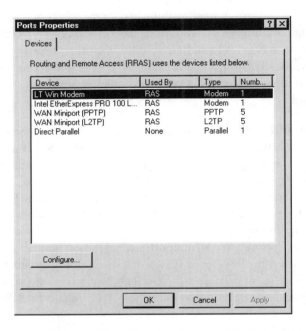

Notice that both port types (PPTP and L2TP) are listed and the number of ports of each type is indicated. To configure the properties for a port type, select it from the list and click Configure. This opens the Configure Device dialog box shown in the next illustration. Using this dialog box, you can specify whether the port type is allowed to accept incoming connections. Disabling the Remote Access Connections option essentially turns the ports of that type off. You can also specify whether or not the port type can be used for demand-dial connections. You need to disable this if you do not want your server to be able to connect to other servers using the port type. You can use the Phone Number field to enter the IP address of the public interface VPN clients use to connect. This would be necessary, for instance, if you had policies in place that accepted or rejected access according to the number dialed by the client. Finally, you can use this dialog box to indicate the number of ports you want available for the port type. By default, you get five of each type, but you can set the number of ports to anything in the range 0–1,000.

Configure Device - WAN Miniport (PPTP)   ? ✕

You can use this device for remote access requests or demand-dial connections.

☑ Remote access connections (inbound only)

☐ Demand-dial routing connections (inbound and outbound)

Phone number for this device:

You can set a maximum port limit for a device that supports multiple ports.

Maximum ports: 5

OK   Cancel

Objective 13.02 Troubleshoot Routing and Remote Access Policy

In earlier versions of Windows NT, remote access was granted to users on the basis of a single option configurable in User Manager or the Remote Access Admin tool. When this option, named Grant Dial-In Permission To User, was enabled for a user account, that user could dial into the remote access server. In Windows 2000, the granting of remote access privileges is more flexible and more complex. Each User object in the Users and Computers tool (or the Active Directory Users and Computers tool if a member of a domain) has certain dial-in properties.

Remote Access Policies (RAPs) are used to configure conditions under which users may connect using a specific remote access connection. These restrictions are based on criteria such as time of day, type of connection, and authentication.

While user accounts define settings for an individual user, remote access policies define settings for a whole group of users. A policy is made up of rules that the system evaluates when it is determining whether a connection is accepted or not. User accounts and policies work together to provide dial-in capability. A policy may be used to define the overall settings for users' connections, but individual settings in a user's account determine whether the user's access is controlled using RAP or not.

Remote access policies are managed through the Routing and Remote Access Service snap-in, where they are found in a container named Remote Access Policies, shown in the following illustration. As you can see in the illustration, only one policy is listed in the container by default: Allow Access If Dial-In Permission Is Enabled. This most basic of policies simply tells the RRAS service that if dial-in access is granted in a user's profile, it may grant that user remote access to the server.

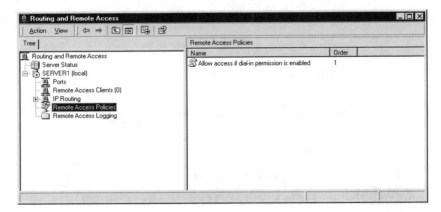

Creating a New Remote Access Policy

To create a new policy using the RRAS snap-in, right-click the Remote Access Policies container and select the New Remote Access Policy command from the shortcut menu. This launches the Add Remote Access Policy wizard.

The first step in the wizard is to name the policy. Once you've done this, you'll see a page that lists the conditions for the new policy. Initially, this page is blank, but each new condition you add updates the list, as shown here:

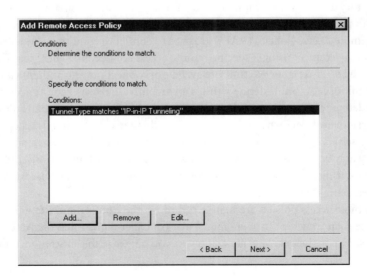

To add a new condition, click Add. This opens the Select Attribute dialog box, in which all available conditions are listed. These conditions are detailed in Table 13-2. Once you pick a condition from the list, a dialog box opens that lets you set configuration parameters that vary depending on the type of condition you choose. For example, choosing the Day-And-Time Restriction opens a dialog box that lets you pick dates and times to restrict access.

After choosing the conditions you want to apply in the new policy, the next step in creating a policy is to choose whether the policy you are creating grants or denies dial-in access.

The final step in the Add Remote Access Policy wizard allows you to modify the remote access profile attached to the policy. You can do this when you set the policy up or come back to it later if you want. Configuring remote access profiles is discussed a bit later in the chapter. Once you finish the wizard, the new remote access policy is created, you are returned to the RRAS snap-in, and the policy goes into effect.

TABLE 13.2	Remote Access Policy Attributes
Attribute Type	**Description**
Called-Station-ID	Phone number dialed by user
Calling-Station-ID	Caller's phone number
Client-Friendly-Name	The simple name of the client
Client-IP-Address	IP address of the RADIUS server attempting to validate connection (IAS only)
Client-Vendor	Manufacturer of RADIUS proxy or NAS (IAS only)
Day-And-Time Restriction	Time periods and days during which connection attempts are accepted or rejected
Framed-Protocol	Remote access protocol (PPP, SLIP, etc.) used for framing incoming packets
NAS-Identifier	The name of the NAS that accepted the original connection (IAS only)
NAS-IP-Address	The IP address of the NAS that accepted the original connection (IAS only)
NAS-Port-Type	The physical connection type (phone, ISDN, etc.) used by the caller
Service-Type	The type of service the user has requested. Types include framed for PPP or login for telnet
Tunnel-Type	The tunneling protocol that should be used (L2TP or PPTP)
Windows-Groups	Windows groups that the user belongs to

Policies are evaluated in the order that they appear in the Remote Access Policies container in the RRAS snap-in. You can rearrange this order by right-clicking any of the policies and using the Move Up and Move Down commands on the shortcut menu. This ordering is very important, as each condition of each policy is considered in order to determine whether a user can access the system or not. Once a policy is found where the conditions of the connection match the conditions of the policy, the policy is used and no further policies are evaluated.

Exam Tip	
When troubleshooting RRAS policy problems, remember that the order in which policies are applied is extremely important.	

Configuring Remote Access Profiles

Remote access profiles are an important part of a good remote access policy strategy. The first thing, of course, is not to confuse remote access profiles with user accounts. User accounts, which we covered previously, are the collection of settings that pertain to an individual user and are stored in Active Directory. Remote access profiles determine the remote access settings that are applied to users when they meet the conditions in a policy and are granted access. Each policy has one associated profile. You can open and edit the profile for a policy on the last page of the Add Remote Access Policy wizard or later using the property page for the policy. Either way, you'll click a button named Edit Profile to get in and use a host of settings across a number of tabs to implement the policy.

Implement and Troubleshoot Terminal Services for Remote Access

Objective 13.03

Terminal Services is a feature of Windows 2000 that lets a server host the operating system and applications used by clients. This allows the server to do the actual work of running the applications and processing data, while a low-end client computer is used simply to display the interface to a user. Another great advantage to using Terminal Services is that it enables you to remotely administer your servers from various locations, even over an Internet connection. The terminal emulation client can be run from most desktop operating systems under current hardware. Terminal Services can work especially well for Windows-based terminals (WBTs), which are true thin-client devices. Terminal Services can even run on many of the Windows-based handheld systems on the market.

Overview of Terminal Services

Terminal Services is based on a protocol named Remote Desktop Protocol (RDP), which provides the communications link over TCP/IP between the terminal client and the server. Input from the client (from keyboard or mouse strokes) is sent to the server through RDP and then the video is sent back from the server to the client. RDP is structured in such a way that even over modem connections, the terminal emulation will work. Terminal Services is capable of running in one of two modes: Remote Administrator mode or Application Server mode.

Remote Administration Mode

Administrators can remotely manage Windows 2000 Servers from anywhere on the network when Terminal Services is installed in Remote Administration mode. Administrator mode is a secure method of administering a network on minimal hardware, making the mode great for administering remote (long-distance) networks. When using the remote administration mode, only two administrators can connect remotely at a time. In addition, administrators must be members of the Administrators group to have remote access.

In Remote Administration mode, you can install software and handle basic administrative functions—even make changes within your Active Directory. Remote Administration mode does not require any additional licensing (see the discussion on licensing later in the chapter).

Exam Tip

A problem with remote administration can arise if more than one administrator attempts to manage a server at the same time. You can use the QUSER command-line utility to see if other administrators are currently connected to a server. QUSER works only if the server is running Terminal Services.

Application Server Mode

If Terminal Services is installed using the Application Server mode, the clients access the server to use the Windows 2000 desktop and Windows applications installed on the server. For example, you could use Terminal Services to allow users to connect to a custom corporate application from a remote location. Application Server mode can be implemented so that low-end clients can have access to the Windows 2000 desktop and applications installed on the Terminal Services server.

When using Application Server mode, you will need to be sure you are properly licensed, a topic that is covered a bit later in this chapter. For each user that connects to the server, a folder is created that allows the user to store information separately from other users. Users also have a profile within the Terminal Services session that maintains user settings such as background wallpaper. These options are configured using the Properties dialog box for a user's account.

Installing Terminal Services

Because of the system overhead of running Terminal Services, it is recommended that it be enabled on a Member server, and not a Domain Controller. For security, it also should be used on a system where the system and boot partitions are secured on an NTFS volume. To enable Terminal Services on a server running Windows 2000, use the following steps:

1. Log on as an administrator and click Start | Settings | Control Panel.

2. In the Control Panel window, double-click Add/Remove Programs.

3. In the Add/Remove Programs dialog box, click Add/Remove Windows Components.

4. From the list of components, select the Terminal Services check box and click Next.

5. Select whether you want to enable Terminal Services in Remote Administration mode or in Application Server mode and click Next.

6. If you select Remote Administration mode, the wizard begins copying files (if you chose to install clients) and then the wizard finishes. If you select application server mode, you will be asked whether you want to use Windows 2000 permissions or permissions that are compatible with version 4 of Terminal Services. Make your choice and click Next to finish the wizard.

Travel Advisory

Choosing the Windows 2000 permissions option when enabling Terminal Services is the better choice, as it is much more secure. Choosing the Terminal version 4 permissions option requires that all users be given unrestricted access to the Registry and file system locations on the Terminal Services server for compatibility.

Once you have installed Terminal Services, you can manage it using the Terminal Services Manager, a snap-in for MMC that is shown in Figure 13-5. You can use this snap-in to manage all of the Terminal Services servers on a network and to view users, servers, and running processes.

Terminal Services Licensing

Each client connecting to a Terminal Services server in Application mode needs to have a client access license; this is separate from the normal Windows 2000 licensing method. There are four components to Terminal Services licensing:

- **Microsoft Clearinghouse** This is a database maintained by Microsoft for the purposes of tracking, activating, and maintaining license servers. A license server receives the licenses it is allowed to grant from the Microsoft Clearinghouse.

- **Terminal Services Licensing server** This server is separate from the actual Terminal Services server. The licensing server is responsible for storing all the Terminal Services client licenses that have been issued to clients. A Terminal Services server must be able to connect to an activated license server before clients can be issued licenses.

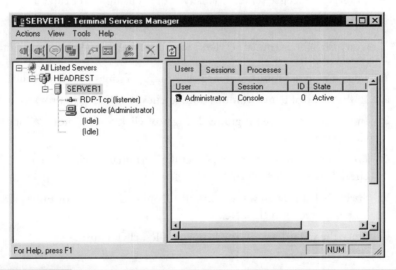

| FIGURE 13.5 | Use Terminal Services Manager to manage all aspects of Terminal Services. |

- **Terminal Services server** This is the server on which Terminal Services is running. When a client logs on to the Terminal Services server, the server validates the client license by checking with the Terminal Services Licensing server.

- **Client licenses** Each client computer that connects to a Terminal Services server must have a client license. The license is stored locally and presented to the Terminal Services server each time the client logs on.

If you are planning to install Terminal Services in Application mode, you must provide access to a Terminal Services Licensing server. This may mean installing one yourself. You do not have to run Terminal Services Licensing on the same server as Terminal Services; in fact, many people run Terminal Services Licensing on a Domain Controller.

There are two types of licensing server that you can install:

- **Domain License server** This is the default setting for a new license server. Its scope is a domain or a workgroup, which is appropriate if you want to keep a separate license server for each domain you maintain. If you install Terminal Services Licensing during Windows 2000 setup, you can select only this option.

- **Enterprise License server** This type of licensing server can serve terminal servers in any domain in a site.

You can install the Terminal Services Licensing using the following procedure:

1. Log on as an administrator and click Start | Settings | Control Panel.

2. In the Control Panel window, double-click Add/Remove Programs.

3. In the Add/Remove Programs dialog box, click Add/Remove Windows Components.

4. From the list of components, select the Terminal Services Licensing check box and click Next.

5. Specify whether you want to install a Domain Licensing or Enterprise License server and click Next.

6. Once the wizard has finished copying files, click Finish.

Once you have installed Terminal Services Licensing, you must enable the service within 90 days using the Licensing wizard available in the Terminal Services Licensing snap-in (available in the Administrative Tools folder).

Providing Client Access to Terminal Services

After the licenses are purchased, each client that connects to a Terminal Services server must have Terminal Services client software installed. Since Terminal Services is emulating the server's desktop, there is little load on the client; the server handles most of the processing. The client software used is normally provided on a floppy disk (or network share) or in the firmware of true thin clients.

The client software can be installed using installation disks or from a shared network folder:

- You can create installation disks using Start | Programs | Administrative Tools | Terminal Services Client Creator. The wizard displays options to create Terminal Services client software for 16-bit or 32-bit Windows. Follow the Setup wizard on the client computer to complete the installation.

- To install the client over the network, you could share the systemroot\system32\clients\tsclient folder on the Terminal Services server, though it would be a better solution just to copy the installation files to another folder and then share that. After a client is connected to the network share, run the setup.exe program and follow the wizard to complete the client software installation.

The client can be run on a range of desktop hardware, including

- Windows-based Terminal devices (embedded)
- Intel computers running Windows 95, Windows 98, Windows NT 3.51, and Windows NT 4.0; and Intel-based computers running Windows 2000
- Computers running Windows 3.1 or Windows for Workgroups 3.11
- Handheld devices using Windows CE

Exam Tip

It's important to know which clients are supported and which ones require licensing. If an unsupported client, such as a Macintosh system, were used in your organization, you would need third-party software (Citrix, for instance) to handle terminal service support. You would also need to have the proper Citrix extensions installed on the Terminal Services server.

A Terminal Services client computer also must have TCP/IP and the Terminal Services client software installed. The client software can be installed using installation disks or from a shared network folder.

Connecting to a Terminal Services Server

After a user has the correct permissions to log on and the client software is loaded, a user can start the Terminal Services client. The client connection screen is shown in Figure 13-6. Notice in the figure that the user then connects to the server by selecting it, choosing the area of the terminal emulation screen, and then clicking Connect. After the user has authenticated, the terminal emulation session begins.

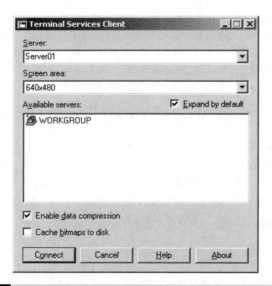

FIGURE 13.6   Connecting to a Terminal Services server

CHECKPOINT

✔**Objective 13.01: Configure and Troubleshoot Remote Access and Virtual Private Network (VPN) Connections** This objective provided an overview of the remote access capabilities in Windows 2000 and then looked at how to install and configure the Routing and Remote Access Service. You learned to configure RRAS at the server level and to enable specific user accounts with remote access. You also learned how virtual private networking works and how to enable it on an RRAS server.

✔**Objective 13.02: Troubleshoot Routing and Remote Access Policy** This objective examined the policies available for controlling remote access. You learned how to view and create policies and how to create a remote access profile.

✔**Objective 13.03: Implement and Troubleshoot Terminal Services for Remote Access** This objective provided a basic overview of Terminal Services and showed how it is installed and implemented on a Windows 2000 network.

REVIEW QUESTIONS

1. You want to ensure that all user authentication information passed between remote clients and an RRAS server is encrypted. Which of the following authentication methods should you disable?

   A. PAP

   B. CHAP

   C. SPAP

   D. MS-CHAP

2. Which of the following methods can you use to grant users dial-in access?

   A. Create a remote access policy that allows access to the desired users.

   B. Add the users to the Dial-In Users group.

   C. Modify the group policy for the users' container.

   D. Grant access to the users on their user accounts.

3. You need to set up RRAS callbacks for a single group of users who work from home. You could do this by going to the Dial-in tab of each user's profile and enabling callbacks, but what would be a better way?

> **A.** Create a Windows 2000 security group and then configure a remote access policy for these users.
>
> **B.** Create a Windows 2000 security group and then configure a remote access profile for this group.
>
> **C.** Move the users to a server that has callbacks enabled for all users.
>
> **D.** Enable callbacks for all users on the current server.

4. Several of your users who work at home have access to inexpensive ISDN lines and would like to combine multiple ISDN lines so that they can have a broadband connection to the RRAS server. What must you do to allow this?

> **A.** Enable the Multilink Connections option on the PPP tab of the server's Properties dialog box.
>
> **B.** Enable the Link Control Protocol (LCP) extensions option on the PPP tab of the server's Properties dialog box.
>
> **C.** Configure a remote access policy that allows users to dial into the RRAS server more than once.
>
> **D.** Configure a remote access policy that enables the Multilink Connections option for those users.

5. You would like to administer a server through a Terminal Services session. You enable Terminal Services on the server. Which operation mode should you choose?

> **A.** Application mode
>
> **B.** Remote Administration mode
>
> **C.** Licensing mode
>
> **D.** Remote Control mode

6. Which of the following directories is the default location for the RRAS authentication and accounting logs?

> **A.** %systemroot%\System32\RRAS
>
> **B.** %systemroot%\System32\LogFiles
>
> **C.** %systemroot%\System32\RRASLogs
>
> **D.** %systemroot%\System32\RRASEvents

7. You are configuring clients for use with PPTP. The client computers are running the following operating systems. Which of these do *not* include built-in support for use as a VPN client?

> **A.** Windows 95
>
> **B.** Windows 98

    C. Windows 98 Second Edition

    D. Windows NT 4.0

8. You have an Active Directory domain named "braincore.net" with five Domain Controllers and ten Member servers. You install Terminal Services on one of the Member servers in Application mode. Where should you install the Licensing server and using which configuration?

    A. On a Domain Controller using the Domain License Server option

    B. On a Domain Controller using the Enterprise License Server option

    C. On a Member server using the Domain License Server option

    D. On a Member server using the Enterprise License Server option

9. You use a number of remote access policies to govern remote access practices. You have just created a new remote access policy that restricts the time of day that connections can be made to your RRAS server. However, the policy does not seem to work. What is the first thing you should suspect?

    A. The policy has not yet been replicated throughout the domain.

    B. The policy does not have a high enough priority. Other policies that are processed before the new policy are being used first.

    C. The policy is too high on the list.

    D. The policy is not linked to a proper remote access profile.

10. You are deciding on a tunneling protocol for use on the VPN you are planning. You want the protocol to support both authentication and encryption for connections. Which protocol would you choose?

    A. PPP

    B. PPTP

    C. L2TP

    D. EAP

REVIEW ANSWERS

1. **A** The PAP authentication protocol transmits authentication information in clear text, meaning it is unencrypted. SPAP, CHAP, and MS-CHAP all use a system to encrypt authentication information.

2. **A D** You can grant a user dial-in access by going to the Dial-In tab of a user's account and giving the user permission to dial in. A more efficient way to provide access to users in a native-mode domain is to create a remote access policy.

3. **A** Remote access policies allow you to create rules governing specific groups.

4. **A** The Multilink Connections option must be enabled for the RRAS server. This option is enabled by default, but you must make sure it is turned on to allow aggregate connections. In order to provide the best control, you should also configure a remote access policy that provides permission to use multilink to the appropriate users, but this step is not mandatory.

5. **B** Administrators can remotely manage Windows 2000 Servers from anywhere on the network when Terminal Services is installed in Remote Administration mode. Remote Administration mode does not require any additional licensing.

6. **B** The default location for authentication and accounting logs is %systemroot%\System32\LogFiles.

7. **A** Windows 98, 98 Second Edition, Me, NT 4.0, 2000, and XP all include built-in support for use as VPN clients. Windows 95 does not, but there is an add-on product available.

8. **A** When you install Terminal Services in Application mode, you should also install the Terminal Services Licensing on a domain controller (which may or may not be your TS server). The scope of an Enterprise License server is an entire Windows 2000 Active Directory site. The Domain License server is the default setting for a license server. Its scope is a domain (non-AD) or a workgroup.

9. **B** Policies are evaluated in order. If another policy matches the conditions of the connection before the time-of-day policy, the other policy will be used before the time-of-day policy has the chance to deny the connection.

10. **C** Of the protocols listed, only Point-to-Point Tunneling Protocol (PPTP) and Layer 2 Tunneling Protocol (L2TP) are actually tunneling protocols. L2TP supports both authentication and two levels of encryption for connections (IPSec and a higher level of encryption); PPTP supports authentication and only one higher level of encryption, but not IPSec. In addition, L2TP is always used with IPSec, a mode of encryption that is more secure than that used by PPTP, and Microsoft Point-to-Point Encryption (MPPE).

Configuring Network Address Translation and Internet Connection Sharing

Objective 14.01 Configure and Troubleshoot Network Address Translation (NAT) and Internet Connection Sharing

Network Address Translation (NAT) is a protocol that provides a way for multiple computers on a network to share a single connection to the Internet. NAT works by altering the information in the headers of IP packets as they pass through the server, translating between the private IP addresses of the local network and a public IP address on the Internet. In Windows 2000, the NAT protocol comes in two variations. The full implementation of NAT is available on computers running any edition of Windows 2000 Server. A simplified version of the protocol, named Internet Connection Sharing (ICS), is available on Windows 2000 Professional and Server editions. ICS is easier to set up and manage than the full implementation of NAT, but it is less configurable.

This chapter begins with an overview of address translation and the differences between ICS and NAT. From there, the chapter moves into the actual configuration and management of both these services.

> **Travel Advisory**
>
> Since NAT is designed to translate IP addresses and route TCP/IP traffic, this chapter talks about a number of TCP/IP concepts and features, as well as features of Windows 2000 Routing and Remote Access. For this reason, it's best if you have already studied Chapters 3–6 and Chapter 13 before tackling this chapter.

Overview of NAT and ICS

Traditionally, a home computer is configured to use a dial-up connection (like a modem or ISDN adapter) or a persistent connection (like a DSL line or cable modem) to connect to an Internet service provider. If you have more than one computer, say on a small home or office network, you are forced to configure a separate connection for each system or purchase a third-party proxy program to allow those computers to share access.

With the advent of Windows 98 Second Edition, Microsoft began incorporating a simplified version of the Network Address Translation (NAT) protocol into the operating system so that no third-party software was required to share

Internet connections. They named the service Internet Connection Sharing (ICS). Windows Millennium, Windows 2000, and Windows XP also support ICS. In addition, the various editions of Windows 2000 Server support the full version of NAT, which offers a good deal more flexibility than ICS and is designed for use on small and large networks.

Throughout this overview, we are going to talk about the NAT protocol in its full implementation, and basically treat ICS and NAT as though they were the same. Following the overview, we'll talk about the actual differences between the NAT protocol and ICS.

Exam Tip

Microsoft regards Small Office/Home Office (SOHO) networks to be the main beneficiaries of ICS and NAT. Though SOHO networks vary a great deal in configuration, Microsoft normally considers a SOHO network to have one network segment, use peer-to-peer networking, and support TCP/IP. For larger networks, Microsoft generally recommends a separate product, such as Microsoft Internet Security and Acceleration Server, to provide address translation services.

Benefits of Address Sharing

So, why share addresses in the first place? Address sharing really provides four benefits:

- **Security**   Since translation is used instead of routing, there is an inherent security benefit provided by using address translation. Hosts on the Internet see only the public IP address of the external interface on the computer that provides address translation—not the private IP addresses on the internal network.

- **Cost**   Another big reason to share addresses is that it's cheaper to configure one computer with a high-speed Internet connection than to provide a connection to every computer on your network.

- **Simplicity**   It is easier to set up one Internet connection (especially with some of the more complicated connection options out there today) and then share that connection than it is to configure a connection for every computer.

- **IP address availability**   For the most part, it is impossible to get a range of public IP addresses large enough to run a network these days. NAT solves this problem by requiring only one public IP address for the NAT computer (though you can use more than one). The local network uses IP addresses in a private range. See Chapter 3 for a complete discussion of private and public IP addressing.

How NAT Works

A NAT server is basically an IP router that translates the IP addresses and TCP/UDP port numbers of packets as those packets are being forwarded between the public and private interfaces of the NAT server. Throughout this section, we will examine the actual NAT process in more detail.

Static and Dynamic Address Mapping   When NAT receives a packet from a private IP address and translates that packet to look as though it comes from the NAT server's public IP address, this process is called *mapping*. Two forms of mapping are available in NAT:

- **Dynamic mappings**   Dynamic mappings are created when users on the private network initiate traffic with a public Internet location. The NAT service automatically translates the IP address and source ports, and adds these mappings to its mapping table. The NAT server refreshes these mappings each time they are used. Dynamic mappings that are not refreshed are removed from the NAT mapping table after a certain amount of time. For TCP connections, the default time is 24 hours. For UDP connections, the default time is one minute. An example of a dynamic mapping would be when a user tries to connect to an Internet Web site using a Web browser.

- **Static mappings**   You can define in advance how certain addresses and ports should be mapped instead of letting it happen automatically. Although you can create static mappings for outbound traffic, the most common reason to use a static mapping is if you want to host some form of Internet service (a Web server, an FTP server, and so on) on a computer on the private network (behind the NAT server) that is accessible from the Internet. In order for hosts on the Internet to reach that server, a static mapping must be defined so that the NAT server knows where to route the incoming requests. You cannot host any Internet services on your private network using dynamic mapping.

NAT Editors   In order for NAT to directly translate packets between a private network and a public one, two things must be true of those packets. The packets must have an IP address in the IP header, and they must have either a TCP or UDP port number in the header. While this works fine for the majority of protocols and applications that send IP traffic (since many of them use TCP or UDP), some do not fulfill these requirements and could not be translated by NAT without a little help.

This help comes in the form of a NAT editor, an installable component that modifies packets so that they can be translated by NAT. Windows 2000 includes built-in NAT editors for the following protocols:

- File Transfer Protocol (FTP)
- Internet Message Control Protocol (ICMP)
- Point-to-Point Tunneling Protocol (PPTP)
- NetBIOS over TCP/IP (NetBT)

In addition to the built-in NAT editors, the NAT protocol in Windows 2000 includes proxy software for the following protocols:

- H.323, a protocol for voice and data transmission
- Direct Play, a protocol used in multiplayer gaming
- LDAP-based Internet Locator Service (ILS) registration, a protocol used by NetMeeting
- Remote Procedure Call (RPC)

Currently, the NAT protocol does not support either the Kerberos authentication method used in Windows 2000 or the IPSec protocol used to encrypt data communications.

Exam Tip

It is important that you know the protocols that NAT can translate directly, those that require an editor or proxy, and those that NAT does not support.

DHCP Allocator   Both NAT and ICS can automatically assign IP addresses to computers on the private network using a Dynamic Host Configuration Protocol (DHCP) *allocator,* a simplified version of a DHCP server (DHCP is covered in detail in Chapter 4). This works well on small networks, since most clients are set up to receive IP addresses automatically by default.

When a client starts up, it broadcasts a message looking for DHCP allocation, and the NAT server assigns it an IP address and subnet mask on the same subnet using a private addressing range. In addition, the NAT server configures the default gateway and DNS server for clients to be the IP address of the NAT server. Note that there is no WINS server allocation.

As you will learn later in the chapter, the DHCP allocator in ICS is enabled by default and cannot be disabled. Although you can assign static addresses to the other computers on the network if you want, the ICS server will always respond to DHCP requests. When using NAT on a Windows 2000 server, you can disable the DHCP allocator and either assign static addresses from the NAT server or let another DHCP server on the network handle requests.

Exam Tip

Remember that an ICS server always responds to DHCP requests, causing potential problems if you already have DHCP services set up on your network. If you plan to use NAT on a network using DHCP, you should use the full NAT implementation.

Host Name Resolution   When using the DHCP allocator, clients are configured to use the NAT server as their primary DNS server. This allows both local and remote host names to be resolved. DNS proxying is used to resolve remote host names on the Internet. In this process, a client submits a name resolution request to the NAT server. The NAT server then queries the DNS server specified in its own configuration for the resolution. Once it receives a response, it forwards that response to the originating client.

Differences Between NAT and ICS

Since both ICS and NAT use the same protocol to translate addresses, this overview has treated the two services as though they were basically identical. However, each of these services implements the NAT protocol in different ways:

- ICS is available on Windows 98 Second Edition, Me, 2000, and XP. NAT is available only on Windows 2000 Server editions.

- ICS is configured in Windows 2000 by selecting a single option on the Sharing page of a network adapter. Installing and managing NAT requires that you use the Routing and Remote Access snap-in, but many more configuration options are available for it.

- ICS allows only one public IP address. NAT can expose any number of public addresses.

- ICS can link only one private network to a public network. NAT can link many private networks that are directly connected to the NAT server.

- ICS does not allow you to disable the DHCP allocator or the DNS proxy. NAT does. This means that ICS should not be used on a network already using a DHCP server or DHCP relay agent.

Installing and Configuring Internet Connection Sharing

Installing and configuring ICS is actually one of the simplest things you'll do in Windows. As you learned previously, though, this ease comes at the cost of a good deal of flexibility. ICS is primarily for users who have a small home or office network on a single network segment and who have a single Internet connection to share. In addition, unless you are running a Windows 2000 server with an Internet connection, ICS is your only choice.

Installing ICS

There are only a couple of requirements that you must meet before enabling ICS. First, you must make sure that the computer on which you are going to enable it (we'll call it the ICS computer from now on) actually has a functioning Internet connection, whether that connection is a 56K modem, a cable modem, or whatever other type. Second, you must make sure that you have a network adapter installed in the ICS computer, that it is configured and functioning properly, and that it is connected properly to the other computers on the network.

Once these requirements are met, you can install ICS by opening the Properties dialog box for the Internet connection (you can find it in the Network and Dial-Up Connections container in the Control Panel). Switch to the Sharing tab, shown in Figure 14-1, and select the Enable Internet Connection Sharing For This Connection option. If you want the connection to be automatically started whenever other computers need to connect to the Internet (and you probably do), also select the Enable On-Demand Dialing option.

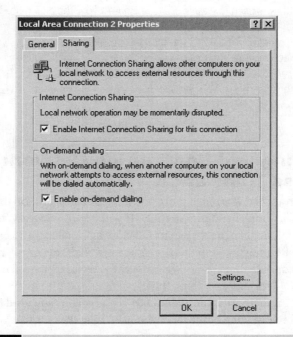

FIGURE 14.1   Enabling ICS is as easy as clicking a single check box.

When ICS is enabled, several changes take place on the computer, including these:

- The network adapter in the ICS computer is assigned the IP address 192.168.0.1 and the subnet mask 255.255.255.0.
- The ICS service is started and is configured to start automatically each time the computer starts. You can change this behavior, as well as stop and start the service manually, using the Services Control Panel.
- The DHCP allocator service is started and configured to start automatically with Windows. The allocator dynamically assigns IP addresses to other clients on the network using the IP address range 192.168.0.2 through 192.168.0.254 and the subnet mask 255.255.255.0.

Once the ICS computer is configured, all you have to do is ensure that all other computers on the network are configured to obtain IP addresses automatically, and everything should work just fine.

Travel Advisory

You can do a little tweaking of the ICS service by clicking the Settings button on the same tab you used to enable ICS (see Figure 14-1). The dialog box that opens has two tabs. The Applications tab is used to create static outbound mappings, which are predefined routes for Internet services you want users to be able to access. The Services tab is used to create static inbound mappings, which allow you to host resources on the private network (such as FTP or Web servers) that users on the Internet can access.

Installing and Configuring Network Address Translation

The NAT protocol offers much more potential for configuration than you have just seen in its implementation by ICS. If you are running a Windows 2000 server, you can implement NAT in its full glory by installing it as a routing protocol in the Routing and Remote Access snap-in. This, of course, requires that the Routing and Remote Access Server (RRAS) service is enabled on the server. See Chapter 13 for more on using RRAS.

As with ICS, there are some preliminary requirements you need to make sure are met before installing NAT. First, you need to make sure that your Internet connection (or connections, since NAT supports multiple public interfaces) is working. Next, you need to make sure that any adapters connected to internal networks are configured properly.

Installing the NAT Service

Once the preliminary requirements are taken care of, it's time to install NAT. If you have not already configured RRAS for remote access or routing, you can use a simple wizard to guide you through the process of setting up RRAS with NAT enabled and configured for Internet sharing. To do this, use the following procedure:

1. Log on to the server as an administrator and click Start | Programs | Administrative Tools | Routing and Remote Access.

2. Right-click the server on which you want to install NAT, and select Configure And Enable Routing And Remote Access from the shortcut menu.

3. Click Next to skip the opening page of the Routing and Remote Access Server Setup wizard.

4. From the list of Common Configurations, select the Internet Connection Server option and click Next.

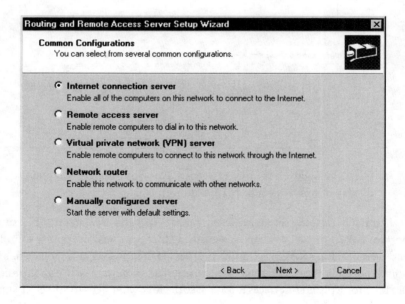

5. The next page asks whether you want to set up ICS or NAT. If you select ICS, a dialog box pops up that tells you to use the Network and Dial-Up Connections folder to configure ICS, the procedure for which we covered previously. Select the NAT option and click Next.

6. The next page in the wizard asks you to choose the Internet connection that you want to share. You can choose a connection from the list (you can always set up additional connections later), or you can create a new demand-dial connection. If you choose an existing connection (as we will in this procedure), just pick one from the list and click Next. If you choose to create a demand-dial connection, the Demand Dial Interface wizard opens and allows you to configure the interface before proceeding.

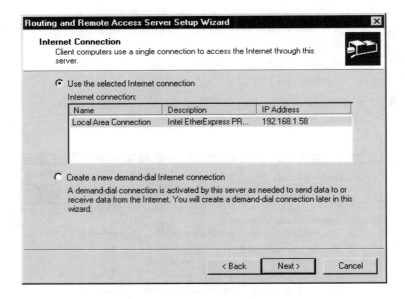

7. Next, the wizard sets up NAT according to your preferences and then displays a summary screen. Click Finish.

If you have already set up and configured RRAS and now want to add support for NAT, you will do so by first ensuring that your server supports routing and then installing NAT as a routing protocol in the RRAS snap-in. Once this is done, you'll add the NAT protocol to the interfaces you want to use and configure the protocol and interfaces for use. Use the following steps to add NAT support to an existing RRAS server:

1. Log on to the server as an administrator and choose Start | Programs | Administrative Tools | Routing And Remote Access.

2. Find the server you want to configure, right-click it, and choose Properties from the shortcut menu.

3. On the General tab, make sure the Router option is selected. Also, select whether the router should handle LAN routing only or both LAN and demand-dial routing. Click OK when you are done.

4. Next, expand the container for the server in the left-hand pane.

5. Inside the IP Routing container for the server, right-click the General container and select Properties from the shortcut menu.

6. In the New Routing Protocol dialog that opens, select the Network Address Translation item from the list of routing protocols and click OK.

7. The IP Routing container should now contain a new object named Network Address Translation.

Configuring NAT Interfaces

Before you can use NAT on your network, you must make sure that a NAT interface is configured for any network interfaces the server has on your local network and any public interfaces on the Internet. It is best to follow one simple rule when setting up your interfaces, though. Create the interfaces for the local network first and the public network second.

Adding an interface is a straightforward procedure that simply involves right-clicking the Network Address Translation container in RRAS, choosing a New Interface command, and then selecting the appropriate network adapter to create the interface for.

Right after you create the interface, a Properties dialog box for the interface opens so that you can provide further configuration. You can also open these pages later by right-clicking the interface object (shown in Figure 14-2) and choosing Properties from the shortcut menu.

There are three tabs for a public NAT interface: General, Address Pool, and Special Ports. Each of these is discussed in the next few sections. For a private NAT interface, only the General page is available and is identical to the same page for the public interface.

Configuring General Properties   The General tab lets you choose the type of interface. You have two choices. The first is to create an interface connected to the private network. The second choice is to create an interface connected to the public network. The Translate TCP/UDP headers option controls whether the

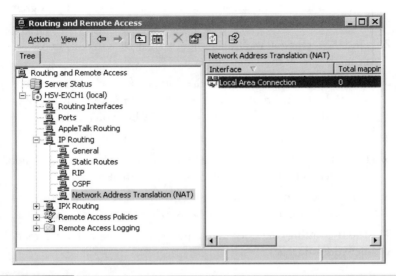

FIGURE 14.2   Configuring a NAT interface in the RRAS snap-in

built-in NAT editors (discussed earlier in the chapter) are functional. This should always be turned on if you want computers on the private network to communicate with the outside world.

Configuring Address Pool Properties   The Address Pool tab, shown in Figure 14-3, is used to control the public IP addresses associated with the interface. The window lists any ranges of addresses you have specified. To create a new range, click Add and supply the starting and ending IP addresses and the subnet mask for the range. To specify a single IP address, just enter it as the starting address and leave the ending address out.

The Reservations button lets you reserve individual IP addresses from the public range and add static mappings in the NAT table that point to particular hosts on your private network. In other words, this gives you a way to let a specific computer on your private network have a static IP address that is exposed to the public interface. This allows you to, for example, create a Web server and register a domain name for that Web server using the public IP address.

Configuring Special Ports Properties   The Special Ports tab provides another way to edit the NAT mapping table: it allows you to specify which ports inbound traffic should be mapped to. For example, you could set up a public NAT interface so that all incoming traffic on port 110 (the POP3 common port) is routed to a specific port number on a specific host on the private network—a

FIGURE 14.3   Configuring Address Pool properties for a NAT interface

POP3 server, most likely. For each protocol listed in the Protocol drop-down menu, you can specify any number of public port numbers that you want channeled to special private hosts. Just select the protocol and then use the Add button to open the Edit Special Port dialog.

Configuring NAT Properties

In addition to setting up and configuring the individual NAT interfaces, you can set a number of global parameters for the NAT protocol itself. You can access these parameters by right-clicking the Network Address Translation container in the RRAS snap-in and choosing Properties from the shortcut menu. There are four tabs on the Properties dialog box for the NAT protocol:

- **General**   Used to configure the level of event logging that the NAT protocol sends to the Windows 2000 system event log. The default is to log only errors, but higher levels of logging may be useful in troubleshooting problems with the protocol.

- **Translation**   Lets you set the lifetime for both TCP and UDP mappings in the NAT table. The default behavior is to keep TCP entries for 24 hours and to keep UDP entries for one minute—and for most applications, these defaults should work just fine. The Applications button opens a separate dialog that lets you add, remove, and edit application mappings. This dialog works the same as the Applications page described for editing ICS properties earlier in the chapter.

- **Address Assignment**   Controls whether the DHCP allocator should be used or not. If the option is enabled, you can specify the range of addresses the allocator can assign by entering a starting IP address and a subnet mask. By default, the same range used by ICS is used: 192.168.0.1 through 192.168.0.254. Use the Exclude button to specify IP addresses within the range that should not be assigned by the allocator.

Exam Tip

If you do not have some other form of DHCP service on your network and you do not select the option on the Address Assignment page for the NAT protocol, NAT will not work unless you configure static addresses for all computers that use the NAT service. This is something to look out for on the certification exam and in the real world.

- **Name Resolution**   Controls whether the NAT server should resolve DNS names to IP addresses for connecting clients. When the Clients Using Domain Name System (DNS) option is enabled, the name resolution component of NAT is active and the NAT server is specified as the default DNS server for clients on the private network via the DHCP allocator. When the option is disabled, another DNS solution needs to be present on the network. The other option on this tab, Connect To The Public Network When A Name Needs To Be Resolved, specifies whether a demand-dial interface should be invoked just for resolving a DNS name.

CHECKPOINT

✔**Objective 14.01: Configure and Troubleshoot Network Address Translation (NAT) and Internet Connection Sharing**   This objective looked at the two forms of NAT available in Windows 2000: ICS and NAT. Both provide translation between a private IP network and the Internet. Internet Connection Sharing (ICS) is available on several versions of Windows; NAT is available only on Windows 2000 Server editions. This objective provided details on installing and configuring both services under Windows 2000.

REVIEW QUESTIONS

1. Which of the following protocols will not work over a NAT connection?

   A. TCP/IP

   B. IPSec

   C. FTP

   D. PPTP

2. You have configured NAT on one of your Windows 2000 servers so that all the clients on your network can share an Internet connection. One of the servers on your network is a Web server that hosts a private Web site. You have configured the Web server to use the TCP port 3356 instead of the default TCP port 80. You need to configure your NAT server to direct all incoming requests on that TCP port to the Web server computer. How would you do this?

   A. By modifying the special port value in the Properties dialog box for the public NAT interface

   B. By modifying the special port value in the Properties dialog box for the private NAT interface configured for the subnet the Web server is attached to

   C. By creating a static mapping using the NAT Properties dialog box

   D. By creating a dynamic mapping using the NAT Properties dialog box

3. Which of the following does *not* happen when you install ICS?

   A. The local network adapter's IP address is set to 192.168.0.1.

   B. The DHCP allocator is enabled.

   C. The local network adapter's subnet mask is set to 255.255.0.0.

   D. The ICS service is configured to start automatically when Windows starts.

4. What is the Translation tab of the Properties dialog box for the NAT protocol used for?

   A. To create application-specific port mappings

   B. To specify which NAT editor should be used

   C. To create port mappings for individual hosts

   D. To specify which port filters should be applied

5. You have a small network with two network segments and want to keep different subnet addresses for them. How would you do this?

   A. Add NAT interfaces for both networks.

   B. Disable the DHCP allocator.

   C. Define two static address pools with the subnets you want to use.

   D. Manually assign IP addresses to the server's internal interfaces.

6. What is the default lifetime of a TCP connection entry in a NAT mapping table?

   A. 1 minute

   B. 1 hour

   C. 1 day

   D. 1 week

7. For which of the following protocols does Windows 2000 include a built-in NAT editor?

   A. FTP

   B. ICMP

   C. IPSec

   D. PPTP

   E. Direct Play

8. Which of the following statements is true?

   A. You can create static outbound mappings with ICS.

   B. You can create static inbound mappings with ICS.

   C. ICS supports multiple private networks, but only one public interface.

   D. ICS supports multiple public interfaces, but only one private network.

9. If you are using a modem rather than a dedicated Internet connection on your ICS server, which of the following options should you enable?

   A. ICS automatic dialing

   B. On-Demand Dialing

   C. Automatic dialing

   D. Dynamic linking

10. Which of the following IP addresses was likely assigned by an ICS server?

    A. 10.35.202.1

    B. 169.254.0.54

    C. 192.168.0.36

    D. 192.168.1.62

REVIEW ANSWERS

1. **B**   Currently, the NAT protocol does not support either the Kerberos authentication method used in Windows 2000 or the IPSec protocol used to encrypt data communications.

2. **A**   The Special Ports tab of a NAT interface's Properties dialog box provides a special way to edit the NAT mapping table; it allows you to specify which ports inbound traffic should be mapped to.

3. **C**   Since the IP address 192.168.0.1 (a class C IP address) is used for the network adapter in the ICS computer, a subnet mask of 255.255.255.0 is configured, *not* 255.255.0.0.

4. **A**   The Translations tab of the NAT Properties dialog box lets you add, remove, and edit application mappings. It also lets you set the lifetime for both TCP and UDP mappings in the NAT table. The default behavior is to keep TCP entries for 24 hours and to keep UDP entries for one minute—and for most applications, these defaults should work just fine.

5. **A**   You must make sure that a NAT interface is configured for any network interfaces the server has on your local network and any public interfaces on the Internet. And remember, you should always configure the interfaces for the private network first.

6. **C**   Dynamic mappings that are not refreshed are removed from the NAT mapping table after a certain amount of time. For TCP connections, the default time is 24 hours. For UDP connections, the default time is one minute.

7. **A** **B** **D**   NAT translates TCP and UDP traffic directly. Windows 2000 includes NAT editors that allow for the translation of FTP, ICMP, PPTP, and NetBT. C is wrong because IPSec translation is unavailable. E is wrong because Direct Play translation requires a separate proxy and not a NAT editor.

8. **A** **B**   ICS enables you to create static inbound and outbound mappings. However, ICS allows only one public interface and only one private interface. To use multiple public or private interfaces, you must use the full implementation of NAT.

9. **B**   The On-Demand Dialing option allows the ICS server to initiate an Internet connection whenever another computer on the local network makes an Internet request. You can enable this option on the Sharing tab of the Properties dialog box of the Internet connection on the ICS server.

10. **C**   When ICS is installed, the ICS server is given the IP address 192.168.0.1 and is configured to allocate IP addresses using DHCP. Clients are given IP addresses ranging from 192.168.0.2 through 192.168.0.254. A and D are incorrect because, although these addresses fall within private address ranges (see Chapter 3), they are not used by ICS. B is wrong because this is an address assigned by Windows 2000's Automatic IP Addressing feature, in which a computer assigns itself an address if no DHCP server can be located. See Chapter 3 for more on this, as well.

Appendixes

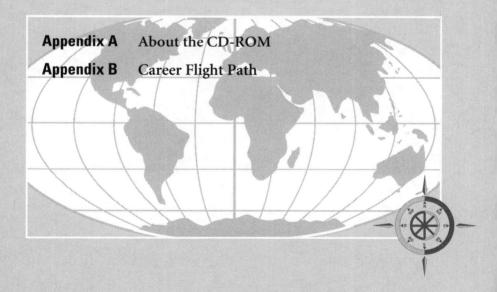

About the CD-ROM

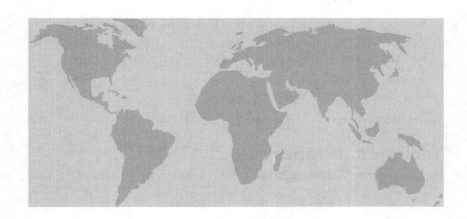

Mike Meyers' Certification Passport CD-ROM Instructions

To install the Passport Practice Exam software, perform these steps:

1. Insert the CD-ROM into your CD-ROM drive. An auto-run program will initiate, and a dialog box will appear indicating that you are installing the Passport setup program. If the auto-run program does not launch on your system, select Run from the Start menu and type **d:\setup.exe** (where d is the "name" of your CD-ROM drive).

2. Follow the installation wizard's instructions to complete the installation of the software.

   You can start the program by going to your desktop and double-clicking the Passport Exam Review icon or by going to Start | Program Files | Passport | MCSA.

System Requirements

- Operating systems supported: Windows 98, Windows NT 4.0, Windows 2000, and Windows Me
- CPU: 400 MHz or faster recommended
- Memory: 64MB of RAM
- CD-ROM: 4X or greater
- Internet connection: Required for optional exam upgrade

Technical Support

For basic Passport CD-ROM technical support, contact Hudson Technical Support:

- Phone: 800-217-0059
- E-mail: mcgraw-hill@hudsonsoft.com

For content/subject matter questions concerning the book or the CD-ROM, contact MH Customer Service:

- Phone: 800-722-4726
- E-mail: customer.service@mcgraw-hill.com

For inquiries about the available upgrade, CD-ROM, or online technology, or for in-depth technical support, contact ExamWeb Technical Support:

- Phone: 949-566-9375
- E-mail: support@examweb.com

Career Flight Path

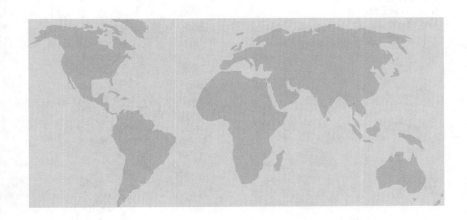

The Microsoft Certified Systems Administrator (MCSA) certification is a relatively new certification that focuses on the real-world skills you will encounter as an administrator of a Windows 2000 network. Exam 70-218, Managing a Windows 2000 Network Environment, is the exam for which you hold the passport in your hands right now.

In total, passing four certification exams is required to obtain an MCSA—three core exams and one elective exam.

Core Exams

There are three core types of exam that every MCSA candidate must pass. These include one server operating system exam, one client operating system exam, and one networking exam. These core tests are presented in Table B-1.

TABLE B.1	Core Exams for the MCSA Certification	
Exam Type (Pass One Exam of Each Type)	**Exam Number**	**Exam Title**
Client Operating System	70-210	Installing, Configuring, and Administering Microsoft Windows 2000 Professional
	70-270	Installing, Configuring, and Administering Microsoft Windows XP Professional
Server Operating System	70-215	Installing, Configuring, and Administering Microsoft Windows 2000 Server
	70-275	Installing, Configuring and Administering Microsoft Windows .NET Server (available sometime in 2002 or 2003)
Networking	70-218	Managing a Microsoft Windows 2000 Network Environment
	70-278	Managing a Microsoft Windows .NET Server Network Environment (available sometime in 2002 or 2003)

Travel Advisory

If you have taken exam 70-240, Microsoft Windows 2000 Accelerated Exam for MCPs Certified on Microsoft Windows NT 4.0, you are already considered to have fulfilled both the 70-210 (Windows 2000 Professional) and the 70-215 (Windows 2000 Server) exams. Unfortunately, this exam is no longer offered, so this is only good for you if you've already taken it.

Elective Exams

In addition to passing three core exams, you will have to pass one elective exam to become an MCSA. Suitable elective exams include

- 70-028: Administering Microsoft SQL Server 7.0

- 70-081: Implementing and Supporting Microsoft Exchange Server 5.5

- 70-086: Implementing and Supporting Microsoft Systems Management Server 2.0

- 70-088: Implementing and Supporting Microsoft Proxy Server 2.0

- 70-216: Implementing and Administering a Microsoft Windows 2000 Network Infrastructure

- 70-224: Installing, Configuring, and Administering Microsoft Exchange 2000 Server

- 70-227: Installing, Configuring, and Administering Microsoft Internet Security and Acceleration (ISA) Server 2000, Enterprise Edition

- 20-228: Installing, Configuring, and Administering Microsoft SQL Server 2000 Enterprise Edition

- 70-244: Supporting and Maintaining a Microsoft Windows NT Server 4.0 Network

- Two CompTIA Exams: You must pass the CompTIA A+ and one additional CompTIA exam. The additional exam can be either the CompTIA Network+ or the CompTIA Server+.

Choosing Your Path

Since there are so many exams available that can provide you with an MCSA, you will want to plan your exams carefully. And don't think about getting just this certification; think about other certifications that may help you out and plan them all together. Consider the following tips when planning your MCSA:

- List any exams you have already taken. Even some of the older exams still count as electives.

- Consider products you use regularly. There is no requirement that you make all of your core exams focus on Windows 2000 or on Windows .NET. You can mix and match versions to suit your needs.

- If you have no plans for future certification and want the shortest possible route, take the three core exams and pick the one elective with which you have the most experience.

- If you are willing to do some extra work for two certifications instead of one, consider taking the CompTIA exams as one of your electives.

- If you are thinking of getting an MCSE in addition to your MCSA, you can make things easier on yourself with a little planning. For example, the 70-218 exam for which you are now studying is a core exam for the MCSA and also an elective exam for the MCSE. That cuts the electives required for the MCSE from three down to two. The 70-216 exam (network infrastructure) is a core MCSE exam and an elective MCSA exam. Take this one as your elective for your MCSA and you're one step closer to the MCSE.

Travel Assistance

For a complete description of all available exams, certifications, available courses, and study guides, make sure you check out Microsoft's Training and Certification site at http://www.microsoft.com/ traincert.

Index

remote access, 379–381
routing. *See* TCP/IP
(Transmission Control
Protocol/Internet Protocol),
troubleshooting
server performance. *See* server
performance
trusts, Active Directory, 252–253
TTL (Time To Live) value, 61,
113, 131

U

U (universal) groups, scope,
262–263
UDP (User Datagram Protocol),
60–61
universal (U) groups, scope,
262–263
Unlock User Accounts, 257
Up-to-Date (UTD) Vector, 336
updates, 19–24
dynamic, 139
hot fixes, 22–23
replication convergence and
latency, 136–138
service packs, 20–22
Windows Update, 19–24
upgrades
IIS installation, 219
storage management, 196
Upgrades tab, software
Properties dialog box, 296
user accounts, 254–261
built-in, 254–255
creating, 255–256
defined, 250
domain, 254
local, 254
managing, 256–257
organizational units, 258
permissions, 263
remote access, 372–374
user profiles, 258–259
user authentication
remote access, 362–363
RRAS properties, 369–370
Web/FTP sites, 236–237
User configuration settings, group
policies
applying, 286–287
configuring, 299
overview of, 282–284
User Datagram Protocol (UDP),
60–61

user profiles, 258–260
Users group, 266–267
UTD (Up-to-Date) Vector, 336

V

Verify Caller-ID option, Dial-in
tab, 374
virtual directories, 230–231, 239
virtual servers, 223–225
VPN clients, 341
VPN Servers, 341–343
VPN (Virtual Private Network)
components, 375–376
installing and configuring,
376–379
overview of, 374–375
remote access with, 359–360

W

WAM_*computername*, IIS user
account, 255
WAN (wide area connection)
links, 143, 323–324
Warning event, 34
Web folders, shared, 169–172
Web server, IIS, 218
Web Site Creation Wizard,
224–225
Web Site Identification, Web Site
tab, 226
Web site information. *See also*
Microsoft Web site
DHCP/BOOTP broadcasts, 98
well-known port numbers, 61
Web site management. *See* IIS
(Internet Information Services)
Web site tab, Web site
properties, 226
Welcome message, FTP sites, 235
WFP (Windows File
Protection), 13
wide area connection (WAN)
links, 143, 323–324
*Windows 2000 Active Directory
Design and Deployment*
(Olsen), 336
*Windows 2000 Group Policy,
Profiles, and IntelliMirror*
(Moskowitz), 313
Windows 2000 Installation
CD-ROM, 18
Windows 95, 98, and Me
ipconfig, 72
NTFS partitions, 187

Windows Component wizard
IIS installation, 219–220
WINS installation, 114–115
Windows File Protection
(WFP), 13
Windows Installer Service, 21,
137–138, 293–294
Windows NT. *See also* NTFS (NT
File System); NTFS permissions
policies, 290
service packs, 22
Windows Registry, System State
data, 344
Windows Settings, Group Policy
snap-in, 283
Windows Update, 19–25
hot fixes, 22–23
overview, 19–20
service packs, 20–22
using, 23
viewing and removing updates,
23–24
winipcfg.exe utility, 72
WINS (Windows Name
Resolution)
clients, 115–117
name registration and renewal,
112–113
Name Resolution, 111–112
NetBIOS names, 108–111
non-WINS client, 114
overview of, 108
proxy agents, 113
review answers, 120–121
review questions, 118–120
servers, 111–113
WINS service installation,
114–115
WinSock interface, TCP/IP, 59
winver.exe command, 20
Write permission, 228, 268

Z

zone transfers, 143–145
full, 144
incremental, 144–145
zones, DNS
creating new, 135–137
DDNS configuration, 139–140
delegating, 138
overview of, 127–129
resource records, 131–132

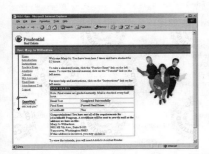